D0872345

Praise for *After 9/11*

"Hovitz shows us, for the first time, what it was like for families in New York City who suddenly had to live like other war refugees, with no idea where their loved ones were or when the next attack might come. *After 9/11* is a moving and remarkable testament to a time that changed our country, told beautifully by a young woman who never gave up hope that she could reclaim her life, no matter how grim things looked."

—Sean Elder, *Newsweek*

"Helaina Hovitz has written that rare kind of book that combines a poetic sensitivity to detail, the stark emotion of memory, and a searing glimpse of the human spirit as it suffers, struggles and learns to heal. In her story are the seeds of hope for anyone who has survived trauma and seeks to truly live again."

—Michele Rosenthal, *Heal Your PTSD: Dynamic Strategies That Work*

"Helaina Hovitz's first book is a brave, honest, and fast-paced personal account of the ways in which one day can change the course of our lives forever. Her story is an example of how trauma and addiction become part of a life, not someone's entire life, and how we can take the wheel and change that course if we are willing to work for it. By combining her own personal experience with interviews and journalistic research, Hovitz shows us, every step of the way, what it is like to finally move towards the light after so many years of darkness."

—Maia Szalavitz, bestselling author and journalist for *TIME*

After 9/11

After 9/11

ONE GIRL'S JOURNEY THROUGH DARKNESS TO A NEW BEGINNING

Helaina Hovitz

Foreword by Jasmin Lee Cori

Afterword by Patricia Harte Bratt

CARREL BOOKS

Carrel Books may be purchased in bulk at special discounts for sales promotion, corporate gifts, fund-raising, or educational purposes. Special editions can also be created to specifications. For details, contact the Special Sales Department, Carrel Books, 307 West 36th Street, 11th Floor, New York, NY 10018 or info@skyhorsepublishing.com.

Carrel Books is a registered trademarks of Skyhorse Publishing, Inc.®, a Delaware corporation.

Visit our website at www.carrelbooks.com.

10 9 8 7 6 5 4 3 2 1

Library of Congress Cataloging-in-Publication Data is available on file.

Cover design by Rain Saukas
Cover photo credits: Skyline - iStockphoto; Author photo - Carlos Luna; childhood photo - Author's collection

Print ISBN: 978-1-63144-062-5
Ebook ISBN: 978-1-63144-063-2

Printed in the United States of America

Author's Note:

To protect the identity and privacy of the people in this book, I have used their first names or last initials only, and, in some cases, changed names. The few exceptions to this rule are those who have given consent to the use of their full names.

While PTSD and other mental health conditions can become a big part of someone's life, these things do not make up an entire life. They do not define a person, and they cannot account for all of the choices we make. Therefore, all I can do, and what I have done honestly, is show you how just one day can change someone's experience of the world around them forever, and how that looks in the context of a life as it goes on.

Dedication

To anyone who lost a piece of their heart or a part of themselves on September 11th.

This is the greatest gift God can give you:
To understand what happened in your life.
To have it explained.
It is the peace you have been searching for.
      —Mitch Albom, *The Five People You Meet in Heaven*

Acknowledgments

Thank you . . .

To the team at Skyhorse Publishing, who banded together to make this book possible.

To Michael Lewis, my editor, who believed in my story enough to give me the one "yes" I needed and help me bring this baby home.

To Joelle Delbourgo, my agent and advocate, who took the time to tell me what worked and what needed work, and who patiently answered all of my questions as a first-time author. You truly saved the day.

To Abby Sher, who helped me bring Grandma Lucy to life again.

To Amye Rosenberg, who told me to keep going and going until I found an agent who cared and a publisher who "had balls."

To Kyle Pope, who told me I could do better and then helped me do it.

To Mark Statman, who agreed to work with me on the beginnings of this project as an independent study back in college, even though it was not, in fact, a collection of poetry or book of Spanish translations.

To Rakhel Shapiro, who helped me find the last missing puzzle piece that put me back together again.

To all of the women in the program who helped me navigate the world "one day at a time."

To Lindsay Champion, who, despite my instructions to "tear it apart," gave me constructive feedback in the delicate way only a very dear friend would.

To Farrell Kramer, who always gives it to me straight and who took the time to assure me that, despite the surprising lack of sex scenes, I really had something here.

To Donna Campione, who helped me get on a plane to Disney World and who, to this day, continues to provide long-term support to children struggling with trauma.

To Dr. Arielle Goldklang, who held me to a higher standard and led me to my new beginning.

To Dr. Jennifer Hartstein, whose guidance and support over many years has consistently helped shape me into the person I've always wanted to be.

To all of the family members who have cheered me on: Aunt Fran, Aunt Libby, Uncle John, and the rest of the clan that always keeps the invitations coming.

To my parents, for loving me when I was at my most unlovable and for never giving up as we tried and tried again to find the answers that would help me become the daughter I was meant to be.

To Lee, for never letting me give up on my dreams, for being my best friend, my biggest fan, and everything that you are. I feel so lucky each day that I get to share my life with you.

Finally, to my grandmother, who showered me with unconditional love right through to the end, love that I felt even when there were no longer any words. You were the sunshine that warmed my heart through the darkest of my days, and you will always be the love of my life.

Contents

PART FOUR

Foreword

Life through the Lens of Trauma

September 11th, 2001, was one of America's most visible shared experiences of trauma. Although the whole country was traumatized—most of it vicarious trauma—those in Lower Manhattan were most directly affected, as thousands were sent running for their lives.

There were hundreds of children living and going to school near the World Trade Center on that day, many of whom were caught in the chaos that you saw on television (or perhaps you've Googled the footage, or seen it at the 9/11 Memorial Museum). A handful of children were caught directly underneath the Towers from start to finish as the turmoil unraveled, and that chaos continued to live on inside of them for years.

One of the further damaging factors of this large-scale trauma was that it did not have a definitive ending. There was the uncertainty of who would be found alive, whether or not more attacks were coming, and when people who were displaced would be able to return to their homes. For Helaina, the physical aftermath went on for months, between the toxic particles lingering outside her front door, the presence of the army and police, and the lack of transportation and access to food, medicine, and phones in her neighborhood. Ground Zero was just blocks away—there was no escaping it.

Orange Alerts and anthrax scares further perpetuated the state of emergency. The presumed sense of safety that makes normal life possible was wiped out as quickly as the towers fell. *Why did this happen? What will happen next?*

Understanding Trauma

Trauma, by nature, is terrifying and completely overwhelming. To be technical for a moment, *trauma* refers to the impact of a *traumatic stressor* on a person, although we often use it to refer to those horrifying events. We are rendered helpless at such times, and the most common imprints are feelings of being trapped and helpless. (Those who have a more active response generally fare better than those who can do the least.)

The most common misconception people have about trauma is that it is simply a one-time event to "get over." Yet for those with post-traumatic stress disorder (PTSD), it's *not* over. It's not over in the nervous system, not over in the body, not absent from dreams or daily interactions. In PTSD, the trauma is stuck inside, staining every part of our lives.

With PTSD, over both short and extended periods of time—years later, even—we experience panic attacks, a pervasive feeling of impending doom, a fear that we are going to die or that we will do something crazy or uncontrolled. Our dreams are stalked by ghosts of the horrifying event, which intrude into waking memories as well, sometimes taking us over completely, as in flashbacks.

Our nervous systems continue to respond to cues similar to those that occurred in the trauma in ways similar to how we originally responded. These reminders are called "triggers," and our out-of-proportion response is often called "reactivity."

We can all be reactive at times, but people who suffer from trauma-related disorders become reactive a lot of the time. Not because they're choosing to be dramatic, but because something is hitting a raw nerve, and they're already permanently wound up, exhausted, or depressed. We react in a "bigger" way than the situation calls for, whether it is with more fear, more insecurity, more anger, more mistrust, more of any emotion. We do this even in response to the most ordinary elements of our lives, like work, school, relationships, or our morning commute.

Disturbing thoughts and images may intrude into consciousness from out of nowhere, startling us with their negative content. It may be an image of hurting an animal, or the thought of someone we love being hurt. We could have trouble focusing or concentrating, become highly distractible, lack good judgment, become disorganized, and have poor impulse control. Many trauma survivors feel confusion, self-doubt, and shame about the inability to pick up and carry on.

The lingering effects of trauma also wreak havoc on our relationships. There's emotional volatility, a desperate need for safety (paired often with an inability to register safety), the fear of being hurt again, the rupture of the trust that allows us to go through our lives in a normal sort of way. Symptoms escalate, continuing a life of chaos and desperate attempts to find something—or someone—to hold onto, and ways to escape what is too intense and terrifying to live with.

With PTSD, we struggle with simple things others take for granted—a good night's sleep, seeing common images in the media, attending a sports event in a large crowd. Our hyper-arousal keeps us on the defensive, ever alert for danger.

Even when life may be going well, we often don't notice the positive. We only notice how hurt and victimized we feel as our minds create crises from situations which would be innocent enough were it not for our filter. The body sensations we experience are no longer warnings of truly impending danger but are like reruns of past events captured on film.

Unresolved trauma is like a creature with many heads, each tormenting us. Although PTSD is thought of as the classic trauma disorder, it seldom appears alone. It often co-occurs with depression, anxiety disorders, addiction, eating disorders, various types of dissociation, and rigidities. People we might consider "control freaks" are often trauma survivors desperately trying to create safety for themselves and escape the helplessness they carry inside.

Trauma survivors are also hard hit on the health front. They suffer physical diseases that commonly accompany unresolved trauma, like irritable bowel syndrome, chronic fatigue, chronic migraines or headaches, chronic lower back pain, high blood pressure, and fibromyalgia.

What is perhaps most disturbing is that some people live with trauma for decades before they ever come to understand what they've been living with and where it all began. Helaina did not know any of this until her ninth therapist explained it to her eight years later!

To Helaina's tremendous credit, as soon as she learned about trauma, she began reading everything she could find, interviewing experts in the field, and reaching out to her former classmates to find out if any of them had experienced the same horrible things. It was during that time that she first reached out to me.

Why Do Some Suffer More?

As if there isn't enough baggage with trauma, people often feel shame or self-blame when they see others recover more quickly from the same traumatic stressor. It is important to remember that many factors shape our response to traumatic events— factors that both precede such events and follow them.

Age is one of these factors. I would argue that Helaina and her classmates, who were just heading into adolescence, were less resilient than adults who had more stability and coping under their belts, and more vulnerable than children too young to fully cognize what had happened. Adolescents are just starting to understand the world around them. For Helaina and her friends that world was deeply shattered by the terrorist attacks, a sudden calamity that was more than they could take in and integrate, especially with the fight-or-flight response being activated frequently in the aftermath.

Then of course there are individual differences. Some children have stronger psychological foundations than others, related to factors like how secure their attachment is to their parents, what kind of physiology they come in with, how much stress their tender nervous systems have already been under, and how strong their sense of self and safety are.

How needs are responded to after such an event also plays an important part. If fears are met with understanding, grounded reassurance, and feelings are normalized, that helps mediate the damage.

As 9/11 also demonstrated, in moments of fear, we reach out for those we love. Resolving trauma may not always require formal therapy if there is sufficient support from one's community, but, too often, family, friends, and even well-meaning professionals do not know how to provide that support. Further complicating it for the kids near Ground Zero, their whole community was in a collective haze.

The Cost on Young Lives

Trauma is everywhere. Studies show that half of all American children have experienced severe life trauma, and that eight million adults live with PTSD during any given year. That number likely continues to go up as we see an uptick in climate-related disasters, school shootings, and acts of terrorism. Add these to the standard staple of traumatic events like sexual and physical abuse, medical trauma, and sudden loss, and we see a severely traumatized nation.

Many of these traumatized young ones may not seek help at all, or even talk about their troubles with another person. Or, like Helaina, they may try and try to get better, only to find that nothing "works." Their brain will not give them any relief. For these reasons, and many more, suicide is the second leading cause of death for people ages fifteen to twenty-four in the United States.

The account you are about to read is not entirely the direct consequence of 9/11. (Life is never so simple.) Some of what Helaina lived with could be categorized as normal teenage angst—surely, as teenagers, many of us rebelled, or had sex with people we shouldn't have, or got drunk one time too many.

For Helaina, these normal adolescent challenges were filtered by a brain that had been chemically reconfigured to respond to the world in a way that made almost everything in her life seem dangerous and sad. She experienced her most formative years through a lens of fear and panic, from her first love to her final midterm exam, and the slow, painful loss of the one person who meant everything to her.

There Is Hope

Fortunately, *After 9/11: One Girl's Journey through Darkness to a New Beginning* ends on a very hopeful note. Helaina's relentless dedication to healing paid off. After years of stumbling through the wreckage of her own psyche and a string of therapists and medications that, for the most part, fell far short and failed to identify the role of trauma in her suffering, she found the help she needed. Through tremendous effort, she was able to pull herself out of that rubble and become the young woman she always hoped she could be.

Helaina was able to find relief, happiness, and peace of mind, becoming strong enough to hold herself together even when the world around her crumbles, which the world will do for all of us from time to time.

Please know: A new beginning is always possible. There is healing after trauma.

It's just that we have to work hard for it. Harder than we've ever worked before.

Only then do we find the light.

—Jasmin Lee Cori, MS, LPC, psychotherapist and author
of *Healing From Trauma: A Survivor's Guide to Understanding Your Symptoms and Reclaiming Your Life*

PART ONE

PART ONE

CHAPTER ONE

"The sky is falling, the sky is falling," said Chicken Little.
"Mommy," I said, "How can the sky fall?"

Aaaaaarrrg!"
I let out a loud cry of frustration as I ran the round brush through my hair, trying to get that one stray piece to stay put.

I slammed the hand mirror down so hard that I broke it.

Great, I thought. *Seven years of bad luck.*

It was already 8:00 a.m., and I had to leave for school, so I picked up my bag and fumed past my mom. She was sitting at the dining room table finishing up her bran muffin like she did every morning, before she left for work a few minutes later. There would be a slab of butter smeared on the plate, a few crumbs clinging to the knife, and she'd drop it into the sink before she left, carrying her purse and her tote bag with her.

"Have a good day," she said as I passed by.

"Thanks. I hate you," I responded, slamming the door behind me.

Her crime that day was a leftover from the day before: she hadn't reminded me to take an umbrella, and as school let out on the first day of seventh grade, the skies over Battery Park City had opened up into an uncharacteristic monsoon. I ran across the flooded ball fields to catch the bus home, the same field my best friend Gina and I had stubbornly sat on the sidelines of at Downtown Day Camp for so many summers, refusing to run around and play, designating ourselves as "water monitors." I got home soaking wet, which, of course, was my mother's fault.

But that morning was a beautiful day, like so many other beautiful days you don't really notice when you're twelve years old.

Normally, I walked to school with my neighbors Charles and Nadine, and Charles' mom, Ann. That morning, Charles and Ann were already long gone, since he had taken the first dentist appointment of the day. Nadine and I ambled along our usual route through City Hall Park and were through the school doors by 8:15 a.m.

Before class, I stopped to plunk my backpack in my locker, taking two composition notebooks and my pencil case with me, the one with the dog's face pictured from a funny angle, making his eyes look huge.

Eventually, I walked down the hall, past the green lockers, to my first period class, science with Mr. H.

He began the lesson on biomes and ecosystems.

"An ecosystem is a community of living organisms that interact with nonliving components of the environment like water, air, and soil."

Vrrrooooooooooooom.

Boom.

The floor shuddered and the shelves rattled.

Then, there was silence.

Everyone looked around wide-eyed, more with curiosity and surprise than fear. I thought maybe it was a truck tire popping, and looked over at Devin, who was almost smirking. Behind him, the clock read 8:46 a.m.

A few kids ran to the window that faced Stuyvesant High School, directly across the street, but saw nothing unusual.

"Sit down, guys," said Mr. H.

I went over to the other window, which faced the West Side Highway, looking out over Chambers Street, but there was nothing to see there, either.

"Guys, if you don't get away from the windows, you're all getting detention."

We ambled back to our tables.

"This is New York City," said the teacher, who was from Canada. "Loud noises are everywhere."

He turned toward the white dry erase board to continue, but Ivan interrupted, because he was one of those kids who always interrupted.

"What if they bombed the World Trade Center?" he asked.

The room stayed quiet for a split second, until Allison shouted, "My mom works in the World Trade Center!"

As if on cue, the wailing of sirens began echoing against the classroom walls, the lights flashing across the whiteboard. When we went back to the windows, we could see firemen hopping out of trucks and walking downtown along the West Side Highway. The side of the truck said Engine 6, the station one block from my apartment, but we couldn't see where they were going. They just walked until they disappeared.

Mr. H sighed, and continued.

"Biomes are different areas of the world that have similar climates, weather, and living things."

Through the small window of the classroom door, we could see teachers running back and forth in the hallway. Two minutes later, there was a knock at the classroom door.

Mr. H went into the hallway and returned seconds later, all signs of color drained from his face.

"They've bombed the World Trade Center," he said.

They? They who?

"We're sitting here to wait for further instructions."

Allison's hands flew to cover her eyes. I had only met her two days before, but I got up and dragged my lab stool next to hers. I rubbed her back, not knowing what else to do.

Okay, they bombed the World Trade Center, but we're not in the World Trade Center.

Mr. H did his best to keep composed as he stood silently at the front of the room with his hands clasped in front of him.

After another knock, and another step into the hallway, Mr. H announced, "Gather your things, and don't stop at your lockers. We're having an emergency assembly."

We didn't go to the auditorium, where an assembly would have normally been, but to the cafeteria.

"Nobody leave the building under any circumstances, and stay away from the windows."

Don't have to tell me twice.

I looked around at the tables full of kids, then over at Patty, who always wore the same big black trench coat. Gina and I had made fun of her at camp for being "big," and I was pretty sure she hadn't forgotten about it.

"A plane flew into the Twin Towers," she was telling everyone around her.

That's impossible. I blew it off like someone told me the walls were made of candy.

A second thought flickered by like a flash of lightning. *What if it's true?*

"There's no way it's a plane," I said. "It was obviously a bomb. We'll probably just get the day off. It won't be a big deal."

She looked at me like I was an idiot.

"I'm telling you what I heard," she said, rolling her eyes and turning away from me.

I walked over to Devin, who was listening to the radio on his Discman. He was one of the few students who had a cell phone, which he was holding in the palm of his hand.

"It's not working," he said, looking down at it. "But the radio is saying that a plane hit the building."

I sat down next to him, fidgeting with my pencil case, zipping it open and closed and sighing, impatiently, wishing I knew what the hell was going on. I looked over at Christine. We weren't especially friendly—she was closer to Nadine— but we said hello in the halls, and I knew that we lived a few blocks from each other. She was wearing two big T-shirts to cover her enormous chest and was talking to some other kids I didn't know.

"Today is my birthday," said Shane as he walked by all of us to go to the bathroom.

All I wanted to do was go to my locker to get my bag, my MetroCard, and the rest of my books. I just wanted to write, to do something other than just sit there, absorbing this weird energy.

I'd done that day's writer's notebook assignment the night before and dated it 9/11/01. I had written about the MTV awards and ice cream and how excited I was to get my braces in a few months.

The next time I looked up, a group of men with large helmets and green uniforms had burst through the cafeteria doors.

"That's the bomb squad!" Devin said loudly.

Thirty seconds later, he made another announcement, but only a few of us heard it.

"A second plane just hit the other Tower."

Nobody in the cafeteria heard the second plane hit, but as soon as the bomb squad started speaking with teachers, the chaos began.

The principal, Ellen, announced that everyone was to be evacuated within five minutes. Parents began rushing into the building, frantic, screaming.

Suddenly, Ann and Charles appeared in the doorway of the cafeteria.

Instinctively, I ran over and said, "Ann, can you believe this?" The idea of her taking me home flashed through my mind, but I didn't like to ask anyone but my parents for anything.

I looked at the men in the large helmets with the tiny visor windows over their eyes and then at the parents shoving their way into the building, crying and rambling incoherently.

Where are my parents?

My mom worked at Rockefeller Center, and my dad taught in Staten Island, so they certainly weren't going to show up here.

But what if they're on their way down here?

What if I'm not here when they get here?

They wouldn't get down here that quickly. You can call them from home to let them know you're okay.

"Take me with you, please," I said to Ann, interrupting my own string of thoughts.

"We're not supposed to let anyone go without a parent," Ellen said.

Her eyes darted from Ann to me, then flickered wildly over the crowd in front of her.

Grandma.

What about Grandma.

At home, you can make sure Grandma and Grandpa are okay, too.

"I walk her to school every morning. I can take her home now," Ann said reassuringly, nodding in a way that conveyed authority.

Ellen gave her approval with a tentative nod before being swallowed into a sea of people. The last person I saw inside was Alex, the sixth grade global studies teacher, who was craning his neck near the window and looking up.

He stayed in the cafeteria until the building was evacuated five minutes later.

He stayed with the students as they were shepherded away from the school, screaming, crying, and running up the West Side Highway.

He stayed, even though his brother was on the 101st floor of Tower 2.

When the three of us pushed open the double doors of the school building and walked out onto the street, something stung my nostrils, causing a burning sensation.

What's that smell?

It looked like we had stepped out onto the movie set of a disaster film.

Police cars and fire engines had parked in all sorts of places.

Peoples' screams were fading in and out as they clambered into each other. Cars were stopped dead along the West Side Highway, bumper to bumper. Camera crews were barking orders at each other. Ambulances were receiving people bleeding on stretchers. Everyone else was standing still, looking up, as plumes of smoke and ash billowed from the gashed mouths of both towers.

I looked up then, too, watching as the building vomited paper, feeling the heat across my face.

"Let's go, kids," Ann said, and we headed up Chambers Street with one objective: get home.

CHAPTER TWO

You never do get to go back to anything, but it really takes a long time to learn that.

—Diane Di Prima, *Memoirs of a Beatnik*

The World Trade Center is one of many things I wish I'd known to remember more clearly before it was taken away.

They were two very tall buildings, just like all of the other very tall buildings in our neighborhood. The walk over to them was all concrete and tricolored streetlights, hot dog carts and business people, taxi cabs and horn-honking traffic jams, smells that cycled between cologne, exhaust fumes, leather, and burnt hot pretzels.

To me, it was just another big space we walked through to get to Hudson River Park, with its sandboxes and swings and the cement elephant sprinkler whose thin stream was always shockingly cold. It was where we went for Krispy Kreme doughnuts, my mom's favorite, or to read stories in the book nook of Borders bookstore. The lobby had endless windows, a Sam Goody—they sold CDs, which, at one time, were used to play music—and my favorite clothing store, the Children's Place.

Nearby was the World Financial Center, which hosted all sorts of fun events with hayrides, characters in costume, and musical shows. The ceiling was made of glass, and from it hung strings of shimmery lights, which cascaded downward like vines, tickling the rows of palm trees that reached up toward the sky from below.

What I remember most clearly is the plaza between the two buildings, the one with the fountain. In the middle of the vertical spouts of water was a big gold circle, and I always tried to get away with touching it as the water trickled down the side. The sun would hit the sphere and make it look like a magical, glistening ball of light that I just had to get near.

"You'll get a disease," my mom, Denise, always said when she caught me moving toward it, gently yanking my arm away.

I'd settle for sitting right alongside it, eating some sort of snack, maybe watching an outdoor performance, trying not to be too annoyed that someone decided to send water dancing down a big shiny ball if you *weren't* supposed to play with it. To me, it seemed like a big sprinkler that adults didn't know how to use, and wouldn't let *me* use.

The way I remember that sphere most clearly now, though, is on the back of a truck, demolished, being carted down the West Side Highway.

Completely destroyed.

* * *

Ask my parents why I'm an only child, and they will tell you to take a look at the tape.

Actually, they'll direct you to a giant box of tiny videocassette tapes under the bed, all starring me.

The other reason I am an only child, they will tell you, is because that's the way I wanted it.

"You didn't want to share anything, including Grandma."

It's a wonder that I didn't grow up to become a reality TV star, having been raised with my every move on camera, my father or myself narrating my life for the viewer. There I was at age two, crouching in the corner to make a poop in the potty and reciting nursery rhymes.

At age three, singing "Puff the Magic Dragon," tossing around plastic food from the plastic play stove, playing, in a rare moment of quiet, with my sticker books, dragging around a yellow-and-red microphone attached to a tape recorder, singing and hosting talk shows or reading books out loud.

At age four, picking up my dress with a spiteful smile while I danced around to some movie soundtrack, my dad's voice interjecting from off screen, "Helaina, if you do that again I'm turning the camera off."

At age seven, singing the entire score of *Cats* like a seasoned Broadway veteran who was about to hang up her feathered hat for one final performance, brow furrowed as she unleashed a ballad in an impassioned falsetto.

One of my favorite videos takes place at a petting zoo on a farm. I'm two or three years old, wearing white frilly socks and a pink dress with a pineapple print. I'm slowly chasing after some kittens, asking, "Are you hungry, little baby?" and emphatically tossing hay in their respective directions.

"I have some food for you, baby!" I said, teetering after this one, then that one, trying to pick them up.

I look at the camera in sad confusion.

"He doesn't want to love me, Daddy."

Right at that moment, the camera is turned off, and when the picture comes back on, I'm holding a kitty up in front of my face, smiling.

Daddy to the rescue.

In the next shot, my mom and I are watching as another child takes a pony ride, undoubtedly waiting for my turn, or my fourth or fifth turn. I'm standing up on the white fence, and my mother has one hand on my back to keep me from falling. Her other hand finds its way to my head of full black curly hair, which she starts fluffing. My tiny arm shoots straight up in the air and lands gently, palm down, on her shoulder, accompanied by a very accusatory "Hey!"

"Uh-uh," my mom says, glancing over my shoulder with her lips pursed and her eyebrows raised from behind her big, red-framed glasses.

"Daddy took a picture," she said.

"Of the horsey?" I ask innocently, not turning around.

"Of you hitting Mommy," she says, to no further comment from me.

Even before then, when I was teeny tiny, my dad would swaddle me in a bunch of blankets, wrap me up tight, and even when it was cold out, take me out onto the terrace and tell me that I was a papoose. I loved this more than anything, feeling safe and snuggled on this adventure that existed just a few steps away.

"Make me a papoose!" I would say. "A papoose!"

As soon as I learned to talk, it was clear that I would never be shy.

Everyone around me knew that I'd be more than happy to engage them in conversation, offering some tidbit I'd learned about caterpillars in preschool or some advice about their own lifestyle choices, like the time I informed a woman in the elevator that she was "just a little bit heavy." I would tell people, as a three-year-old, "that age is just a number" when they asked. I emphatically chatted up neighbors like Tony, an old man who wore a fedora and smelled strongly of the aftershave that clung to his thick white gristle. Tony would give me a dollar for being so smart—on the days he gave me five dollars, I damn near lost my mind.

"We'll put it in her college fund," my dad would say.

My dad is a short man, about 5'8" and thin by nature. He still has a full head of hair, which cycled from black to salt and pepper and, finally, gray. His weight fluctuated at times, increasing when he quit smoking, decreasing when he started going to the gym religiously. His brown eyes and thin lips pop against his naturally tan skin, and he always dressed in "cool" jeans, tank tops, or well-made suits with shiny ties. He always smelled of expensive cologne, which he sprayed generously when he got ready for work in the wee hours of the morning. Along with his naturally booming voice and big smile, it helped him command a much bigger presence than his height ever could.

My father grew up in Brooklyn with his father, a baker—who was also an alcoholic—his mother, and his two sisters. In Lower Manhattan, specifically, absolutely everyone knew him. He was active on the Southbridge board, where we lived, on Community Board 1, and on other volunteer committees, including a youth committee that he stayed on long after I graduated from middle school, high school, and college. If you needed a hand, he was your guy. People stopped him to talk to him about noise outside of their window or if they were having trouble getting their kid into a school. I thought he was the mayor of everything, capable of fixing everyone's problems. My mom would get annoyed when he went out of his way for people, occasionally saying, "Why are you helping them? It's not your job."

"That's not why we help people," he'd say, and she'd roll her eyes.

Dad was also very generous. Whenever we passed a homeless person, he always stopped, if he had spare change. So, it got to the point where I would see them from a block away, and say, "Daddddy," prompting him to start patting down his pockets. On one family trip to Washington, DC, on our way to some colonial museum, we passed a woman who said she only needed fifty cents to get a sandwich. "Oh, sure!" I told her, looking expectantly at Dad, who obliged. My mother said, "She's not going to get a sandwich."

"Oh yes, she is! She said she was," I pointed out, matter-of-factly.

When we left the museum, a city bus passed by, and there she was, sitting on board, eating a sandwich, smiling, and waving at us.

Daddy knew *everything*. He always knew the twist in the movie plot and that "Directed By" was the last of the credits before the show started. He knew how to make a squirt gun with his hands in the pool, how to make Play-Doh out of baking soda and flour, and how to make sure that the costumed character at the party came over to take a picture with me, even if it looked like we'd never make it through the crowd. He never missed a school or camp play and stuck my report cards right on the wall, whooping for joy, shouting, "All right! That's my girl!" and kissing me on the cheek.

He was the originator of names like sugarshack, sweet-heart, and baby, whereas my mom simply used Helaina, and more often, "Helaina Natalie" because I was usually in trouble. He was the hero who always believed me when I said I felt sick and needed to stay home, who, later on, respectfully challenged the teachers at school when he felt I wasn't being given a fair shake. My mother never learned how to drive, so he drove us everywhere: on vacations, shopping, to shows, to birthday parties, or to the hospital, when intense stomach viruses struck.

My dad worked at a print shop and as a choir teacher at a special education high school in Staten Island. In the early days before Photoshop, he literally "cut and pasted" our faces on cartoon characters or movie stars, writing funny or sweet messages for our birthdays or anniversaries or Christmas, copying the cutouts and then printing and laminating them. He also made collages, cutting out baby photos of me and adding captions on large rectangles of red or black Plexiglas, which hung proudly right in the entryway to our apartment.

My dad was the spoiler, the one who understood why I just *had* to have the $75 princess dress for Halloween or another Barbie to add to the pile because *that* was Grocery Store Barbie. When we went out to eat at all sorts of restaurants, he said, "Don't worry about what it costs, honey. Get whatever you want." Not in a "big shot" way, but in a generous way, because that's who he was.

"You thought we had money growing up because you always had what you wanted, but it only looked that way," my mother later told me. "We took out a lot of personal loans."

They both worked, and they must have saved smartly.

My mother was the "silent" hero, who always found fun things for us to do. She took me to our very first Broadway show, *Beauty and the Beast*, and even though we could only afford tickets in what she called "the nosebleed section," I sat still, not moving, for nearly three hours. Holding up my little yellow binoculars and wearing my yellow Belle dress, I was completely mesmerized by what was happening on stage.

We went to see everything under the sun at Madison Square Garden, most often there were shows where people in costume acted out movies while ice skating. We went to the Big Apple Circus, and we went to see shows that the kids at Borough of Manhattan Community College put on. We went to the Renaissance Fair upstate, and we went to the zoo, where my favorite exhibit was the one that was set up to feel like a rainforest. She managed to find all of these fun activities, however people tracked those things down before the Internet or smart phones. Sometimes, she got creative locally: there was a tiny patch of park directly under the Brooklyn Bridge, right by the water, where we went to barbecue. We would bring tinfoil, burgers, buns, charcoal, marshmallows, and a lighter, a city family "going camping."

To this day, the taste of Pepsi reminds me of Manhattan Beach, where we'd take our beach chairs and sit out, marching past the Puerto Rican families whose barbecues by the parking lot sent smoke and charcoal fumes billowing out into the crowd. The small yellow hot dog huts served Pepsi, but at home, we only had Diet Coke.

My dad didn't drink soda, but he didn't drink alcohol either—just water, which was fine with me, because drunken people made me nervous. I didn't want to be around them, and I would stand in the doorway of a restaurant refusing to go farther if people were being loud and smoking at the bar by the entrance. I didn't like that these people were belligerent and acting boisterous, and I didn't like that they couldn't be stopped. They were out of control.

"Why do people drink when it makes them sick and smelly and scary?" I'd ask.

"I don't know, honey," he'd say.

Actually, I'd later learn, he knew exactly why: because they couldn't stop, and he had been one of those people who couldn't stop. In fact, he still was, which was why he didn't start.

I loved "the arts," and Mom somehow found ways to afford drama class, music class, art class, swim class, singing lessons, and the cutest outfits you ever saw on a kid—all on a very modest, middle-class income. What I wanted most of all though were mother-daughter outfits.

Every month we got this clothing catalog, and I would go through with a red marker and circle what I wanted. In addition to tops and dresses, I would always fold down the corner on the pages where mothers and daughters wore matching dresses, or top and bottom sets, then keep my fingers crossed as we went through it together.

Never, not once, did we get one of those mother-daughter outfits, no matter how much I tried to convince her that they were beautiful, or that everyone who saw us would just *love* it.

But she did bring me to the Newport Mall in New Jersey, where my favorite store, the Limited Too was always waiting like a tiny Disney World, and I could barely wait to get through the doors, never knowing where to start. It was stocked with preteen versions of trendy outfits (think fur-lined polyester jackets, velvet baby-doll pajamas, and leopard leggings) that I couldn't wait to show off to all of the boys in school who couldn't care less . . . plus, furry pom-pom pens, neon-colored candy, pillows you could insert your own photo into, and training bras that, at eleven, I actually needed.

I usually got everything I wanted, at least from that store, but the one thing I didn't get was a dog, no matter how frequently I asked.

"When can I have a dog?" I would demand, stomping around the playground or marching up to my mother while she was doing something in the kitchen.

"When you're old enough to walk it."

"I'm old enough now!"

"I don't think so," my dad would somehow enter the conversation and chuckle, turning back to his computer, which I wanted to throw out the window.

* * *

You would never, ever, have seen either of my parents wearing turtlenecks, sweatshirts, corduroys, loose T-shirts in dull colors, anything with a college logo plastered across the front, "mom jeans" or "dad jeans," visible white socks, or chunky sweaters. Everything was smartly accessorized, well put together, fitted, and stylish. That's how this family did things, with my mother at the helm.

She was just five feet tall, a size four with short, dark, loosely curly hair, which she always had cut just above her ears, styled and highlighted by the trendiest salons in the city. They would color it for free if she sat as a hair model for two hours as part of a class to teach young stylists. She had a few piercings in each ear and wasn't like the other mothers who had long hair and wore long skirts with flowers on them and baked cookies. She also wasn't a high-powered business type, either. She fell somewhere in between, a travel agent who changed agencies fairly often and worked only part time, three days a week. Bosses were always trying to get her to work more often, but she wouldn't do it.

Her skirts, blouses, and jewelry were modern, always a stone's throw away from something you'd see on the runway or in a fashion magazine. She knew how to shop and never pay retail, finding one-of-a-kind accessories that caused people to reach out and touch them and coo, "Ooooh, where did you get this?" She never wore a pair of sweatpants anywhere except to the laundry room within the apartment building, and never went outside without makeup on. Over the next twenty years, she would look like she hadn't aged a day.

On special occasions she wore contact lenses, but mostly she wore glasses, which she switched out every few years depending on what was in style. Her nails were always manicured, and she was always ready ten minutes *later* than we were supposed to leave, which caused my dad to sigh loudly and threaten to sit back down on the couch, and if more time ticked by, to get undressed, and ultimately, to "just forget it."

I grew up to share my father's urgency for being on time and impatience for "waiting around," and when I was still little, I always felt that I had to lay claim to him, since everyone else got to share him too.

He hosted the Halloween parties for kids in the community room, and I trailed him like a member of the Secret Service, a duty that took precedence over running around with my friends, Charles, Gina, and Julie. Sure, I said hello to them, posed for some pictures, and shoveled a candy corn–covered Entenmann's cupcake into my face, but ultimately, my most important mission of the night was making sure everyone knew that Paul was *my* dad. I handed out the "best costume" certificates my dad had printed at his job—everyone was a winner, very progressive for the mid-'90s—and smiled condescendingly at each kid when they reached my dad at the front of the line.

"Wow, look at you! And who are *you* my dear?" my dad would say and he held the microphone to their tiny painted faces. "A witch!" the kid would exclaim, like a huge mystery had just been solved.

"Congratulations, here you go!" he'd smile, and that was my cue to hand over the paper.

He's just being polite, kid. You're a store-bought witch. I'm an enchanted woodland fairy. Move along.

It's a miracle that the witch didn't scare me, even in her lame costume, because I was scared of everything.

Unfortunately, my mother felt the best way to convince me to do things on a day-to-day was by scaring me into them.

"If you don't brush your hair, the birds will make a nest in it."

"If you don't hold Mommy's hand, someone is going to take you."

"If you put dirty things in your mouth, you're going to get 'trench mouth.' Your jaw will look like *this* and it'll stay like that forever."

She also tried to get me to face my fears through her own brand of "exposure therapy." I was supposed to watch the scary TV show on Nickelodeon because it was meant for kids, "So how scary could it be?" I was supposed to climb through the colorful tube-like tunnels at kids play places, because "All of the other kids are having fun, look!"—which she often said in a way that indicated something was wrong with me because I was not.

In the first of many years of seeing the play *A Christmas Carol* at Madison Square Garden every December, there was one scene that I couldn't handle. A seemingly endless plethora of bellowing, green-lit ghosts in chains swarmed the stage and the audience, if memory serves me—instead of just one plain, old Jacob Marley—and without fail, I trembled and screamed, climbing up my dad's body.

"I wanna go home!"

He stood up to take me out of the theater, but my mother stopped him, saying, "Don't you take her out of here. No! Paul, no. She has to learn not to be afraid."

Year after year, I never stopped being afraid, a scenario they often brought into an ongoing discussion of how they felt the other person was inconsistent in their approach to raising me, which they often had in front of me.

At Disney World, we spent a lot of time in the gift shops and taking pictures with characters. I was afraid of rides, naturally. When the Wicked Witch popped out during the Great Movie Ride at MGM Studios, I covered my eyes, crying, "I want to go home!" This was my catchphrase, because home was safe. Nothing bad could happen at home. The scary stuff would stop, the ride would always end, I would walk out into the sunlight holding my parents' hands. I would lead them to the safety of It's A Small World for the seventh time, and everything would be ok.

It's not real.

This did not make it any easier for me to sleep at night, though. My fear of the dark was crippling, and, most nights, my mother would lay down with me until I fell asleep, or until she got too bored to wait any longer. Sometimes, my parents were like soldiers that I ordered to be stationed at my bedroom door. Ironically, I was too busy vigilantly waiting for them to walk away from the door to actually sleep. If they tried to leave, I would call them out on it, and come stomping out after them like a warden in a red flannel nightgown. Sometimes, I'd sing to my stuffed animals to try to calm my fear, but, like clockwork, after I fell asleep—or I'd killed two hours until they went to bed—I would march right from my room into theirs and nudge my way into their queen-sized bed next to my mom.

There were times, it seemed, when I was supposed to be scared—or rather, as my mom would put it, "alert"—like when taking the subway.

When I was two and a half feet tall, she began testing me.

"Would you have gotten in that car if I wasn't here with you?" she'd ask as she guided me toward the next silver car with scratched windows marked up in black graffiti.

"Did you see who was in that car? Half of them were home-less. When you're a teenager, you're going to have to take the subway by yourself, you know."

I knew how to identify a homeless man by age four, and always felt sorry for them. Sometimes people asked for money, and we had money. They asked people for food, and we had food. Why didn't they have food?

My mom never gave to them.

"There's help for them if they want it," she said.

But one night there was an exception. It was around Christmas, and a man who was shaking pretty badly came into our subway car. He spilled his cup of change, sending quarters and nickels and pennies rolling everywhere. As people bent to help him pick it up, my mom quietly added a dollar.

"It's Christmas," she said.

In a conventional sense, I grew up very well versed in keeping myself safe by New York City standards. If I got lost, I was to find a police officer or go over to the guy in the little plastic box by the subway turnstiles and tell him I was a lost child, giving him my name, my address, my phone number, and my mother's name. I wasn't supposed to step on the sewer grates in the street—in fact, I supposed to stay very far from them, especially if they were smoking, because that meant they were probably going to explode. I was never allowed to wear a nameplate necklace, because someone could pretend that they knew me or my mom and try to kidnap me.

I was never told what terrible things would happen after I was hypothetically kidnapped, but I had an active enough imagination to fill in the blanks.

Mom taught me always to walk with confidence, especially when I got older.

"Keep your head up, and look straight ahead. Take meaningful strides. Don't let anyone see that you're scared, or think that you are. You're tough. Never keep your head down," she said.

"If you think you need to cross the street, do it, but don't make it obvious. If you need to change subway cars, wait until the next stop. But do not look afraid."

At the same time, I was also brave, or at least, that's what people told me.

There was the time in preschool that I got a splinter on the jungle gym at Washington Market Park on Chambers Street, right behind the Borough of Manhattan Community College and across the street from P.S. 234.

The class gathered around to watch as the teacher, Heather, tried to get it out. I cried silently, and she told me, "You are so brave!"

How am I being brave if I'm crying? I thought. Besides, what other choice did I have? I could let her get the splinter out, or I could walk around with a splinter for the rest of my life.

In third grade, when I got a stomach virus so severe that I had to be hospitalized, the night nurse took me into a room to try and give me an IV. The nurse, who had orange colored, fanned-out hair and wore crimson lipstick, kept poking at my vein and making me bleed but failed to insert the IV.

"Damn it," she said under her breath, sending a trail of blood down my arm.

I wasn't bothered, it was just blood, but Mom had to go sit in the hallway so she didn't faint.

"You're a brave kid, you know that?" the nurse smiled through yellowing teeth.

What am I going to do, run away? I thought. There was nothing to do but wait for her to fix it and make it better.

* * *

My mother and her sister, my aunt Fran, grew up on Orchard Street, in a building next to what is now the Lower East Side Tenement Museum. They were raised near streets you weren't supposed to walk down after dark, streets that are now full of clubs and bouncers guarding red velvet ropes that you can't get behind without forking up a fortune or showing some serious cleavage. The people around Mom and Aunt Fran inspired the characters in movies like *Donnie Brasco* and *Goodfellas*. In large groups, they went out to eat at Little Italy's Mafia-run restaurants and sometimes had the check picked up with the wave of an arm by "Big Sal" whose life was later made into a movie you may have seen.

They moved into Southbridge Towers in 1971, until my aunt later moved into a condo on East Sixty-Fifth Street on the Upper East Side. Grandma had given them each a choice: an apartment or a wedding. They made their respective choices quickly and easily.

Southbridge Towers is a residential community in the Financial District near the South Street Seaport, an affordable housing complex comprised of nine buildings, four tall ones and five short ones. The tall ones have twenty-seven floors, the short ones have six. There's a community room in the middle of the square block where people hold small parties or art classes for kids and holiday parties for the seniors. It is a little community that very few people knew existed downtown, an area best known for its Wall Street stock brokerage firms and law offices. In the '90s, little communities were coming up downtown, and a few schools also arrived to meet the need. Buckle My Shoe was one of the first to debut, and the things I remember from my days there are clear and random, the way most early memories are.

* * *

It was the early '90s, before Tribeca was *Tribeca*. I went to preschool to try to be "socialized" and to get a head start on learning—I didn't need the child care, because Grandma was home all the time, and she lived in our apartment building. But my poor mom held hope that preschool would remedy certain things and give me a leg up on others.

As a three-year-old, I didn't walk around in a purple pom-pom hat looking to hit random kids on the playground, but if someone shoved me on the slide line, they sure as shit were getting a shove back. And if they didn't want to play Princess Helaina Leads the Way, I might have had to aggressively snatch their jump rope away. Instead of giving me the dirty looks, parents and babysitters would glare at my mom and usher their children away from me. I peed in the inflatable pool and then immediately announced in someone's ear, "I peed in the pool," and laughed when all the kids had to get out as someone's mom drained and refilled it. I climbed the bookshelf at the library. When I was three, I was asked not to return to Gymboree because I abused my Noodle privileges by whacking the other kids over the head with it at a birthday party.

Enough said.

My mom would roll me into preschool the three days a week before she went to work, and I cried every single time, clinging to her legs, like someone who was never going to see her mother again.

"You'll see Mommy again after school. You have to let her go now," one teacher, or three teachers at once, would say.

"Okay, now say, 'Bye, Mommy! See you later! Can't wait to tell you everything I learned today!'"

I had to be removed, literally detached from her, finger by finger, completely inconsolable.

I eventually managed to get through the day well enough, learning the value of chewing with my mouth closed and raising my hand instead of calling out every single answer, which I always knew, but those mornings were rough. They stayed rough until I entered the third grade.

We'd occasionally go on field trips, and the teachers would use these multi-child leashes with Velcro cuffs that closed around our wrists to keep us all attached to each other. If one person decided to sway back and forth, it threw the whole group off balance, so we looked like a bunch of teetering Weebles. This was their best effort at making sure that nobody got lost or taken.

We'd walk down Church Street or West Broadway in this swaying blob of tiny pink jackets and glittery shoes, and I'd watch pieces of the sidewalk sparkle. If I looked straight down at them while I walked, these sparkles seemed to pop right off the ground and twinkle in front of my eyes.

"What is that?" I asked Sandy, the teacher, one day.

"That's recycled glass," she said.

I was disappointed, not only because I didn't really understand what that meant but because it didn't sound very magical.

"What about those black spots?" I followed up, noticing all of the dark, raised circles that covered the sidewalk.

"That's peoples' gum," Sandy said.

That, too, struck me as odd, because gum was supposed to stick to your shoes, not the sidewalk, and gum was obviously not black.

I liked Sandy. She had short brown hair and tiny brown eyes and wore berry-colored lipstick. She seemed warm, and I always competed for a spot on her lap during story time. This competition often resulted in my pushing someone else out of my way, or sulking if I didn't win, which ultimately caused the outcome of nobody getting the lap.

I also refused to sleep during naptime, so I crawled around to other kid's mats, usually starting with Shane, who had dark skin and only had a mommy who had white skin. Sometimes, my father would take his choir students to sing for my class—but God help him if he sang one of "our songs." One day, he sang "Puff the Magic Dragon," and I stormed off to the corner of the rug with my hands over my ears, facing the wall, until it was over.

My grandpa usually picked me up at the end of the day, from the sandbox where Shane and I shuffled around. Typically, we were usually the last two kids to be picked up, after begging whichever teacher was there to "make some of it wet sand," which they treated like a luxury, as though tossing a cup of water into the sandbox was akin to shaving black truffles onto our jelly sandwiches. When my grandpa tried to get me to put my socks and shoes on, I'd refuse to exit the sandbox, or I'd wiggle and worm around defiantly.

"Ah, c'mon now," he'd say, frustrated.

"Don't give your grandpa a hard time," the teacher would say.

Sometimes, she'd have to resort to the threat of, "We're going to let him leave you here."

That didn't scare me—no, sir. There was no universe that existed where my mom would let me be abandoned at school, or on the street, or anywhere.

I don't know where my grandpa found the patience for this. He had been a jeweler and a gambler—one that my grandma had to bail out of jail twice—and there he was trying to shimmy a sock onto a wiseass four-year-old.

His name was Charlie, but actually, his name was also Gregorio. When his Italian-speaking mother brought him to school here in New York, the teacher couldn't understand what she was saying, so she offered a list of names. "Michael, Anthony, Charlie . . ." Apparently, she nodded, and said, "*Sì*, Charlie!" and that was that.

Eventually, Grandpa Charlie would manage to strap me into the stroller, kicking and huffing, and pushed down Chambers Street, across City Hall Park, and, finally, home.

* * *

Sometimes, I learned, not listening to your parents was a great move.

When I was four years old, while we were coloring at the table, I heard someone in the hallway of our building screaming, "Help! Help!"

"Mommy," I said, "Someone needs help."

My mother walked to the door, looked out the peephole, and said, "There's nobody there."

I went to open the door, and she put her hand over mine, over the knob, keeping it closed. "Uh-uh," she said in warning. "That's how people kidnap children. Look, there's nobody there."

She picked me up by the waist and held my eye up to the peephole so I could see that nobody was in the hall. She walked away, looking back purposefully over her shoulder to indicate that I should not open the door.

As soon as the back of her slipper was out of sight, I opened the door.

There, sprawled on her stomach, hands reaching out in front of her, was Jean, our older neighbor who lived directly next door—a view not visible through the scope of the peephole.

"Please get help!" she said to me in a strained voice.

"Mommy!" I yelled.

My mother ran over and immediately called 911.

As it turned out, Jean was having a stroke—somehow she had managed to push the door open but couldn't get back up to use the phone.

When she came home a few days later, she said to me, "If you hadn't had opened the door, I might not be alive."

After that, Jean would bring me little presents, a straw doll from her trip to the Caribbean, a real nutcracker at Christmastime.

"You're the little girl who saved my life," she would say.

* * *

I had inherited a singing voice from my dad, who was a musician in his younger, wilder days and even played with Jose Feliciano (the guy who sang "Feliz Navidad") at a club in Brooklyn. I would sing for pretty much anyone, but it was the one thing I was shy about, so I usually started out hiding behind my mom or a piece of furniture. I sang for the women sitting in front of the building or in the pizza place, I sang for the people eating their lunch in the food court at the South Street Seaport, I sang for the camera, and, most important, I sang for Grandma, who thought—no, *knew*—I was God's gift to the universe. She was definitely the gift in mine.

Grandma Lucy lived two flights up from us in our apartment building. Her home, just like her heart, was a warm place full of unconditional love.

She was always cooking something and wearing a colorful housedress. She must have had about twenty of them: some had shiny gray buttons, some had pastel floral prints, some were striped, and some felt hard while others were hardly like fabric at all, baby soft from so many washes with fabric softener. She always wore lipstick and perfume, and her hair was done up in a round, blonde "bulb," almost like a helmet, on top of her head. She smelled like cotton, hairspray, and that sweet smell that grandmas have that you can never quite put your finger on.

She was also short, with light gray-blue eyes and what you might call a round potbelly, but slender otherwise. She had a big bunion on each foot, which she hid in high heels and underneath stockings and house slippers.

She was in her late seventies when I was born, and her arms were the only arms that would make me, a colicky baby, stop crying. She would have to walk through the garage in the middle of the night when my mother, who lived in the next building until I was two, called her in hysterics so that I, and everyone, could finally get some sleep. From the time I could walk on two feet, she diligently watched me put on shows, clapping and making a big fuss. I was her everything, and she was mine.

I often ran away from home when my parents said or did something I didn't like, dragging my Minnie Mouse suitcase up two flights of stairs to her apartment, where she was always waiting with open arms.

Whenever I left Grandma's apartment, I always said, "I love you," and sometimes we'd say it ten times back and forth as I waited for the elevator. "Love you!" we'd call out across the hallway, dragging out the syllables.

"I love you, a bushel and a peck, a bushel and a peck, and a hug around the neck!" we used to sing, and she would scoop me up and never give me one kiss but fifteen or twenty.

If I knew I was being bad, which I most often did, I would ask, "Grandma, are you mad at me?"

"No, my dear," she would say. "Only dogs get mad."

Whenever my parents got mad at me, I would call Grandma.

"Grandma, I'm coming up," I would say.

"So she could spoil you," my mom pointed out.

Every Friday she would walk to the beauty parlor in Chinatown to get her hair done, and at dances, everyone could count on Lucy and Charlie to be dancing up a storm, dressed to the nines. But though she was fiercely loyal to my grandfather, she was also fiercely independent. She would walk a mile round-trip to Pathmark, the grocery superstore down on Cherry Street near Chinatown, all by herself, with her little red shopping cart in tow.

One day, after she brought home what turned out to be a carton of "strawberry-less" Turkey Hill strawberry-flavored ice cream, she promptly mailed a letter to the company expressing her disappointment, telling them they should call it "Lucky if You Find a Strawberry." She was very satisfied with herself when she received a calendar and coupons in the mail good for years to come and posted them proudly on the refrigerator.

We often cast Grandpa away to the little room where he could watch the horse races in his blue recliner, so Grandma and I could be alone. Or, if we wanted the little room, we sequestered him to the living room. He'd busy himself in the bathroom combing over the few strands of his white hair that still hung around, cleaning crumbs off of the dining room table, and shuffling around in slippers and a T-shirt that had several holes in it, refusing to wear the new ones everyone bought for him. Often, he could be found chasing me around with a comb trying to brush my giant mop of curly hair, or pick lint off my clothing.

Grandma and Grandpa never seemed to get along—she was usually pushing him out of the way with her arm and saying, "Get away, yeah?" One time, they were yelling so loudly at each other—I must have been four then—that I grabbed the phone, called my mom, and told her she had to come upstairs, quick, because Grandma was going to get a heart attack and die from all of the yelling.

I preferred when it was just she and I up there, in the warm house that always smelled good, where she praised me and clapped and laughed and watched and tickled and hugged and kissed. We would read the same books over and over—there was this book about an ice cream shop on the beach that only had three flavors—vanilla, chocolate, and strawberry—and the main character, some kid or an animal who could talk, kept asking for all of these alternative flavors, driving the ice cream man crazy. I can still hear her voice as she read it, with so much life, me squealing with delight. I found it so hysterical, for some reason, most likely because that main character was such a pain in the ass.

Grandma always made oatmeal the best way, with the flakes floating around in the milk among a good amount of sugar. I always complained when my mom made me lumpy old regular oatmeal; no matter how much sugar or milk I added, it wasn't the same. I didn't like red sauce, so while my mom and uncle fought over who got to take home the leftovers, I insisted on having plain bowtie pasta with butter.

Grandma let me sit on the countertop and grate the cheese for the Sicilian pizza she made every Friday. I would kick my little legs against the cabinets below and reach out and hug her around the neck and just babble on and on about whatever it is that goes on in the life of a five-year-old who is too smart for her own good.

We always picked up our Italian specialties from Di Palo's, because that was the only real, authentic Italian deli around. They had thinly sliced, velvety prosciutto sans the funny aftertaste, mozzarella, soppressata, and Italian bread that was just the right amount of crusty on the outside and soft on the inside.

The only time Grandma ever said anything that wasn't coated in sugar was when I somehow hurt myself while I was "acting out."

"God's punishing you," she'd say.

It felt so awkward and uncomfortable inside, I had to refute it immediately.

"No he's not!" I would cry, and launch into a Celine Dion song like some sort of panic move. My grandmother loved when I sang Celine Dion songs. Even now, I remember what it felt like inside my stomach to be able to hit those notes with total abandon, something I could never do now.

She took me to auditions for commercials and for singing parts in something or other, but I didn't take it too seriously. At the end of one audition, the woman came out and told my grandma, "She was great, but when I asked her what she wanted to be, she said 'a teacher.'"

Despite her disappointment at my lack of a showbiz career, I was still the constant light of her life. She read with me, practiced script writing with me, and dealt with the wrath of my frustration when I "didn't get it." She took me to Burger King before my ballet lessons, and we made friends with a girl named Isabel who worked behind the counter. Isabel used to sneak me free Hershey dessert pies. My grandma would give me five dollars to give to her, and when she wouldn't accept it, we made a fun game of trying to get her to take it.

* * *

As much as I didn't want to share my father with anyone, that went double for mom. My mother, by then, was no longer touchy-feely, fussy, or very affectionate at all. I did have one thing left, though: her attention.

Whenever we walked to the 2/3 train in the morning to head to kindergarten at the Early Childhood Center on Greenwich Street (which only went up to second grade then) I'd think, *we better not run into the fuzzy-haired man*. We'd pass shiny aluminum carts that left just enough space for someone standing inside to sell bagels, coffee, and pastries—"don't eat those, they're exposed all day," my mom would warn. We were always rushing, because I had spent twenty minutes jumping on the couch and tossing around my wardrobe options.

More often than not, on the subway platform, right at the bottom of the stairs, we *did* indeed run into the fuzzy-haired man, a guy who took his two sons to school at P.S. 234. He wore black glasses with thick frames, had wild, curl gray hair, and sometimes wore a black beret.

Here's why I hated the fuzzy-haired man, with his stupid conversation about schools and the weather: he would impose on my time with mom, and our train ride together.

"I'm going to tell Daddy," I would threaten, as if she were having sex with him right there in front of me.

We'd exit the train at Chambers and bustle down Duane Street, where the wind was so strong it almost blew me away.

When I got to kindergarten, there was more crying and clinging and consoling. By then, my mother had practically become like Houdini, having mastered the art of making her escape and quickly slipping away in a cloud of Jean Paul Gaultier perfume. After I was finished crying, I would meet with my reading buddy named Telly, who, to me, seemed the size of Chris Farley but was probably just a chubby second-grader at the time. We would fly through any number of picture books, and I'd loudly declare that we had to "pick up the harder books from the other classrooms," because I was so smart. Then, I'd tickle him.

Each week, we took the time to write and illustrate a page about one of our classmates. My book looked like this:

Helaina likes to hide in the bathroom during clean up time.

Helaina tries to kiss Lukas but Lukas doesn't like it.

Helaina likes to color her lips in magic marker and pretend its lipstick.

In my defense, those magic markers, the ones with the fat caps that smelled like Oranges or Chocolate, were begging for a run-in with my mouth. After my lipstick was in place, I would stand two-feet tall in a flower dress and sneakers that were filled with goo that changed into different colors when you pressed down—and I'd point to a boy.

"You're my boyfriend!" I would declare confidently, sidling up to sit on his lap as he tried to build a Lego-something-or-other on the desk.

I still remember the smell of the art room, the scent of dried paint and those brown paper towels you pulled out of the metal dispenser. It's a smell that years later, when I returned to the school to work as an after-school counselor in college, would bring me back to a time when I was completely enveloped in that world. The shimmer of sequins on the floor, the faded magic marker lines on the table—it was an all-consuming place that held great potential for a creative genius. Everyone else's drawings were good, and took them a long time, while I made ten drawings that were hastily scribbled, shouting "done!" each time.

At recess, I'd wander from group to group, always disinterested. I only wanted to be with the adults, and really, I only wanted to be with Grandma. This school stuff was all just a ridiculous placeholder. I had to take the school bus home even though Daddy easily could have picked me up, and I hated the bus. It was hot and loud, and we had to make all these stops before going home, which was so close. Sometimes people's parents weren't there and you had to wait *extra*, and sometimes I was hungry, or had a headache, and really needed to make it home in time to watch my shows.

Once in a while, Shane came over after school to play circus or Power Rangers, and, on one occasion, he broke my brand-new Skip-It. For some reason, I didn't cry. I just tied him to a chair and then tried to ride him like a pony. In hindsight, I guess it looked like some sort of weird dominatrix scene, which I'm sure explained the look on his grandfather's face when he came to pick him up. I did better with Shane than I did with most of the girls who were around, most likely because he would listen to whatever I said and did whatever I wanted. He was happy to watch *Zoobilee Zoo*, a show I was obsessed with, featuring a bunch of actors dressed as animal versions of themselves, singing their way through life's most complicated dilemmas.

The actor Ben Vereen played Mayor Ben, a tiger who existed to "lend a helping hand," but my favorite character was the pink musical kangaroo named Whazzat, who was kind of the coquette of the group. A close second was the thespian fox named Bravo who was always calling out, "Attention, please!" or "Places, everybody!" and clapping his paws together. Mayor Ben would explain things like how "movies weren't real, they're just pictures with stories." When the Zoo crew was about to embark on their own movie project, he broke into a song that went, "Did you make a mistake? Did you do something really dumb?" took a thirty-second choreographed solo dance break, and resumed by prancing around and crying, "People make mistakes!" He purred with joy, like the realization that people were fallible was the most exciting news he'd ever heard.

I lived by the motto, "play it again," when it came to tapes like the ones Mary-Kate and Ashley Olsen made. Their first video opened with them explaining how they're twins but that there was an easy way to tell them apart, because one of them was the cute one. They proceeded to launch into one a series of many tone-deaf songs, like "I Am the Cute One" followed by "Someday, I'd Like to be President," where they wreaked havoc on the town with a Bill Clinton look-alike. In other videos, the trench coat–clad twins solved mysteries as "super duper snoopers," and I watched them solve the same mystery over and over. I listened to the soundtrack to *The Lion King* on a loop. I felt deeply moved by songs like "Can You Feel the Love Tonight," relating, at age six, to the love in that song and counting down the days until I could feel it about someone.

* * *

My favorite place to sleep was at Aunt Fran's house.

Aunt Fran coached me, from a young age, to know that her neighborhood was "far more glamorous" than where we lived downtown. Her building had a doorman and carpeted hallways and pretty elevators. The sidewalks were cleaner, wider, and there was less garbage scattered around them. Her stove didn't work, which didn't matter because she never cooked anything, and my uncle's side of the bed, where I'd cuddle up to her to watch movies, always smelled like cigarettes. Aunt Fran had no kids of her own, so she'd take me out to lunch at places like Serendipity, and I always managed to come home with some new stuff, a book or a toy or a headband. At night, she would put all kinds of creams and powders on me after my bath, and I felt like a princess. I slept in her bed and she cuddled with me, holding me tight like a little spoon and a big spoon, until I fell asleep.

Aunt Fran met Uncle John at my parents' wedding at the Vista Hotel, right in the World Trade Center.

"You're going to hate him," my mom told my aunt about John, my dad's best friend, a veteran who had been deployed everywhere but Vietnam during the Vietnam War.

"You're going to hate her," my dad told John about Fran, my mother's maid of honor.

My parents were right—they kind of hated each other, but they also must have really loved each other, because they stayed together. After being engaged for fourteen years, they ended up getting married, without any of us there, at an Elvis chapel in Las Vegas.

I was ten at the time, and when I came home from school and saw how upset my grandmother was, I was furious.

"They eloped," she said sadly.

How *dare* they make Grandma sad, I thought.

"It's okay," I said to Grandma, putting my head on her shoulder. "You'll be at *my* wedding!"

Uncle John still loves to talk about the time we spent in the reclining chair in the small bedroom of my grandmother's apartment when I was a toddler. I'd sit on his lap while he watched football. I was mostly mesmerized by the moving colors, raising my hands in the air and shouting, "Touchdown!" whenever he grabbed my wrists, even though I had no idea what was happening.

He had a slim build and a tiny beer belly, lots of freckles, blue eyes, and pale skin. Like my father, he still has a full head of hair, even though he's pushing his seventh decade. It was always a surprise whether or not he'd have his mustache at the next get-together, and I could always count on him to fly me around the living room or the bar where he worked, his arm holding my tiny body up between my legs, his hand on my chest to prop me up. That flight never lasted long enough.

He loves to tell the story of how, when I was baptized, the church was about ninety-five degrees, and I was crying, and he had a broken rib from something or other, and he held me the entire time because I was quiet in his arms. His second favorite memory is of the time he and my parents went to Belmont Race Track, and my "mom and aunt were supposed to be watching me," and I started running downhill on a gravel ramp.

"If it wasn't for me grabbing the collar of your jumper and yanking you up just in time, you might look like a different person today, young lady," he says. "Your face was less than an inch from the floor, and you were going in for a nose dive."

Later, when I asked him questions about his time in the Army for a school paper, my uncle told me about the time he was driving an eighteen-wheeler truck on the Autobahn highway in Germany. A man in a smaller car next to him looked up at him, smiled, and drove right underneath him, using the truck to kill himself. He told me, also, about the time that he held his friend in his arms while he burned to death after a truck explosion.

On one occasion, we were walking down East Sixty-Fifth Street after dinner at John's Pizzeria (no relation) when a Chinese delivery person on a bike whizzed passed us down the sidewalk.

My uncle said, "Excuse me," and started to go down the sidewalk after him.

"John, not now, not in front of the baby," my aunt called out after him, even though I must have been eight years old.

He stopped, turned around, and came back with an angry look on his face.

"You're supposed to ride that in the street, asshole," he yelled back behind him. Then, just a bit more quietly, "I can't stand those fucking gooks."

After second grade, I transferred to an elementary school called P.S. 116 on Thirty-Third Street that had a gifted and talented program, and I referred to the other classes, the regular ones, as "the stupid classes." The "popular girls" wanted nothing to do with me in third grade, and I preferred to spend my time writing stories on our personal computer by using a story-building program with random stamp graphics. "Sexy Teenage Girls" and "A Singing Pizza" were among my titles, as well as "A Face in the Fudge," which won an honorable mention in a *Reading Rainbow* story contest. More than kids my own age, I was interested in my friend's baby siblings, whom I wanted to play with, take care of, and throw myself on the floor to make laugh.

I hated my fourth grade class, because this group of girls bullied me, making fun of my "white girl" attributes, criticizing everything I said or did. Worse still, I had contracted mononucleosis without knowing it until it was over. During those months where I had all of the symptoms and no actual diagnosis, I spent a lot of time in the nurse's office with crippling headaches, asking her to call my dad and begging everyone to just believe me, because something was really wrong. It wasn't until a blood test turned up the results months later that we even found out.

My saving grace that year was joining the school newspaper, writing articles about the condition of the girls' bathroom, our recent field trip, and a famous Judge named Leslie Crocker Snyder, who had come to speak to our class.

In fifth grade, I made a friend who had arthritis and got to take the elevator with her after lunch instead of the stairs with everyone else, and I won a research award at graduation for a feature article I wrote called "Hair Care You Can Bare," in which I interviewed two experts and did a ton of investigative reporting about egg yolk scalp treatments and how to detangle knots.

I had an on again, off again boyfriend named Matt, who I married, showed my boobs to, divorced, and remarried over a three-year period.

Back in my pink and white room, I would lie chest-down on the pink carpeting and wait for my favorite songs to come on the radio, pressing record as soon as the radio DJ stopped talking so I could capture the song on my cassette tape. Sometimes, I only got half the song, and often, I ended up with a tape full of song parts, not necessarily whole songs—some songs were on there twice. You had to be diligent about having that finger on the record button, or you missed out.

* * *

I liked Downtown Day Camp much more than I liked school.

I went there every summer from 1993 to 2001. The idea of sleepaway camp was out of the question for obvious reasons, and the camp, held in the P.S. 234 school building between Warren and Chambers Street, was a very close ride, or walk, from home.

In my first year, I "claimed" the coolest looking female counselor for my own. Sarah had what I would describe to my mom as a princess-face, long, curly blonde hair, and a body I knew even at age five was smokin' hot.

"She's sooooo sexy," I cooed.

When she offered to take me rollerblading, I almost plotzed.

She was going to take me for milkshakes at Burger King, and then we were going to skate around the complex like great pals.

When the big day came, I put on my pink kneepads, elbow pads, helmet, and skates, and parked myself right at the table, staring at the front door. It was 5:50, and she said she would come at six.

"Mommy, what time is it?" I asked.

"It's 5:58," she said.

"Mommy, what time is it?"

"It's 5:59."

"Mommy, what time is it?"

"It's six o'clock."

A few more minutes passed, and I started to worry.

"Maybe she was just saying she was going to come to be nice, honey. Or maybe she said she thought it *would* be fun, but she didn't mean she was coming," my mom said.

"No way," I said, secretly afraid that she wasn't coming, but feeling so *sure* she would show up, because she *promised*.

After however many more minutes passed, there was a ring at the doorbell, and I practically tripped over myself to get to the door.

It was her!

"Ok byeeeee!" I called behind me as I wheeled down the hallway, holding the wall as subtly and nonchalantly as possible. *Oh, this wall? Just making sure the internal beams are aligned properly.*

She took me to the Burger King downstairs and got me the large vanilla milkshake, a size I had never held before in my life. Then, we bladed around in circles for an hour on this patch of concrete by the community room.

I don't remember what we talked about, but I know she was paying attention to me the *entire* time, saying "Wow!" whenever I did something on my skates that I considered to be a trick, and laughing at all of my jokes. This was my idea of heaven on earth.

When we got back home—me all flustered and puffing with delirious happiness, clunking down the hallway and dragging my Velcro skates behind me—my parents tried to hand her a $20, for her time and for the milkshakes, but she wouldn't accept it.

Wow, I thought. *She just likes spending time with me!*

As I got older, summers were full of sleepovers in which my dad was delegated to the couch, sitting with the camcorder in one hand as Gina and I performed pop standards of the time, like Monica and Brandy's "The Boy Is Mine," NSYNC's "Bye Bye Bye," Britney Spears's "Baby One More Time," and anything that the Spice Girls ever recorded. Outside of those sleepovers at my house, I couldn't "do" most sleepovers because I was afraid of the dark and didn't want to risk the off chance that there would actually be sleeping involved.

Gina and I made trouble at camp every year, along with Liana, a girl we accepted into our duo in the summer of 1997. We never wanted to stay with our group, so we left the room to go put on performances for other counselors who were taking their breaks, eating french fries, and looking at their beepers. We amused ourselves by dangling counselors' MetroCards out the window and taking our makeup and nail polish to the field during outdoor time and charging five cents for makeovers. When the counselors got wise to our plan and said we had to give the shiny nickels back, we ran to the soda machine in the snack room and shoved them in there before they could stop us, listening to the delicious clank of a Fresca landing at the bottom.

Our little group of Southbridge Towers campers got chauffeured directly to and from camp in a silver van known as Van 4, which they'd call out at the end of the day after the first three yellow buses headed out. I loved that van. It was like a tropical vacation from the stinky school bus I had to take during the school year, the one that made a trillion stops around the city before just getting across town to Fulton Street.

Sometimes, the cute van driver, whoever he was that year, would let me sit up front, control the radio (why was there so much *talking* in the morning?), or kiss him on the cheek.

As much as I enjoyed imprinting on a male counselor every year, it was the girl counselors, like Sarah, that I was really crazy about. I identified so strongly with them because I'd always felt like a teenager trapped in a tiny body, in a tiny life. I may have lived for shows like *Rugrats* and *Gullah Gullah Island* and had way too many Beanie Babies, but while that part of me embraced being a kid, I always wanted to be older. One day at a barbecue with my aunt's drinking, smoking New Jersey friends, I declared, "I want to be an adult."

A roar of, "Oh honey, no you don't!" rose up from the cloud of cigarette smoke and beer breath, and I remember thinking then, even at that young age of six, that they were wrong—I knew exactly what I was saying. I knew that there was responsibility that came with being an adult, and I wanted it. I wanted all of it.

Still, I slept in my parents' bed, waking up every morning to the radio alarm, which played freestyle dance music on KTU. All the while, I knew that being an adult would be better than being a kid, because you had more control over what you got to do.

* * *

I was only half Catholic, but I had received my First Holy Communion at age seven. I went to Sunday School at St. Andrew's Church, a ten-minute walk from home, if you were walking at a leisurely pace. My dad often pointed out that since my mother and grandmother never went to church, he didn't necessarily understand why I had to go.

But every Sunday at 10:00 a.m., I met up with Gina and a couple of other friends, took a lesson in a small group, and sat through Mass, all the while hoping I would get to spend time with Gina afterward, that her parents weren't bringing her somewhere else to do something else. I looked forward to seeing her every week, especially after we began going to separate schools after second grade. I loved the Church Christmas party and the Secret Santa, I loved Father Jim, who was a "cool" priest, and I loved putting a dollar in the collection basket as I pondered some of the things I was learning.

Does the wine really turn to blood? The fish, the bread, was it true? Why doesn't he do this now? Why doesn't God send people to do this right now and feed hungry families?

My dad told me that I didn't need to go to church to talk to God, and he was the only one who didn't kneel when he attended services, which I found embarrassing. But when I learned that Jesus was Jewish, it softened the blow.

When I got my first white plastic rosary, I "said it" on the 2/3 train platform on my way to Macy's with my mom. I frantically tried to get through it before the train got there, afraid something bad would happen to me on the way if I didn't. It was exhausting, but I believed that I just needed to get to the cross, and I would be ok. At night, I prayed the same way, like if I didn't, I would be personally responsible for the suffering of the neglected and abused animals, hungry children, and something bad happening to Grandma.

* * *

One day when I was ten, my dad and I were walking down John Street when we passed a sheet over a giant lump, surrounded by yellow caution tape.

"Daddy, what is that?" I asked.

"A jumper," he said.

"What's a jumper?"

"He killed himself."

"Why?" I asked.

"I don't know, honey."

He went on to explain that if you try to commit suicide and it doesn't work, they take you to jail.

"What! Why?"

"Suicide is illegal because you're taking a member away from society, and the government also sees that as taking tax-paying money away from them."

Grandma always used to tell us that when she started to "go" we should just do something called "pulling the plug." My aunt, too, still proclaims that she is going to "take the pills" and "live La Vida Loca" right up to the end. Throughout all of my grandma's cooing and kissing, one thing always gnawed at me: for a small kid, I had this unusually pervasive fear that Grandma was going to die. *What if she dies now, what if she dies tomorrow, what will I do?* Some nights, I would cry and cry, worrying about when Grandma was going to die.

One day in fifth grade, I picked up Grandma's phone when it rang—the cordless one in the small room, as she picked up the white phone in the kitchen.

"There is a lump . . . ." is all I heard someone tell my grandma.

I knew what that meant from some TV show I saw, and I immediately burst into tears when Grandma came into the small room.

"I don't want you to die!" I wailed.

"Grandma isn't going anywhere," she said, kissing the top of my head.

A few weeks later, when Grandma was scheduled for surgery, my mother brought me to school on the subway instead of making me take the bus. I always, *always* had to take the stupid bus, so I knew this was bad. I cried in public on the train, feeling, for the first time, very self-conscious while crying. My mom explained to the teacher why I was upset, and my teacher reminded me that I was supposed to go sit in on another class for an article I was writing for the school newspaper.

"You should go," my mom said, nodding.

I nodded too, took out my notebook, and went. The assignment was the only thing that kept me going, the only thing that got me to stop crying. It was the only thing powerful enough to pull me out of my sadness and into the present.

At the end of fifth grade, I faced my fear and went on a mandatory, two-night trip to Bear Mountain with the rest of the school. We got stuck in the rain, and I had to slosh around in wet socks and sneakers, which made my feet shrivel up and caused painful sores to form. (My mom had tried to buy me special waterproof boots before the trip for eighty dollars, but it turned out the salesman was wrong and they weren't waterproof, so we returned them, after she got a major run-around, between phone calls to the manufacturer and several trips to the store.) We got to see a guy holding a big snake, and on the last night, we had a dance. It started off as square dancing, for some reason—not exactly the official state dance of New York—then turned into an actual dance, where we all shook our butts to Sisqo's "The Thong Song" and Madonna's "Music."

That summer, during our sleepovers, Gina and I danced to all of the female R&B groups: Mya's "Case of the Ex," Toni Braxton's "He Wasn't Man Enough," Brandy and Monica's "The Boy Is Mine." From Gina, I learned what a condom was, I learned that wearing bracelets on your biceps was cool, I learned that a dick looked like a pickle, and I counted down the days until I would have to go to middle school, which I didn't even want to go to. I didn't like *any* of the middle schools I toured, so I figured, why don't I just pick the one that's closest to home?

* * *

I had always loved back-to-school shopping—it helped ease the sting of the sadness of going back. The Lisa Frank folders, the stickers, the pencil cases covered in dogs and unicorns, the brand-new notebooks, the "nice" pens that wrote in liquid ink, the fresh pencils just waiting to be sharpened. I.S. 89 itself, however, was all wrong: for one thing, the kids sat on the floor, in a circle, instead of at desks like they were supposed to. But since my dad had helped get the school built (he was always involved in that community volunteer board stuff, and he knew the principal), I felt like I had a bit of an edge.

Every morning, on the walk to school with Ann, Charles, and Nadine, we left extra time so Charles could feed the squirrels in City Hall Park. Nadine and I would swing our violin cases in place and roll our eyes while he called them over. City Hall Park was still lush then, with winding paths, a fountain, and a statue of Nathan Hale that my grandfather used to point out to me every time we passed it on the way home from Buckle My Shoe.

"Who's that?" he would ask.

"Nathan Hale!" I would proclaim, not knowing who the hell Nathan Hale was.

"Nathan Hale!" my grandpa would cry, and he would chuckle, which he didn't do much of.

Along the way to school, Charles would sing show tunes or recap entire episodes of shows like *The Simpsons*, retelling everything quickly, with more speed and volume as he got more exited and closer to the punch line, and I always said "Heh" to be polite.

Here are the key things I remember about sixth grade.

A kid named Tyler, who I peed my pants with, literally, in kindergarten, made fun of the combination lock I used for my locker because it was pink and used to be my dad's. A Filipino boy named Henry had an insatiable crush on me and I didn't have one back. I had developed a crush on a kid named Peter over the summer while in camp. He used to lick his knees, didn't have a crush on me back, and I got to see him every day.

"Ew," Gina had said. "He's so not your type."

I didn't really have a type, and chose not to "crush" on celebrity boys. What was the point? I wanted someone I could actually have, but the pickins were slim at I.S.89 that year.

One morning, on the way to school, Ann told us a story about how an angel had pushed her out of the way of a falling block of cement while construction was being done on a nearby building. I thought she was kind of crazy, and Nadine made a face, but secretly, I half believed her, because I believed that angels were real.

There was a small special-ed class of about five kids at I.S. 89, and I always got upset when people made fun of them or instigated trouble with them, feeling weird, like something was wrong with me because it deeply bothered me and it didn't seem to bother anyone else.

Nelly's "Country Grammar" was a big song on the radio, as was Missy Elliot's "Work It," but my dad always turned it off in the car, because he hated rap, and I would groan.

The first time we were allowed to go out into the neighborhood for lunch, I went with my new friends, Jasmine and Ali. We headed down Chambers Street, and I suddenly decided I wanted a burrito, even though I had never tried one before. Since they wanted pizza, I told them I'd meet them on the corner in five minutes.

I carefully counted out the cash and waited in the darkly lit, empty Burritoville restaurant.

When my food was ready, I searched for them up and down the block, but they were nowhere to be found.

I sat on a ledge and took a bite of my burrito, and it was awful. I threw it out.

I started to cry, sitting outside the gate of P.S. 234, and a woman came up to me and asked, "Are you ok?"

I told her my friends had left me and that I couldn't find them. She walked me back to school, where the eighth grade math teacher found me whimpering in the lobby. She invited me up to her room and told me I could stay until lunch was over. When I approached them at gym, they shrugged and simply said, "We couldn't find you," making my tragedy seem like nothing at all. I remember feeling, as I always had, that everyone else was friends in way that nobody was friends with me.

It was the year Shane started calling me "Helaina Ho-vitz—'Ho', if you know what I mean." The fact that people happened to keep emphasizing that "o" was clearly being half Jewish's fault.

Later that year I developed a new crush on a kid named Will, who was at my "math table" and didn't believe in anything. His family, he said, were Atheists, and just celebrated holidays for fun.

"Do you really think there's someone in the sky watching over you?" he laughed.

Yes, I did. In fact, to me, God was the only thing that was hypothetically keeping everything ok in the world. He watched over you and protected you and kept you safe, if you were good.

It made me uneasy when Will laughed at me, and being uneasy made me even more uneasy. *If I truly believe, can he make me feel doubtful? If God doesn't exist, who's protecting me?*

When it was time for me to receive Holy Confirmation, my teacher told me I'd have to renounce all other religions. I said I wasn't going to do that, I liked being both. Despite the crisis over the pronunciation of my last name, I was not going to "renounce" my father's traditions, my dead grandfather's

Haggudah, the electric menorah perched on the window by our dining room table in December.

"Well, then, you'll go to hell," she said.

After Mass was over that day, my mom walked me home past the J&R music store, where a bunch of people were waiting in line.

"What are you guys waiting for?" my mom asked.

"NSYNC tickets," someone said.

"Oh, Mommy, can we?" I asked. I had never been to a concert before.

"Sure," she said. After about an hour, my dad showed up— my mom had just gotten a cell phone, so she must have called him—and I told him, while we waited, "Daddy, I don't want to go back there. I don't need my Confirmation."

"Okay, honey," he said, without asking questions, and we were second in line from the front when they announced the tickets had sold out and they wouldn't be adding any more shows.

We had our own rituals, as a family. Friday night was when we ordered takeout, usually Chinese food, sometimes pizza. Mom and I watched TGIF on ABC, which had *Boy Meets World*, some show called *Popular*, *Sabrina the Teenage Witch*, and a show about a Genie who becomes human and is totally baffled by everyday things, like the mind-boggling urge to pee that he has no idea how to address. Saturday night was for SNICK, or Saturday Night Nickelodeon, which had shows like *All That*, *Keanan and Kel*, and *The Amanda Show*. I was starting to also really enjoy a show called *The Saddle Club* about a group of equestrian preteens just trying to navigate the throws of life while growing up in the horse world.

What I did not enjoy was Disney's version of the diary of Anne Frank, which aired in May 2001. It was Disney, so I figured it would be educational and "safe," even if they did plan to tell "The Whole Story" picking up where her diary left off.

I loved that diary when I read it in fifth grade. Anne Frank said that despite everything, she still believed there was good in people, and there would be many times in the years to come that I picked up the book and read parts of it.

> *Writing in a diary is a really strange experience for someone like me. Not only because I've never written anything before, but also because it seems to me that later on neither I nor anyone else will be interested in the musings of a thirteen-year-old school girl. Oh well, it doesn't matter. I feel like writing.*

Anne knew any day could be the day—and then, it was—and she still had hope in the world.

> *It's difficult in times like these: ideals, dreams and cherished hopes rise within us, only to be crushed by grim reality. It's a wonder I haven't abandoned all my ideals, they seem so absurd and impractical. Yet I cling to them because I still believe, in spite of everything, that people are truly good at heart.*

As soon as Anne and her father, played by Ben Kingsley, were torn away from each other after arriving at the camps, the violence with which I burst into spastic tears shocked even me. My mom tried to call me back in and get me to finish watching, but I knew plenty about the Holocaust and knew I wouldn't be able to watch anymore.

That night, I pictured them ripping me away from my parents to starve and die alone, watching others suffer. I spent the night curled into a ball, crying, and rocking back and forth, raw with grief.

The next day at school, this girl, Paige, said with a laugh, "Did you see when they were all barfing in the cattle cars?" She was kind of weird, kept to herself, had Argentinian parents who lived in a huge SoHo loft and let her and her friends write in Sharpie on her wall and eat whatever junk food they wanted.

Her reaction to the movie disturbed me for the rest of the week.

In early September 2001, we were coming back from a trip to Colonial Williamsburg when I pointed out the Twin Towers as they came back to view.

"There they are," I said. "Almost home!"

"You're right, baby, that means we're almost home," said my dad.

As we inched toward the Holland Tunnel, the news on the radio recounted that a singer named Aaliyah died in a plane crash, the president, George Bush, had just detailed his defense priorities at the American Legion, and I thought dreamily about how I was just a year away from finally becoming a teenager.

CHAPTER THREE

We are going to go live right now to a picture of the World Trade Center, where I understand—do we have it? No we do not. We have a breaking story though, we're going to come back with that in just a moment.
First, this is Today *on NBC.*

—Matt Lauer, *Today*,
September 11, 2001, 8:51 a.m.

Don't look up, don't look back, just keep going!" Ann shouted as we jostled through the crowd. I was tiny, so I had to fight my way through walls of people. At eye level, all I saw were peoples' backs, their arms, their necks. Cameras and backpacks were slamming against my face. That feeling of being knocked around in a crowd was one that I'd experienced so many times as a small child in a big city, but it had never felt like this before. Before, it was fun. An adventure.

Now, it suddenly felt like I couldn't breathe, and maybe I couldn't. In fact, I felt like I was going to faint.

Charles kept turning around to look at the Towers over his shoulder. When I tried to look away, my gaze met people packed shoulder to shoulder, looking up and taking pictures, watching dark things falling off of the sides of the buildings.

As we pushed through the crowds of people, I kept wondering, *Why are they all just standing there, watching?*

We were at the corner of Chambers Street, standing almost underneath the Towers when I turned right and saw something fall and hit a car, making a snapping noise on impact.

"Oh my God, they're jumping!" Ann said.

What? Who's jumping?

I kept hearing similar sounds, but still couldn't see much. Some reminded me of the crashing and grinding of garbage trucks, others, of a heavy box suddenly dropped on the ground, others still, hail hitting a window, only heavier, like a giant bag full of nails, creaking, slamming, booming.

Maybe they're small explosions. Are bombs being dropped on us?

Eventually, the crowd disbursed a little, and we began to change direction on Chambers Street, going straight toward City Hall, while everyone else moved to the left to head uptown. Ann suggested we duck into a pizza place to get a plastic bag for my notebooks and pencil case, so we did, then tried to continue down Chambers Street, which would lead us to the Municipal Building.

I had no idea what we were going to do, but I knew I had to stay close to Ann.

A policewoman standing in the center of the street abruptly stopped us, shouting along with other police, "You can't go down there! We don't know if there are bombs in the cars!"

If you need help, find a police officer. Tell him your name and address.

It was close to 10:00 a.m. when we tried the next block, but another officer who saw my plastic bag, barked, "Suspicious package!" and stuck her hand out to stop us. She didn't even bother looking in the bag.

"But we live this way!" I said in disbelief. "We live there!"

"Too bad," she said. "You have to go uptown."

Just then, a sound—one, then another—rumbled and rippled through the street. The noise shifted, erupting into millions of sharp pieces of chalk screeching in unison against the black-board of the sky.

Boom.

Boom.

Boom.

The sky was suddenly full of gray smoke, and it was gaining on us.

Where is it coming from?

"Kids, pull your shirts up over your faces and run!" yelled Ann.

We turned and ran without looking back. People everywhere were doing the same. Middle-aged men ran alongside seven-year-olds and toddlers, all screaming and crying in unison. My entire body was throbbing, my feet, my face, my stomach, one huge pulse. *More buildings are being bombed. Fighter jets are shooting at us.*

I felt very dizzy, and suddenly I could feel my heart pulsing on the outside of my shirt at a speed so fast it scared me. *I shouldn't be able to feel that without touching my hand to my chest.* My vision suddenly blurred into nothingness as I tried to run as fast as I could. Confused, I ran a few more steps, cursed myself for wearing a skirt, and turned to see one lone woman in a magenta-colored skirt-suit covering her mouth and running toward us, screaming, "Oh my God!" abandoning her high-heeled shoe, her purse knocking against her side as she ran.

You'll see Mommy again after school. You have to let her go now. Say, "Bye, Mommy! See you later!"

* * *

The next few minutes are blank in my memory, a void where the next part should be—but Ann and Charles remember.

Voices shouted, "Get inside! Quick!"

A group of maintenance men and janitors pulled the three of us inside a building with a giant lobby, where we waited a few minutes for the smoke to clear.

When we stepped back outside, we saw people running, stumbling, and sobbing. I looked down and saw what everyone was tripping over: underneath at least three inches of beige ash were dozens of shoes, bags, and backpacks. Everything had been abandoned.

That's how fast everyone is running.

For the first time since we left school, I saw my face reflected in a dark store window, and only then did I realize I was crying, that the top of my shirt was wet with tears. For a moment, all of the noise stopped. There was a look in my eye I had never seen before, whites of my eyes that I didn't know existed. I looked so grim and so forlorn amid the white ashes whirling around us. Seeing my reflection didn't make anything feel real; it confirmed that this had to be a nightmare. I looked like I was already dead, a ghost coming to a terrifying realization.

As the three of us began to run again, my ankle-length khaki green skirt constricted my steps to six-inch strides and my clogs irritated the skin on the sides of my feet and my toes. I tried to move faster. *I'm going to die because of the outfit I picked out today.* We slowed, then started running, then slowed down again.

Mobs of people were running past Church Street and Broadway, women and men, black and white, too old to run and too young to understand. Some of them were bleeding, some were wheezing, a few were vomiting, but many were just screaming, covered in white, splattered in red. They all ran uptown together, arms flailing. I desperately tried to cling to Ann. We could barely push through all of them—we were the only ones going the opposite way.

If you leave me, I'll die.

There was an unspoken understanding between us all that no matter how dangerous it was, we had to get home. Grandma and Grandpa were home. Home was the only way Mom and Dad would be able to find me.

If they're still alive.

All of those years of my mother coaxing me out of her arms as I cried and grabbed at her before school started, came down to this moment.

"We're all going to die," Charles kept saying. "We're all going to die." He stated it, then he screamed it, then he mumbled it, and then he would start over again. Each time he said it, my fear became more and more real. Soon, I believed him. All signs pointed to the end, and I finally started to accept that it was all over.

Ann and Charles will die quickly, and I'll be all by myself bleeding from my head.

No, we're going to be taken hostage by the people who are doing this, sent to concentration camps to be tortured, like in The Diary of Anne Frank.

We changed our route once again and headed down Duane Street to police headquarters, right by the courthouses and St. Andrew's Church. We passed firefighters and police officers dragging battered people, holding them upward. I couldn't tell if they were alive or already dead. We arrived at another checkpoint near the Municipal Building to find seven or eight police officers standing there.

"We want to go to the church," Ann insisted, thinking it would be a way in.

"You have to go uptown," the police barked, motioning frantically with their arms.

Under any other circumstances, we all would have turned around, authority-respecting folks that we were. But scared, exhausted, and desperate, we persisted, trying to move past them. In turn, the officers all locked arms and formed a human wall, creating a barrier with their bodies to protect Police Plaza from the three of us. We turned back toward the courts, lost with so many others in a whirlwind of dust, pieces of paper, shoes and screams, screams unlike any that I had never heard before.

I had also never heard God's name said aloud so many times, and yet it seemed that he was the first to go missing in so many people's lives.

* * *

As everyone else ran *from* whatever was happening, I was still determined to run *to* it, whatever it was, because I had to get to Grandma.

Did I remember to tell her I love her?

I thought I was going to somehow protect her when I got there, and, at the same time, I had a horrible feeling that it would be too late.

"Helaina, keep your shirt over your face," Ann kept reminding me. There was dust and ash everywhere.

Parents and big kids were stuffing little kids' heads underneath their shirts. A man ten feet in front of us on the street clutched his arm, his face twisted up in pain, fell to his knee, and then hit the floor.

Who's going to call 911 for him? How's he going to get help? He's going to die alone, in terror, buried under ashes, to the sound of screams.

Ann came up with a new plan to try and sneak down Worth Street through Chinatown and circle down to the East River. At the corner of Oliver and Madison Streets, a few blocks from the Smith Public Housing Projects, we stopped at a bodega, a small hole-in-the-wall store that sold lottery tickets, brand-name baked goods wrapped in cellophane, and cigarettes. The store was still open. Ann said we should buy water—I hadn't realized I was thirsty until then, but my throat was aching from the dust and the running. At that point, I could have been missing a foot and I'm not sure I would have noticed.

Through the doorway, we saw another plume of smoke fill the sky.

Then, we heard what seemed to be the entire city shaking and rattling as if hit by an earthquake. The lines of the doorframe became wavy, the way that gasoline makes everything on the horizon behind it appear fluid like waves.

Mobs of people ran past the store, screaming, "Run for your life!"

We stayed in the store, each one of us frozen. I looked at Ann and swallowed hard. It was like an icy cold hand suddenly grabbed the back of my neck and began to squeeze.

For some reason, at that moment, I declared, "I'm going to become a nun if I make it out of this alive!" I didn't fully understand what a nun did or didn't do, but I knew that they were somehow close to God, special and protected. I reached for Ann's hand. Charles held her other hand, and we waited for the smoke to clear, though I don't know for how long, and then left the store.

The procession of people covered in blood and ashes, mouths open and limbs thrashing in all directions, continued to hurry past. Whatever had happened seemed like it had ended—it was quiet except for the sound of coughing and sirens.

My hands were wet and I was sweating, but I suddenly went cold. My muscles tightened, and I felt many things at once. I felt like I was holding my breath for an eternity. My shoulders tingled as the fear rippled down my back. I felt dizzy but startlingly alert. I had never been more awake, more aware, in my life. I felt like I had been kidnapped, blindfolded, tied to a chair, and forced to listen to other people screaming out in pain and the sound of chainsaws gearing up, not knowing what was next for me.

We sat on a bench in a small park in the Smith Projects, waiting for Ann to tell us what to do next. Everything was blurring together: gray smoke, cement, cops, cars, wallets, shoes, water bottles. We still had no idea what the hell was going on, and we were, as we had been the whole time, so close to home.

My thoughts returned to my parents.

Are they alive?

Is this happening all over the city?

There was nothing to do but wait where we were; we could not, for a while, run toward our buildings, because that was the direction that the smoke was coming from.

My grandparents were so close and yet worlds away.

I'm not even going to get to say goodbye.

I started to silently pray.

God, I'm sorry I stopped praying, but please . . .

I couldn't get past please. I didn't know where to start. I didn't know what to ask for. Worst of all, I had a feeling it didn't really matter. Whatever was happening was clearly still happening, and whoever *they* were, *they* weren't going to stop until we were all dead.

I used my hands to wipe my eyes and my nose, again forgetting to pull my black shirt back up over my face. Once the smoke began to clear, slowly fading gray to white, we headed to South Street. We couldn't turn back now. I looked up at the FDR Drive overhead as we walked along the water underneath it, squinting to see one abandoned car, then another. Through a gap in the layer of white ash I could make out the color of the convertible: blue. The driver's door was left open and the top was left down. Some people were huddling next to car radios, but most were walking quickly uptown.

There was no traffic on the FDR, under the FDR, on neighboring streets. The day had fallen silent but for sporadic sobs and the faint murmur. The city had stopped. I listened for more sounds, terrified of what I might hear and what it would mean. I thought bombs—or worse—would go off on the Brooklyn Bridge, City Hall, Wall Street, the Courthouses, all within blocks of our buildings. And although I was with Ann and Charles, I felt entirely alone.

We kept walking, hoping there would be no more cops to stop us.

We looked from Peck Slip to South Street, and I shielded my eyes with my hands and linked arms with Charles, who was still holding Ann's hand. I would have given anything to at least know what was happening.

"Helaina, please cover your face, don't breathe this in," Ann pleaded.

I want to go home. I want to go home.

A bald man in spectacles wheezed and coughed violently into a handkerchief as he stumbled toward the East River. He was covered head to toe in ashes, barely able to see. Debris flew off of his shoulders in the breeze he created by rushing past us.

"God bless you," Ann said to him, her lips quivering before her face collapsed in on itself and she let tears fall.

I thought it was only a matter of time before we became part of the ashes that covered the neighborhood, scattered across the water, or brushed onto a curb by a street sweeper, down a drain.

But, miraculously, the path was clear. Ann's building, 100 Beekman Street, was the first one on our square block, near Peck Slip and Pearl Street, but she insisted on taking me home first.

I didn't know what home meant now, or what it would look like, but I knew we were finally going to make it.

We walked past Wolf's Diner, past the trees planted in the middle of the block, past the bar where all the neighborhood drunks gathered, through the tiny tunnel that led right to my front door. People were packed shoulder to shoulder in the lobby. It was dark, and among all of them, I recognized only two people. Everyone looked like they had rolled around in sawdust. We headed for the stairs, and I ran up the steps that I had climbed so many times before, running away from home up to Grandma's house.

When I pushed open the staircase door, I saw Grandma at the end of the hall, standing in the doorway of her apartment, holding the white chorded phone to her ear.

"She's here, Paul!" Grandma cried into the phone. "She's here! Oh my God!"

She was already sobbing, and I started to cry. So did Ann and Charles.

I ran to her, and she hugged me harder than I thought possible. She kissed me twelve times in a row, just like when I was little. Grandpa was standing next to her, hugging Charles, hugging Ann, hugging me.

"If it wasn't for you, she'd be dead," Grandma kept telling Ann.

"No, I put them in harm's way by taking them out of school . . ." Ann said.

My grandmother gently thrust the phone to my ear, smoothing my hair and kissing my head as I assured my dad that I was ok. There was this sense that time was limited— the dark lobby, the elevators out, Devin's cell phone that had stopped working. We quickly called my mother next. She was still at work.

Through tears she asked, "Are you okay, baby?"

She'd never called me that before, and never would again.

"I'll get down there as soon as I can," she sobbed. Then the phone line went dead.

Charles and Ann kissed my grandmother goodbye. She thanked them again, profusely, and then they were gone.

It was 11:00 a.m., but if you had told me that ten hours had passed, I would have believed you.

I turned toward the TV, which was showing the same images over and over. The planes hitting, from this angle, now that angle, freeze-framed, in slow motion, now from closer up. Over and over and over.

And Over.

And Over.

And Over.

Then, they fell down, one then the other. They just . . . fell.

Finally, I understood. *That's what we were running from all morning. That's where the dust was coming from.*

I picked up the remote and flicked through the stations. My neighborhood was on every single one, and yet, where that same view should have been right outside of the window a few inches away from my face, I could see nothing but black.

Then, new images surfaced, sending a cold, heavy pit of fear into my stomach. The Pentagon had also been hit, and yet another plane had been hijacked. Planes were destroying the entire country.

This is going to go on all day.

The world is ending.

I'm never going to see my parents again.

I stopped on CBS and saw that the *Price is Right* was on, the only entertainment program still running in the middle of everything. I peeled a banana and forced myself to eat it. I tried to look out of the window in the living room, the one that faced Beekman Street and the Twin Towers, but I still couldn't see anything. For an hour that's all I could see. Darkness.

I wandered in and out of each room, and, with shaking hands, picked up the books that I used to make Grandma read over and over: *Bert and Ernie in Don't Forget the Oatmeal, Mad about Madeline, The Book of Mermaids*. Though only a few hours had passed, I saw that my childhood was now far away, millions of years behind me. The safety of these books, and of this house, of this neighborhood, of the city, of the world, had dissolved.

I sat at the table and thought about all of the things I'd never get to do: walk to school or take the subway alone, get the puppy I'd always wanted, get my period, fall in love. Gruesome and horrific images flooded my twelve-year-old brain.

What if I become an orphan?

What if someone dumps my parents' bodies outside our apartment door?

What if Grandma dies first, and I lay dying next to her, and that's how it ends?

I tried shouting "ha!" the way my father taught me to do when I got scared as a child, but it didn't work.

The sky, the air, the view outside the window, and the view inside my head, was black. There was nothing to make the fear stop.

The next two hours, along with whatever Grandma and Grandpa were saying or doing, do not exist in my memory.

* * *

Around 2:00 p.m., the blackness gave way to a dusty beige storm. The first thing I saw was a man wearing a gas mask, standing alone in front of New York Downtown Hospital, handing out flimsy fabric facemasks to whoever passed by. I later found out that ambulances were taking everyone to St. Vincent's on Twelfth Street, but over eight hundred people had walked downtown to this emergency room covered in ashes. The streets were empty of vehicles except for the odd MTA bus letting off groups of people.

Grandma gave me the extra key to our apartment downstairs so I could go close all of the windows, but the damage had already been done. The kitchen table was covered with a fine layer of what looked like sawdust, as were the beds and the floors. But it wasn't sawdust, as we were to discover later. Our couch and our beds were the final resting places for people we did not know, whose dusty remains had blown in through the windows.

The TV had been left on in the living room, and I turned to see the freeze-framed image of a man jumping out of the Tower, a white marker circling his body in case it was in any way unclear that this man was committing suicide.

Was that the man I heard earlier?

I went back upstairs and kept checking for my mother out of the same window I used to look out of when I was little, waiting to spot her coming home from work. I would sit on the thin ledge, Grandma protecting me from falling by standing behind me. We would watch for her every day, and when I finally saw Mom walking toward our building, her red coat, her tote bag, her purse, a shopping bag full of something, I would push my face up against the screen of the open window and scream, "MOOOOOMMM-AYYYY!" and she would look up and wave, along with a few other startled passerby.

I looked, and looked, and looked, and with every passing moment, I grew more afraid that she was not coming home. But around 3:00 p.m., the doorbell rang, and I nearly flew into the other room.

"Mommy!"

There was my mother, looking exhausted, holding her purse and her tote bag. I was expecting her to throw her stuff down and scoop me up in her arms, having thought that I was dead.

When I was little, I always asked my mom what she would do if anything ever happened to me. *"I wouldn't want to live anymore."*

She opened her arms to hug me, holding on for just a second longer than she normally would have, and when she let go, she had an exasperated look on her face.

"You have no idea what I had to go through to get downtown."

* * *

She had walked into her office building on Fifty-Second and Madison to find people sobbing, someone screaming. When she walked into the conference room where the TV was on, she almost fainted.

"That's my daughter's school! My parents are down there!"

She went down the hall to her desk to put her stuff down, and heard everyone scream again. A second plane hit. Everyone began to flee the office.

"If you need to leave, leave," said her boss.

But my mother hadn't heard from me, so she wasn't going anywhere.

She called my dad, who said that the I.S. 89 administration stopped picking up the phones, and that when he spoke to Grandma after rumors started swirling about a first plane, he figured she could walk over and go get me, in case school let out. He, like many people, thought it had been a helicopter. She called Grandma, who, luckily, had not gone to get me, but hadn't heard from me either.

Then came the collapse.

"They're falling! They're falling!" people were screaming.

"What do you mean they're falling?" she shrieked. My mother thought I was dead, and so she, too, was dying inside. Everyone was trying to console her as she cried, holding her head in her hands, but there was no use.

As soon as she got the call from me at 11:00 a.m., she tried to get on the train.

"Sorry, uptown is running, downtown isn't," police told her.

My mother, who is very claustrophobic, braced herself to face her fear, but had to let three MTA city buses pass by on Third Avenue because they were literally packed to the brim. She faced her nightmare and pushed on to a fourth bus when she saw a space open up, between people running off, running on, going in the back way, all sorts of chaos.

When the bus got to Union Square the bus driver said, "Everybody off, no busses past Fourteenth Street."

"How am I going to get downtown?" she asked the driver.

"I don't know, lady," he said. "But it's not going to be by bus."

She began walking, sweating, feeling faint because she hadn't eaten.

In heels, she walked miles down Bowery, where they were giving out cups of water by the Bowery Rescue Mission, a homeless shelter.

She got to Police Plaza, showed her ID, and was told she couldn't go through.

She tried to push through them and they started shouting at her.

"No! No! Get her out of here!" they said as they pushed her away.

She sat on the steps and began to cry again.

Eventually, she looked up at the line of people and followed it until she saw where they were coming from, the Smith Projects, and walked down Pearl Street, the same way we had.

* * *

I kissed Grandma goodbye and told her we'd be back soon as Mom and I walked down to our apartment.

"Don't touch anything," she said when we got there, noticing where I had already ran a finger through the ashes on the table.

We still had electricity within the apartment, so I put in a video tape, Shelley Duvall's "Fairy Tale Theatre." It was *Little Red Riding Hood.* I had this faint hope that a distraction would take my mind off things, but deep down, it seemed absolutely absurd, like trying to mail a package in a burning box.

Five minutes into watching the video, the power went out. It was 4:00 p.m.

We decided to see if, by some small miracle, the payphone across the street still worked so we could speak to Daddy, who was still in Staten Island. We grabbed our pink bath towels and wrapped them around our faces and our heads, so that only our eyes were peaking out. When we emerged from the lobby, the streets were empty. The front desk people had gone. Security was gone. We stood in the tornado of ash that still blew down Fulton Street toward the East River, the only two people on the entire block. What was left of the Towers was still on fire.

Why isn't anyone around? Where are the police? The firemen? The medical workers?

It may as well have been 3:00 a.m. There was nothing but white and darkness at once, the sky black, the air white. We stood in this blizzard, holding kerchiefs over our faces, but it didn't do any good; the wind whipped the dirt around our faces, into our nostrils, mouths, ears. The smell was similar to cooking meat, sweet and acrid, musty and suffocating. The payphone, miraculously, worked long enough for us to call my father, who told us that the Verrazano Bridge was closed, and he wouldn't be able to get home.

"The police keep insisting that you've all been evacuated and brought to holding shelters," he said.

How could the police have told everyone we had all been evacuated when we hadn't been?

That's why nobody's here.

Next, we called Aunt Fran to let her know we were okay.

"I love you, Aunt Frannie!" I said.

Less than a minute into the call, the payphone powered off for good, ceasing to work as inexplicably as it had worked in the first place.

I looked through partially shielded eyes at the silhouettes of steel that still resembled buildings. The skeleton of the World

Trade Center was still partially intact, but caving in and crumbling by the minute. They were still on fire, floors upon floors all ablaze.

A good deal of Manhattan had left the city, including half of our apartment complex, but hundreds of us could not. We were alone, in the way that hundreds of people in individual apartments can be alone, scattered behind close doors. Senior citizens, asthmatics, handicapped people, children, infants, can be alone and yet together, as the fires continued to burn.

Journal Entry, 9/11/01

The poor pigeons were probably dying.

I've been really nauseous and dizzy, shaking, and terrified of more bombs. We don't know who did it.

The people in wheelchairs can't get out because there are no elevators.

It was like gold dust outside.

The beige sand whirled over everything.

Poor Shane, it was his birthday.

We don't know where to go next.

What about people with asthma? Why is my temperature 100?

Daddy can't get home. The Palestinians were celebrating, we heard on the radio. There was a daycare center in the WTC.

The Internet isn't working.

The phones aren't working.

They're not letting people into the city, just out. That means lockdown: nobody gets in or out, uptown or downtown.

We just bought $100 worth of meat that will go bad in the freezer, its 5:30 and the power is out.

I had a silly candle fetish when I was ten that has now saved us.

The smoke is really bad. We have no AC, we filled pots with water just in time.

Me and Mom are pioneers. We have each other and our own flashlights.

Grandma and Grandpa aren't alone; we are here.

We went back outside to see if the payphone worked.

It didn't.

There wasn't a soul around, not even security. There are so many helicopters flying around.

It was around 1:00 a.m. that my mother and I decided to try to sleep—I saw it on her wristwatch, which she left on my father's nightstand.

I took his side of the bed and lay down next to her. We were very warm, but couldn't open the windows because of the debris. My gaze fell to the windowsill where some ash was still visible. I looked outside at the grounds where I had wheeled my baby doll's stroller years earlier, my grandpa following closely behind with my real stroller, the happiest child in a happy little neighborhood.

"I'm scared," I said. "I miss Daddy. What's going to happen to us? Are we going to die?"

"No," my mom said.

Not sure whether I was more afraid to stay awake or go to sleep, I waited, and I waited, and I listened to the dead silence outside, and at some point, I fell asleep, accepting the risk that I might not wake up.

CHAPTER FOUR

Post-traumatic stress disorder was first introduced to the DSM diagnostic system in 1980 to describe a syndrome found in Vietnam veterans who, upon returning from their tours of duty, often experienced anxiety, sleep problems, and intrusive and disturbing "flashback" memories of events that took place during the war.

They were frequently jumpy and some responded aggressively to even the most minor signals of threat. Many had terrifying nightmares and reacted to loud noises as though they were gunshots, and they were still in the jungles of Southeast Asia.

During my general psychiatry training, I had worked with vets who suffered from PTSD, and many psychiatrists were, even then, beginning to recognize its prevalence in adults who'd suffered other traumatic experiences like rape and natural disasters.

What struck me especially was that, although the experiences that had scarred adults with PTSD were often relatively brief (usually lasting for a few hours at most), their impact could still be seen in their behavior years—even decades—later.

How much more powerful, I thought, must the impact of a genuinely traumatic experience be for a child. The developing brain is most malleable and sensitive to experience—both good and bad—early in life. This is why we so rapidly learn language and motor skills. They are also easily and rapidly transformed in traumas.

—Dr. Bruce Perry, *The Boy Who Was Raised as a Dog*

For many, it was all over. Time to go about business as usual.

But the next morning, little pieces of paper were whirling around in the sandstorm, right outside the window, like confetti that announced the end of a parade.

But neither the Giants nor the Yankees had won a championship. Someone was going to claim a victory, but I wasn't sure who, or even what they'd been fighting for.

The rancid fog still lingered heavily in the air, so opening the window was still not an option. The water was off and the phones were down. According to my mother's silver watch, it was 6:00 a.m.

I remember pacing the apartment, asking, "Where's Daddy? Where's Daddy?" A question I knew she wouldn't be able to answer. I tried to keep my body in motion, picking up a magazine, putting it down, picking it back up, looking out the window, and helping my mother clean. I speculated about what might be next as I tried to figure out what to do with myself, feeling like a sitting duck just waiting for a hunter. I contemplated the first thing I would grab if I only had time to grab one thing. Thousands of thoughts jumped from point A to point Z, and nothing made sense, a series of equations that weren't even written with numbers or letters but in some foreign language. A feeling of doom infiltrated every inch of our apartment, from the magazine rack to my bedroom bookcase to the photos hung up on the wall.

Now and then, a scream or a sob made its way in from outside.

For a brief moment, the TV flickered on and revealed Mayor Rudolph Giuliani telling us to "Go about our lives as normal."

He was standing at a command post surrounded by other men in suits, Governor George Pataki among them, in front of a silver clock with triangles instead of numbers and a red and white striped collapsible wall that only reached to the governor's shoulders. The screen was split, with Giuliani in a small screen in the upper left hand corner and various news montages of the attacks and the aftermath in the full screen view.

"The best way for the people in New York to deal with this right now, not only with their own grief which we all feel and have, is to show that we're not going to be affected by it," he said. "We're not going to be cowered by it, or afraid. We're going to go about our business and lead normal lives, and not let these cowards affect us in any way, like they're trying to do, which is to instill fear in us."

The sound of the front door swinging open ripped my attention away.

My father stood in the living room breathing heavily, and I wrapped my arms around his middle. When I pulled away, I was sticky with a film of sweat and dust.

When I looked up, I saw a combination of terror, exhaustion, and relief on his face, something that's impossible to imagine unless you've actually seen it. Wide-eyed and mouth slightly agape, he looked almost stunned, the hair around his face wet and matted to the sides, his body soaked with sweat and covered in gold dust.

Covered in dead people.

When he realized that the police weren't letting people drive into the city, he had tried to hire a boat, looking up boat companies in the Yellow Pages, but none would go near Lower Manhattan.

At 7:00 p.m. they opened the Verrazano Bridge, and he was able to drive to downtown Brooklyn to his school principal, Mary's house, in Carroll Gardens, and found that another of his colleagues, Phil, was already there.

Dad parked the car and, an hour later, tried to walk across the Brooklyn Bridge, but the police held him back, just as they held everyone back.

He told them, "My family is down there," but they replied the same.

"It's too dangerous. We don't know what else could be happening. Everybody has been evacuated."

He tried to tell them that they were wrong, that he had spoken to me and Mom, that we *hadn't* been evacuated, but they didn't listen. He turned back and drove to Mary's house and found out that the subways were running, but not all the way downtown— they were stopping at Phil's house, though, so they traveled together to his apartment in the West Village. Dad began calling all of the emergency numbers that the news stations provided.

"All downtown residents have been evacuated and are now in holding shelters."

But nobody would tell him where these shelters were, or how to call them directly. How would he find us?

After a sleepless night of crying and watching the attacks replay on the news, he gathered the few things he had with him at daybreak, around 5:30 a.m. He began to walk downtown, staying as close to the East River as possible, hoping he'd find a way in past Canal Street. Police and barricades still blocked off every possible way anyone could enter downtown.

"They told me everything was still on fire, so nobody was allowed to go past Canal Street."

Without ever lowering his ID, which he held up to show he lived in Lower Manhattan, my father kept trying checkpoint after checkpoint, holding up his license like a tour guide with an umbrella, herding an invisible group.

"Nobody gets in, nobody gets out," they kept telling him as he tried different routes.

He was finally allowed past Pearl Street, and he started to run, tears streaming down his face, afraid of what he would find when he got there. But he found his way home the same way Ann, Charles, and I had the day before, and the same way my mother had, and he found us, alive.

Journal Entry, 9/12

9:30 a.m.: Daddy's home!

He found out that a man jumping out of the World Trade Center killed a fireman. Couples jumped out holding hands.

The World Financial Center is on fire.

People with asthma should stay inside because of the asbestos. I'm going to help Dad help people.

People who knew they would die called to say I love you.

My dad hadn't been home long before he headed right back out again.

There may have been cops outside, but none of them were checking on the people living in Southbridge—they were busy trying to keep order in the streets. People were still, essentially, trapped, my dad said, without any phones or water or lights, including the old ladies that had trouble walking, that sometimes forgot my name even if they saw me every day.

They can't even call their families.

They're probably so confused.

They're alone and they're afraid.

To forget an entire population of people, and to not know they were there, didn't make sense.

How much chaos is there? How could we not be prepared for all of this?

My father left to join the other men from the Southbridge board of directors and maintenance staff who had stuck around, or somehow also made it back in, in the community room. They compiled a list of everyone they could think of to check on, asthmatic neighbors, neighbors who needed important medication, people with dementia who likely had no idea what was happening. They only had a partial list to work from, and from there it was based on word of mouth, neighbors telling other neighbors, running around in a desperate frenzy to try and help each other. My dad, Joe, John, all the guys I usually said hello to, were running back and forth to the community room to pick up water and bring it to people.

All of the stores and the restaurants were closed.

I mentally filled in the gaps, speculating about the people who might have been forgotten, the people who weren't on that list. *What if all of their neighbors left?*

The sadness that was starting to overcome me felt familiar. It was what I felt whenever I tried to watch movies like *Charlie and the Chocolate Factory* or *Oliver Twist*, a feeling that held on strong and refused to let me move past it to see what happened next in the story, prompting me to leave the room, and staying with me long after the movie was over. I looked over at my Baby Minnie Mouse, the stuffed animal my mother said I would just toss to the side like all the other toys. I had slept with Minnie every night, even when her large plastic eyes began to get scratched up. Now, she was in a garbage bag by the door, along with other dolls coated in the same poisonous dust that spread in sheets across the rooftops and sidewalks.

* * *

After making sure that Grandma and Grandpa were still okay, my mom and I went to join my dad in the community room. Stepping outside was like being swallowed in a physical fog, a smell of burnt metal and rust lingering heavily in the air. The smell, the smog, would rotate in its smell, its color, its density, over the next six months, but it would never go away. The air would turn gray and dull, a feeling of doom lurking everywhere.

I overheard John telling my dad about one elderly woman he checked on.

"She had a blank look on her face, and was just staring out of her apartment window at the burning buildings," he said. "Her hands were shaking. She was cold, for some reason, and just looked out of the window. It was like she didn't realize I was trying to talk to her."

He left after that, bringing an arm full of water bottles back out with him.

I wandered over to a folding table where someone had left a single copy of the *New York Daily News*.

It's War.

That's all the cover said, along with a caption that described the accompanying image, in case somehow someone had missed it: the second plane heading to the second Tower, the first already on fire.

How did they write this?

How is a newspaper out?

How did they actually produce a newspaper yesterday?

Suddenly, I remembered that Grandma had said the same thing the day before.

"This means war," not as if she were declaring it, but as though she knew what would happen next. Those words triggered something in me, waking up another monster that realized it was all planned. Carefully planned. The new monster would go on to fill so many instances of "not knowing" things with a singular message: *Something bad is happening.*

I flipped the cover open to find out that "they" believed that "they" had caught forty of the fifty men who were part of the "diabolical plan."

I closed the paper, unwilling to find out more.

The "what" of what happened is something that would start to make sense in the weeks that followed, fragmented, scattered pieces of facts and speculation forming a collage held together by a very thin and brittle glue. The "why" would never be as clear.

"Helaina, talk to Aunt Fran," my mom said. Someone had brought a working cell phone to the community room, and it was our turn to use it. "She said it's like nothing is happening uptown. People are just eating in restaurants and walking around like normal."

That explained my question about the newspaper.

People in white coats from the hospital began to bring in cardboard boxes full of small milk cartons like you'd get with school lunch and cellophane-wrapped sandwiches.

"How can I help?" I asked my dad.

"Come on back here, honey," my dad said. "Stand next to me, and you can help give out the food."

Standing behind the table lined with cardboard boxes, I explained to the old ladies and the children, "These are peanut butter, these are turkey, these are ham." I wanted to stay there doing that all day, because it made me happy. When I did it, I wasn't thinking about all of the questions swimming around in my head.

Occasionally, someone who was homeless came by, and I gave them the same choice, "Turkey, ham, peanut butter and jelly," but let them have three or four sandwiches, even though I wasn't supposed to.

"We may not have enough," my dad said gently, when he saw me.

I slipped extra baby milk cartons into their hands before they left.

Journal Entry, 9/12:
4:40 p.m.: The TV went out again.
5:20 p.m.: The TV came on again, blurry. Remains are collapsing. Everything is normal everywhere else and we're forgotten. Everyone is hanging their American flag.
6:07 p.m.: I am scared again, they are saying that 5 World Trade Center may collapse.
6:25 p.m.: 5 World Trade Center Collapsed. 1 Liberty is collapsing.
6:45 p.m.: 1 Liberty is collapsing, Millennium Hotel may be in danger.
7:05 p.m.: The Millennium Hotel lost seventy-five windows.
7:20 p.m.: The FBI identified most of the hijackers, they think the mastermind is bin Laden.
7:25 p.m.: I am trying to watch *The Mask* to calm down. It's not working.
8:00 p.m.: The TV went out again.

Shortly after 8:00 p.m., word started spreading that we were all supposed to pack an "emergency" bag, because "they" were afraid that the Millennium Hotel, which was actually a block closer to us than the Trade Center, was going to collapse, and we had to be ready to go if that happened.

Go where?

I retreated to my room to hurriedly pack my bag, trying to figure out what I would need and for how long. I thought of a sleepover at Gina's house back in fifth grade.

We had been eating Chinese food around their glass table, Gina, her parents, and her baby sister in a high chair, when the fire alarm in the building went off.

An automated message came over the buildings' speakers.

We all stayed calm and ignored it, but Gina freaked out, leaving the table to grab her things.

"Mom, what if it's real?"

"It's not, Gina, sit down."

"Mommy, can you just call the lobby to make sure?"

The automated message kept sounding, escalating Gina's panic with every passing second.

"Mom, call the lobby!" she cried.

I chuckled, and her mom and I just continued eating our Chinese food. After a few minutes, her paranoia started to annoy me.

What would you grab if there was a fire and you only had a minute? She'd asked me that night.

Journal Entry, 9/13:

2:00 p.m.: Mom is scaring me because she's saying if the Millennium Hotel collapses, which they think it will, we're dead. C-TOWN [supermarket] by the Smith Projects is open, so we have to get better facemasks and walk over because we don't have any food.

4:00 p.m.: There was nothing left in C-Town, so we tried going to Jubilee on John Street. I had to run for my life again because everyone was running again; they thought 1 Liberty Plaza collapsed. I am going to have a heart attack if this keeps up.

The Borough President Virginia Fields was in the community room hugging me and telling me how brave I am. She's the only one who cares about us. Nadine said the school auditorium collapsed. The lights are still out at St. Margaret's nursing home down the block. What's going to happen to them?

4:50 p.m.: John Street was evacuated. I am throwing my valuables into the middle of the room. I'm scared we're being evacuated. Now they are saying that the atrium at the World Financial Center is crumbling. The debris is coming back. There's a rumor that there is a crack in my building. Nobody is even paying any attention to us. There is a line of ambulances on my block and the army is here.

6:30 p.m.: Oh my God they just caught more people on American Airlines trying to cause more damage, they were using fake IDs and wearing pilot outfits.

7:00 p.m.: We are no longer allowed in the street and are confined to our building.

7:25 p.m.: Grandma came down because she is scared about her window breaking. I can't believe ninety people made bomb threats today. I hope Kyle's mom isn't dead. My friend Liana said one of our old counselors sent her an email about how it's her fault this happened and she's probably happy. She's Brazilian.

9:25 p.m.: There's no more police outside, does that mean it's safer? Dad got Grandma her cancer medicine.

10:25 p.m.: There is more disgusting smoke in my room. How did it even get in here? It smells the worst. . . .

It was to the community room and back in those first couple of days, passing only through the courtyard of our complex's square, to avoid stepping out into the chaos of the caution tape, barricades, and fire engines in the street. The American flag was lowered at something called "half-mast," which I didn't understand.

When we did try to venture out to the corner, I found military posted there, standing still, like those British guards who weren't allowed to move or make a sound. A street sweeper rolled by, and the dust whirled about and then settled again. It was like trying to vacuum a beach during a sandstorm.

On Thursday, my dad started trying to figure out what to do about the people who were dependent on medications, either from Downtown Pharmacy or delivered by mail, who were obviously not going to get them either way.

"Why can't the pharmacy people get here?" I asked him.

"Nobody is going to be at the pharmacy for a while. The pharmacists' IDs show where they lived, not where they work, so they can't get in."

Don't people make fake IDs all the time?

What will people trying to get down here try to do?

How much worse can it get?

My dad had become an unofficial "liaison" to all of the elected officials—Councilmember Catherine Freed, Assembly Speaker Sheldon Silver, and Manhattan Borough President Virginia Fields. Tuesday the eleventh had been Primary Day for elections, so even though they had left, that day, they came back in the following days. While Battery Park City had been evacuated, we hadn't been, and they, at least, knew that. My dad let them know what we needed, and, at the same time, began negotiating with the police to make sure the pharmacists could get into the area and start getting people their medication again.

Back in my room, I did mindless things like re-arranging the hundreds of Lisa Frank and Powerpuff Girls stickers on my night table, which was really two clear plastic storage drawers. The movement matched what was going on in between my ears, frenzied thoughts like angry bees swarming a hive, going in a thousand different directions, all of them bad. Somehow, new smells kept entering the apartment, even with the windows closed.

I looked out the window at the place in the yard where we buried Sally, my first real pet. Sally had been our class hamster, but I had grown attached to her while we took her home to care for her during winter break, so our second grade class voted to let me keep her. As for that "yard," it was a concrete basketball "court" with two hoops, framed by four tall buildings. Sally was buried there in a large, square planter full of dry dirt and small patches of grass.

"Ashes, ashes to ashes, dust to dust," my mother had said when I finished my teary speech, pretending she was only sad because I was sad, or maybe she was. I peered out at the planter and thought about how unsettling it was that Sally was now covered in ash.

The dead were everywhere, I was beginning to learn, whirling around and settling, but they were nowhere to the people looking for them.

Pictures started to go up around the neighborhood, of people in happier times, getting married, having a picnic, on a cruise. The faces of moms and dads, sisters, brothers, and best friends covered the walls of hospital, the lampposts, and the church by what was now being called "Ground Zero."

The people who loved them were torn between grief and hope, unsure of which hurt more and which emotion was more dangerous to give in to.

We had a lot of food that was defrosting, since the refrigerator didn't work, but the gas on the oven worked. We were able to eat what we had in the house, but stores remained closed because nobody could get in.

Some people wore proper gas masks, others walked with their shirts over their faces. Some used towels, but most people wore flimsy paper masks that did nothing.

* * *

Christine, her mother, and her little brother were confined to their building in the Smith Housing Projects for those first two days. The barricades outside did not make her feel safer, and neither did the police. It made her feel more afraid. Police were not a new sight, after all, Christine lived down the block from Police Plaza. But these police were armed, and there were a lot of them, and they stood in the same spot outside for hours. All the stores had already been looted, so that was done. The rest of the stores were closed.

On Thursday, she and her family were permitted to walk over to the Pathmark on Cherry Street. When the automatic doors opened, she felt like she was stepping into a post-apocalyptic movie, watching as people scoured the bare shelves for whatever they could find. Random items lay in disarray everywhere, some bread here, a can there.

On the way back, soldiers asked her and her brother for ID before they would allow them back in the building.

"We don't have ID," her brother said. "We're twelve."

Her mother interjected.

"When can trucks come in with food so we can feed our kids?"

Christine watched as annoyed looks flashed over the soldiers' faces. They ignored the question.

You're supposed to be helping us, she thought. *You're supposed to be protecting us.*

Meanwhile, the violence in the projects was escalating. An old Muslim woman who always sat outside her building had been shot. Bodega owners were being beaten up, their stores looted and broken into. Police escorted the rest of them out of the neighborhood, and they had to close down their stores for the week.

* * *

On Friday morning, I ventured out to the corner where a few people sat outside in front of Burger King, trying not to actually listen to what they were saying.

". . . Biological war."

"They're telling us that we should clean our terraces with a wet rag."

". . . Nuclear bombs."

". . . and Christine Whitman from the EPA is saying that the air is safe to breathe."

Actually, Miss Whitman, the administrator for the Environmental Protection Agency under President Bush, was wrong, we'd later learn. The EPA would go on to detect twenty-two metals in the air: antimony, arsenic, beryllium, cadmium, chromium, cobalt, lead, manganese, nickel, selenium, aluminum, barium, calcium, copper, iron, magnesium, potassium, silver, sodium, thallium, vanadium, zinc, asbestos, benzene, tolene, styrene, propylene, and ethylbenzene. And they hung around for a very, very long time.

The conversation was interrupted by the whirring sound of a plane passing overhead

Vrrrrrrooooom.

It was flying low, too low, which caused me to duck.

"Look at that plane! Did you see how low it was? Right over Lower Manhattan," said my neighbor loudly.

The anger and fear in her voice scared me.

"Daddy . . ." I said through my teeth, pulling at his shirt, wanting to go back inside. "Daddy!" I hissed again.

"What sweetheart?" he asked, but continued talking anyway. I watched as the National Guard pulled up and troops filed out onto the street. My adrenaline was pumping, and all sorts of conflicting messages were flashing through my brain like lightning.

Run.

You can't run.

If you don't run you're going to die.

You can't leave Grandma upstairs.

The army is here.

It's too late.

They're the good guys.

How are they going to keep us safe?

Maybe the adults were able to talk themselves into feeling safe, but I couldn't.

All around us people started and stopped running at random.

It's happening again.

A truck made a noise.

What was that?

A piece of metal hit the floor.

What was that?

Someone clapped their hands.

What was that?

Someone shouted.

Why?

Neighbors embraced us quickly as they hurried past—that was what people did now. They hurried, and they cried, and I grew more nervous.

What were they running from?

My mind became home to ten different TV screens for which I didn't own any remotes, producing programming that scared me just for existing, images and scenes that shook me to my core. No matter what the specifics looked like in my mind, one thing was for sure: it was just a matter of time before something catastrophic happened again.

We had our prayer vigil that evening, which started in the community room, where Joe broke down in tears after someone sang God Bless America. An old lady who liked to knit, Rose, was brought in by the Red Cross. She had been wandering around for days.

We left, as a group, to walk to the Engine 6 fire station across the street. We held lit candles as we walked.

"They lost eight men," my dad said.

"Lost like they're missing, or lost as in, dead?"

"I think they're becoming the same thing."

The faces of the old ladies I knew were twisted in pain.

I had always run up to them and said something sassy to "Make their day." That night, I said nothing.

* * *

On Saturday, Verizon gave everyone a free cell phone (after a few weeks, they started charging people for the phones, which is when my dad wrote to a reporter named Asa Aarons to help us get those bills voided, which he did). The reason we had no phone lines, I learned, was because all the wires coming from the hub at the World Trade Center were damaged. They started stringing new telephone lines right over the sidewalks, and that caused a whole other issue, especially because they didn't even work.

Mom wanted to try to get me away from the smell, to somehow get out of the area, to do something that gave the faintest impression of "normal life."

Trying to find some semblance of normal life by walking past Canal Street was like trying to find a pencil mark under a dribbled mess of watercolors bleeding together into a murky brown. What was underneath was now impossible to bring back.

We had to try three different times, because we couldn't get past Pearl Street before everyone started running and screaming, not unlike how they had that day.

"The buildings are falling! Everyone's evacuating! Go back to your apartments, get your things, we only have a few minutes!"

As we shuffled along, I asked my mom, "Is City Hall a government building? Is it a target? What about the Municipal Building? The Courthouse? Police Plaza? What about the Brooklyn Bridge? What about the Stock Exchange?"

At some point, we made it, and found that what my aunt had said was true—aside from a few people wearing facemasks, things were open above Canal Street. But we couldn't get away from that smell, and I could have been in Hong Kong and not been able to escape the feeling of anxiety vibrating through me with every step. A war was already waging inside of me, where an invisible little girl had taken up a home, acting in constant state of defense and offense, of paranoia, trying to predict where and when the next attack would come from. I didn't want to go back to school, but I didn't want to stay in my apartment, either.

I wanted to be nowhere, because nowhere was safe.

* * *

Journal Entry, 9/16:
I finally took a hot shower today. I'm going down to the community room to help again. We watched the movie ET. I sat in the back with Grandpa. It was a sad movie. Mom and me went to Blockbuster and got six videos.

FEMA, an organization that provided people with coupons to use for HEPA air purifiers and vacuum cleaners—they had to be HEPA, my mom explained, because those were the ones that filtered out asbestos—initially set their boundaries on Nassau Street, cutting Southbridge out by only two blocks. An angry mob went to their office, and the boundary was changed. They also gave us access to a "professional cleaning crew," one that our neighbor described as "one Mexican guy and a few Puerto Rican teenagers."

We had to file with the Red Cross for things that had to be thrown out, curtains, bedspreads, the couch, and the air conditioners, which had been drawing in soot. My dad explained to me later on that some people began to claim they had damage that they didn't have just so they could get new things, and I couldn't understand how anyone could be so ugly at a time like this.

Later that day I ran into my neighbor Franky, who I had rode the bus to kindergarten with years before. Before we could say hello, we heard a boom.

"Was that sound really loud enough to be a dump truck?" I asked.

"What the hell else are they going to do next?" he said, trying to make us both feel better. "The damage is done."

But his shrug was jumpy, and as he opened the front door, he said, "Phew, it still smells like dead bodies."

How many kids can identify the smell of dead bodies?

With every day that passed, "missing" became closer to meaning "dead."

"There's little hope," said a news anchor on the TV that kept flickering on and off. "There's little hope."

They also talked about the anthrax scares, about how chemicals were being mailed to news corporations and senators, killing five people and infecting seventeen others. It became known as "Amerithrax," and the note written to the people who received it looked something like this:

9-11-01
THIS IS NEXT
TAKE PENACILIN NOW
DEATH TO AMERICA

DEATH TO ISRAEL
ALLAH IS GREAT

Chemical warfare.

I pondered this as I sat in the slippery orange booth at Burger King, one of the only places to reopen, one table over from a military man with a rifle. My dad found out that my cousin Melanie, who worked at the Capitol Building in Washington, DC, had begun taking Cipro as a precaution. As I picked at my French fries, I thought about having to join a mass exodus of people fleeing the United States. I was certain that it was just a matter of when, and more so than me, I was worried about Grandma.

What if Grandma is walking around when something happens?

What if she gets lost?

Who's going to die first?

What if Grandma had been on her way to the beauty parlor in Chinatown on 9/11?

I pictured people pummeling over her, her having a heart attack, the cops telling her she couldn't go home. She was too old to run.

Grandma could've died.

Stop.

Grandma is going to die.

STOP.

Grandma is going to die. She's going to die. And you won't be able to save her.

STOP!!!!!

Dead. Dead. Dead. Dead. Dead. Dead.

My CD/Radio/Cassette player was working, so I played the only CDs I had, listening to "Unpretty" and "No Scrubs," the CD single of Mariah Carey's "Heartbreaker" Featuring Jay-Z, and the remix, with Missy Elliot, Britney Spears' "Oops, I Did It Again." I lay on the floor of my room, with its pink carpet, even though I wasn't supposed to because of what was in it, flipping through an old magazine and singing along absent-mindedly, thinking about all the times I'd sung and danced along when there was nothing else to think about but singing and dancing along. It took a week before the thought settled in: there was no more "future" to think about. There was no "eventually" or "one day" or even "soon." Nothing else mattered. We were all going to die.

Journal Entry, 9/19:
Today I stayed waiting for Daddy at the dentist for a really long time. I had such a bad stomachache. We took the bus, then some Spanish woman was talking really loudly in my ear. My dad was in pain from something called a root canal. He isn't mean so he didn't ask her to stop talking so loud.

The elevators were working again, and when I got home, I rode upstairs with a young guy who was holding a clipboard.

He asked me in a very pleasant voice, "How are you doing?"

I sighed.

"Hanging in," I said.

"You know, if you say you're doing great, you'll believe it and feel great," he said.

"Maybe," I smiled weakly.

"So, how are you doing?" he asked again.

"I'm hanging in," I said again, walking right into it, on autopilot.

"No! You're doing great!" he said.

I laughed.

Then I walked down the hallway to our apartment, and stopped laughing.

That evening, they set up a game room for us in the basement of the community room.

Charles and Nadine were playing video games, and I hated video games, so I just watched. I was bored and at the same time on edge, listening to Charles talk about his elaborate escape plans and his ideas about what would be next.

"Next will be the water. They'll poison the water. Do you know what was in those buildings? We'll probably mutate and die of some weird contagious nuclear disease. Biological warfare is coming, I'm telling you. And our city is always going to be the number one target, which makes *us* the number one targets. The next attack will be by land for sure, not air again. And there's no way we're going to be able to survive the next one. No way."

Charles, by now, was already developing sleep paralysis. Essentially, he was waking up from a nightmare, but not actually waking up. His body did, but he didn't, almost like being paralyzed.

"My dad said, 'We should get all of those sons of bitches.'" Charles continued. "I hope we go to war. My grandma said we should do to them what we did to the Japanese and drop an atomic bomb on them."

Charles also had this new "thing" where he suddenly reached out to choke people, just putting his hands around our necks and squeezing, but not hard enough to actually hurt us.

Charles and some other friends in the neighborhood decided to go exploring through the dark garages. For a moment, roaming in the darkness with flashlights, he was able to recapture the feeling of childhood wonderment that now belonged to another lifetime. When security discovered them, Charles shouted back, "We're afraid to go outside because the air is poisonous."

The guard let them stay.

Another day, I went over to Charles's house to try play a computer game called *You Don't Know Jack* and listen to show tunes—his choice, not mine. I noticed a funny contraption, a makeshift cage, in the corner of his room.

"What's that?" I asked.

He launched into a story, because Charles loved to tell stories.

"Well," he said. "On Wednesday morning of last week, it was dead silent when we woke up. I got out of bed needing badly to use the bathroom, like my usual routine. Wake up, bathroom. But the toilet wasn't working. My dad's coworkers had told him that the bathroom at their office would be available. So, we had to walk through a dust storm down Water Street, half awake and in our pajamas, over to Maiden Lane."

"Uh-huh . . ." I said.

"It's usually bustling with people on their way to work, but Water Street was deserted. Like a ghost town. Anyway, on the way back, we found a small bird on the ground. It was injured. My dad picked it up and brought it back to our house. We turned my old wrestling ring play set into a cage for the bird, and fed it water and grains. We nursed it to back to health, and this morning, we set it free. It fluttered off the terrace and faltered slightly before hovering over the Brooklyn Bridge. It picked up speed, flew into Brooklyn, and flew out of sight."

* * *

In the week that followed, the absence of the Towers left a dull, dank feeling in the air. The weather seemed to always be overcast, and even on the rare sunny day, there was nothing to smile about. The heavy smog from the burning pile lingered, and it became our sky. Everyone was worn and haggard. Every loud noise sent a surge of fear through my body. More photos of faces were put up in front of the hospital, and I decided that nothing could be accepted at face value. I knew, not thought, that something else, something worse, was going to happen. It's like watching *Jaws* when they "catch" him the first time. There's too much movie left for that to be the end of *Jaws*.

The dread of going back to school was not the average disappointment of going back to school after a "break." It felt like a legitimate death sentence. By now, I had started sleeping in my parent's bed with them again. When my mom finally got ahold of my pediatrician, the doctor said, "You have to get her out of there," so I wedged myself between a foot of space on the floor between my mom's side of the bed and the wall, using their comforter as a mattress.

I eventually got to see the end of Giuliani's initial speech from the morning of September twelfth, when some station re-ran it.

"Not only are we going to rebuild, but we are going to come out of this stronger than ever," he concluded. "Emotionally, politically, much stronger as a city, and economically stronger too. We're going to work on that right away."

After a while, the beige color of the ash turned to gray, and the first time it rained the gray didn't wash off of Fulton Street.

CHAPTER FIVE

The military checkpoints, the sirens, the rubble. This is all familiar to Ellen Foote, who lived in Beirut for years with her foreign correspondent husband long before she was the principal of a middle school in Battery Park City, in the shadow of the World Trade Center.

Many of the three hundred sixth, seventh, and eighth graders at Ms. Foote's school, Intermediate School 89, felt the seismic shock when two airplanes hit on September 11. From the floor-to-ceiling windows on the school's south side, they smelled the smoke and heard the cries.

These sights, sounds, and smells evoke the days when Ms. Foote and her husband, Steve Hindy, a former correspondent for The Associated Press, lived across the street from the American Embassy in Beirut, in the late 1970s and early 1980s.

In the days after the attack, she located all but two of the families at I.S. 89, despite telephone lines so tangled that calls to

Chinatown sometimes rang in the ticket office of the Mets base-
ball team.

She spent time, daily, with a social studies teacher who saw the
terrorist plane hit the exact spot where his older brother worked at
the World Trade Center, yet stayed with his pupils until the last
was safely at home.

In retrospect, her job in Beirut seems a peaceful one, assem-
bling research material for journalists at the Arab World File.
And, in retrospect, her reason for coming home seems ironic. When
her husband left Beirut, he was offered a new posting in the
Philippines.

But Ms. Foote balked. "I'm tired of being an Ugly American,"
she told him. "I need to go back to New York and feel safe."

—Jane Gross in "Changed Lives: A Principal's World
Suddenly Turned Into Beirut," *New York Times*,
September 26, 2001

One morning, my mother got a call.
"The kids are going back to school at the O'Henry
Learning Center."

"No," I said as soon as she hung up. "I'm not going back."

"Yes, you are," my mother said. "And I'm glad you're going
back."

Things had not been especially easy for us as of late. We were
both irritable, anxious, jumping when we called one another's
name, flipping out if the folded shopping cart started slipping
from its place up against the wall, falling to the floor with a
"clap."

So now, what? We were supposed to magically "forget every-thing" and go back to normal, pretend that it was just school as usual?

This is foolish.

We couldn't go back to I.S.89 because of the realities that still exited in Lower Manhattan. Crews were still digging through rubble and finding bodies, and the entire area resembled a war zone. The air was toxic; they kept testing and retesting it, but those chemicals hung around for a very long time. Simply put, the student population of I.S.89 couldn't go back to their school building because it wasn't safe.

Ironically, there we were, though, Charles, Nadine, Christine, and several others who lived not in Battery Park but in build-ings on the East Side that made up this forgotten population. Everyone knew about Battery Park, but no one knew about us.

It was decided that Charles, Nadine, and I would take the A train to Fourteenth Street to get to the new school relocation. We weren't used to taking mass transit to get to school, so our mothers came with us that first morning. On the two-block walk to the train, a new backpack clunking against my lower back, I peered closely at the Pakistani man in the newsstand, his face framed by cigarettes, magazines, and candy. The men who sold bootlegged copies of CDs and movies would not be out in a few hours, like they normally were, since they didn't have any sort of legal identification at all. The hot dog man was not on the corner.

I couldn't believe I was putting myself back in the same exact situation again, and it also seemed that it was a bad idea for someone like me to be getting on a train.

They were taken to camps in trains.

Somebody could hijack the train and take all of us there.

What are the chances of that happening?

As likely as two planes hitting the same target.

On the subway platform, the sense of dread and doom spread like a bad stomachache. Above us, something rumbled loudly.

What was that?

Charles's eyes widened.

It was only the 2/3 train passing above us on the upper level, but we didn't know that; even if we did, it wouldn't have mattered.

There's absolutely no way I'm going to be able to deal with this.

"Mom, I can't do this," I said quickly, vibrating with anxiety. A surge in my chest sent me moving quickly toward the stairs before I even realized it. "I need to go home."

"No!" said Charles, obstructing my path. "We have to try to get back to normal, or else the terrorists win."

"Terrorist" was a word we had now come to associate with the people who "did it." I was already sick of hearing the new phrase, and it had only been two weeks.

If we don't take the subway, the terrorists win.

If we don't fly, the terrorists win.

If we don't go out to eat, the terrorists win.

What did it even mean to let them "win"?

Thousands of people were dead. Thousands of other lives were ruined. Everything was closed. The Towers were gone. "They" were burning our flags and cheering. "They" already won. In fact, it wasn't even a matter of winning. There was no battle. They just destroyed everything.

The train ride was bizarre. If people riding the train were afraid, they didn't show it. No fear in their eyes or bodies, nothing different about these commuters. Rowdy kids screamed and shoved each other, people pushed and sneered and read their books and went about life as normal. I felt like I was going insane.

We emerged from the subway stairs and walked toward Seventeenth Street and Eighth Avenue. It was narrow and unfamiliar. The delis looked dirty, the streets looked too busy, and the people looked too different. Charles, Ann, my mother, and I all made our way to the middle of the block. Nadine and her mom had gotten off at Canal Street so Nadine could throw up; she was on antibiotics, and her mother had given her chocolate cake for breakfast.

Hundreds of parents and children were mobbing the entrance. My breathing began to quicken, and I froze in place.

"Come on," my mom said.

I wouldn't walk.

"You have to be brave," she said. "You were always so brave."

Everything in my body defied moving forward, but my mother pulled me toward the building anyway. The first thing I heard was Thomas's mother telling him, "Don't worry, its ok, just go." Thomas, who was short, like me, with shiny dark hair and brown eyes, hesitantly pet their dog, Eddie, goodbye. I caught his eye, and we walked toward the double doors of the building entrance. Kyle, whose mother had escaped from the 101st floor of Tower 1, was standing in front of the security desk and pointing to his mouth. He was going to be sick.

As we squeezed our way through the crowd, looking like two backpack-and-sneaker wearing deer caught in headlights, Thomas began telling me what the past two weeks had been like.

He told me about traveling from hotel to hotel, how his mother had bought chicken nuggets from a store and asked the hotel to cook them on his birthday, so he could have something that felt like a homecooked meal. He told me about the giant convention center where people went to figure out whose homes were intact, and who had to go to which hotel and how they would pay for it. He told me about this little kids' area they had at the center, which was run by therapists who provided crayons and paper and told them to "draw how they felt."

"Do you guys have a plan?" I asked him as we were jostled around with the crowd, referring to what they would do when another attack took place.

"If it happens uptown, we meet at the movie theatre down in Battery Park. If it happens downtown, we meet at whichever hotel we're currently staying at. We've already been to three."

There was a little American flag sticking out of his backpack—they were everywhere now, on stickers, on cars, in windows, on T-shirts.

"United We Stand, Never Forget, These Colors Don't Run."

The scene in the auditorium was absolute chaos. The first thing I did was check to make sure everyone I knew was alive. Everyone was. I saw Becca sitting with Henry and gave her a big hug. She looked tired.

One little girl, someone's sister, asked Becca how many people she saw jump.

"I wish I didn't," she said.

"Hey," I said, plunking down in the empty seat on her other side. "No offense, but you look exhausted. You ok?"

"I haven't been sleeping," she admitted. When she did manage to nod off after two or three days straight without sleep, she had recurrent nightmares that people were throwing themselves off of the burning towers and falling on top of her. Sometimes, she was one of the people, trying to figure out whether jumping or burning to death was the quickest way to die.

After we broke off into our classes and found our first room, a random woman gave us paper and crayons.

"Draw how you feel?" Michael said, looking down at the paper. Michael had shown up with blue hair, for some reason, which made me think that his mother was way cooler than my mother. "Nobody's going to take this seriously."

* * *

The reporters found us on day two.

"Did you see people jumping?" they asked us, thrusting microphones into our faces.

"Don't talk to them, just keep walking!" teachers and parents said as they ushered us inside. We had no problem with that. None of us wanted to explain to them what we saw, or ran from, or anything else they asked. But, even inside the building, all eyes were on us. Teachers and parents from the other schools whispered, "Those are the ones. That's them."

A couple of teachers tried to initiate a discussion about what we'd been through in between some semblance of actual lessons about math and English, but it never caught on. Nobody wanted to share their private, most intimate fears with the class, but one person did offer something.

"There are people who died, or whose parents died, so we don't have the right to talk about it," Trevor said matter-of-factly.

That was the end of any group discussion.

* * *

The sun always shone brightly on I.S. 89, reflecting off of the Hudson River and the seemingly endless, glimmering windows of the World Trade Center. The sun was completely unobstructed, the Hudson River on one side and the West Side Highway on the other. Light filtered its way into the classroom, spilling across the tabletops marked up with pen and marker, draping across the carpet.

By contrast, The O'Henry Learning Center was dark and boxed in by other buildings. Across the street was one of the city's "worst" high schools, which had black bars on the windows and cops usually stationed out front around 3:00 p.m. The entire area felt like one big prison.

In the park across the street, homeless people slept on benches and gangs huddled in a circle, smoking weed and waiting to jump younger kids. Within weeks, a few of our classmates—the ones who had suddenly become angry versions of their former selves from back in August—began smoking pot in the park with them and tagging graffiti on lampposts. The rest of us walked quickly past it with our heads down.

Greg refused to join his friends to go out for lunch when we were first given the option and brought our permission slips in. They tried to convince him to go out with them, telling him he was being a pussy, that he was ridiculous. They assured him nothing bad would happen to him. So he did, and nothing did happen.

The next day, he was jumped.

The environment inside of the O'Henry Learning Center wasn't much better. There were kids from three other schools inside: the Lab School, which had both a middle school and a high school, and the Museum School. There was barely enough room for them, and not a lot of room for us.

All of our classes were scattered in random classrooms on different floors. The building seemed to have seven different staircases, and we could never keep them straight; sometimes our classes got relocated, and we wandered through the maze, showing up late and nervous. A few "mock" classrooms were created by putting up partitions, and there was often confusion about which room which school or class was supposed to have. Sometimes we looked for alternate space, and a couple of times, we just merged classes. Our school office was the size of a dressing room, and music class was held in a storage closet.

The O'Henry kids made it clear right away that they didn't want us there.

"Get out of our school!" they shouted at us in the hallways.

Everyone was watching us, looking at us. Older students threw things at us in the cafeteria, beat kids up, chased us around the block, didn't want us hanging out in their parks, didn't like us sitting at their lunch tables, didn't want us eating their lunch food. If we needed to wait for a classroom to open up, we sat down in the hallway and pushed ourselves as close to the wall as we could get, trying not to get pummeled by backpacks or have our fingers stepped on.

They thought that because we were from downtown, we thought we were "special." They had no idea how wrong they were. We wanted to be regular kids, regular students, just like them, but our world was so much different than theirs.

Soon, within the school, a new division surfaced between kids who lived downtown and kids who lived anywhere above Canal Street, outside of the disaster zone; between kids who had been caught in everything and those who got out; between the people who literally lost their homes and those who didn't.

"The other kids can hang out after school," said Sarah, one of Charles's friends. "They don't need to move from one place to another, figuring out where to go next, nowhere to cook, using an ice bucket for a refrigerator."

Sarah was tall and very thin, wore long skirts with t-shirts, round spectacles, and the same long, skinny brown braid over her shoulder, which she usually fidgeted with. One day, Sarah's father came to pick her up in a gas mask, and all of the other kids made fun of him. Sarah began carrying a little over-the-shoulder suede purse with fringe on the bottom around with her everywhere. I thought it was weird until I got to high school and I started doing the same thing.

I need to have everything with me, just in case.

Everything we needed consisted of pocket money, a student MetroCard, some Tylenol, a lipgloss, and a cell phone. Sarah had a cell phone long before I did, and called her mother anytime she heard a plane flying overhead, watching it until it flew out of sight. Her eyes were always darting, her neck always craning. She scanned her surroundings at all times.

That looks suspicious.

Is that supposed to be here?

What was that sound?

What is that guy doing?

Why is there a cop here?

And it also became personal, as it did for me:

Why is she looking at me like that?

What are they saying about me?

What are they going to do about it?

She stayed locked in her room whenever she wasn't in school. She began carrying a flashlight everywhere in her bag too. For her, it was school, home, school, home. She avoided crowds at all costs, and, in the stairway at school, she often waited on the edge of her seat for the bell, hoping to beat the rush. Becca was beginning to have panic attacks in those crowds, though she didn't know exactly what was happening. When I saw her in the stairwell, jostled between hordes of stinky, sweaty older kids shouting and rough housing, she looked like a lost toddler in a crowded department store.

"Rebecca, go to the nurse!" Reena shouted as she hurried to class, being carried by the sea of writhing bodies, clutching her books while people shouted at her to get the hell out of their way. Reena, who was a year older than us, had begun clutching everything she owned, because now she owned very little. She lost her Gateway Plaza home and lived in a shelter along with other Battery Park City residents. She didn't have any of her things, like her Walkman, her DVDs, her sweat-shirts, her books. Soon, she would return to Gateway to see men throwing everything she owned into a dumpster. Her Mickey Mouse doll, her childhood books, so many of her clothes were all gone. She slept in the clothes she did have from that day on, refusing to wear pajamas, believing the terrorists would strike again while everyone was asleep.

Reena asked to see a guidance counselor (apparently, at the time, we had one, but I don't remember being informed of her existence), who ended up leaving us after a couple of months (because, she said, she saw too much and wouldn't be able to bring herself to go back when we returned to the building).

Reena's father had his own ideas about his daughter's ability to "just bounce back," and his misconceptions were the misconceptions of many parents and teachers.

"Children are naturally resilient," he told her. "Everyone should stop coddling you guys. Just move on."

Whoever started that rumor was undoubtedly the same person who came up with, "Sticks and stones will break my bones but words can never hurt me," looking for yet another way to invalidate the very real feelings of young, impressionable people.

And yet what else could we do but try to move on? What did moving on really mean? Putting one foot in front of the other, listening to adults, doing what we had been trained to do, just show up?

I got myself dressed, I put on pink Bonne Belle lip gloss, painted my nails, and wore Versace perfume for girls, but on the inside, I was becoming a neurotic adult. There was no concentrating about anything while cymbals were banging together in my brain. I couldn't make them stop, so my insides danced to this music, flipping and kicking and punching wildly. I spent entire school days nervously looking out of the window and biting my nails, then my cuticles, making my fingers bleed, shaking my foot like I had a motor running, and chewing up my gums. I picked up other people's reactions as if they were contagious. The room was too small, the noise was too loud, and

I was looking for an escape I couldn't find, one that wasn't there, like a mouse in a maze that had been set on fire.

I started feeling dizzy, then nauseous, losing my breath, losing, it felt like, control of myself.

On the outside, we looked like any other group of kids. We weren't wearing our pain on our bodies in any obvious way.

But when we heard the whir of planes overhead, it was clear that breath was being held as we all waited for the sound of the crash.

If we were outside, and not in a classroom, some of us started running, in no particular direction. Obviously, other kids didn't run anywhere.

"Oh my God, what's wrong with you?" they laughed and pointed.

What part of "war" didn't people understand?

They were fools, all of them.

"We just know better," said Sarah. "What do planes do in wars? They drop bombs on people. They don't get it."

In case it wasn't obvious enough already, it became very clear that there was something different about us and the other kids in the O'Henry Learning Center the day the truck tire popped.

We were all in the schoolyard for recess when we heard a huge booming noise that echoed across the concrete yard. Everyone stopped what they were doing, but the I.S. 89ers hit the ground or ran around searching for teachers, sobbing and hyperventilating.

The other kids just stared at us like we were crazy.

"It was just a truck," said one of the adults overseeing the yard activity.

None of us believed her, and, that night, I had a dream that I was forced to watch footage of people being crushed in the World Trade Center on the news.

After that, it became more clear that teachers were dealing with more easily distracted children. People who never used to call out, like Greg, started cracking jokes, getting up and walking around, impulsively banging on the table, wired up, vibrating with hostile energy, and, at the same time, just plain exhausted. Becca's brother, Ivan, always kept talking, or singing, or banging on the desk when Mr. H asked for three minutes of silence. We'd have to start the time over and over, until we were being dismissed fifteen minutes late every single day.

Sometime in those first couple of weeks back, a bowling party was thrown for us at Chelsea Piers, a sporting complex off the West Side Highway on 23rd Street that had an ice skating rink, indoor soccer field, batting cages, and golf range, the only place like it in Manhattan. Outside were all of the boats people took to cruise around the harbor, dance, and drink too much.

I didn't go, because it was still too difficult to get in and out of the neighborhood.

Becca was able to walk over from her apartment on 28th Street—she wouldn't have gone otherwise, since she refused to get on any form of public transportation. She lived in an apartment building complex in Chelsea not unlike ours, which was rent-controlled and had a colorful mix of residents.

"How was it?" I asked her the next day.

She shrugged.

"Bowling alleys are loud," she said.

"But did you have fun?"

"They had a big banner that said *Welcome I.S. 89.* I think it was supposed to make us feel safe, like it was a safe place."

"Did it work?"

She looked at me as if I had asked her if she believed in Santa Clause.

"No."

* * *

Charles always reported new threats as we traveled to school.

"These aren't people we can declare war on and eliminate. They hide within borders. This is an international organization that spans from Algeria to the Philippines. They're more serious of a threat than I first thought. They'll get us, and of course it'll be New York again."

Seek out the danger before it catches you off guard.

But once I catch it, what do I do?

The Internet was a dangerous place for a twelve-year-old back in 2001, even more so than it is now, and it was full of false information. Very few news organizations had begun to develop websites, many did not yet have one at all. There was no way to check the reputability of what was up there, but many of us, not just Charles, had this insatiable need to know everything. Along the way, we found out a lot of really terrible other things that happened to people, in the city, in the country, in the rest of the world. In our own country, people killed other people and weren't even sorry about it. They sexually abused kids, children like my dad's special-ed students. They robbed and hurt innocent old people. Children were shot. Just going outside could get you killed, especially in New York. They hurt animals and left them to die.

The more I opened my eyes to the news of the world, the more awful it seemed.

Like my father, Charles sometimes didn't know how to talk without practically shouting, even if you were standing right next to him. As a result, Charles was no stranger to being bullied. Other kids saw him as weak. They taunted him in the hallways and during lunch, calling him gay, threatening to hurt him. Even in elementary school, a group of Italian boys who lived in our neighborhood ruthlessly bullied him, forcing him to find a new way to walk home. My mom told me Charles would be "protecting me," but really, I felt like I was the one protecting Charles. I tried to look out for him when we took the train together after school, but it made me nervous to be alone with him because he was like a moving bulls-eye, and I was tiny.

On top of the terror report Charles delivered daily on our subway rides, there were the actual last minute MTA transit changes, rerouted trains, delays, policy investigations, and I had no idea how to navigate them. Months ago, whenever the conductor had come on over the loudspeaker on the subway, I had always ignored it, since I was with my mom anyway, or I chuckled, because I couldn't understand a word he said. Now, I jumped every time, and panicked if I couldn't understand what he said. What if my life depended on it?

"Why are we stopping?" I'd ask Charles, who had been stuck in the subway, underground, for an hour after the first plane hit.

"I'll bet it's a bomb," he'd say. After a moment, he'd thoughtfully add something like, "Maybe they hijacked a train. Maybe someone blew themselves up. Maybe our parents are dead."

Journal Entry, 10/7:

I am pretty religious, but when I was running I thought to myself, if I die, am I going to heaven? I strongly believe in it, but what if something else happened?

Today in class, Mary told us people kill abortion doctors. How do you stop murdering by murdering?

I had my friends, Allison, Rose, and Charlotte, who I shared lunchtime with. Allison, like me, was pretty jumpy, but for the most part, they all seemed fine—living, respectively, in the West Village, on Ocean Avenue in Brooklyn, and in the Fashion District uptown. I called them from the cell phone my parents and I still shared to talk about whatever I had read in my Teen People magazine (when the mail started coming again), sharing some embarrassing story a girl had written in, or hair tip that I thought we should both try that night and check in on the next day. I ripped out pictures of boys and taped them to my wall with scotch tape, like I felt I was supposed to.

But spontaneity, lightheartedness, joy, silliness, were slowly draining out of me, as if the part of me that was able to produce them had been deprived of blood and oxygen. When my family and I managed to travel uptown to the movie theater by Union Square, I tried to manage to lose myself in ten minutes of an entire movie, but the low rumbling in my seat caused by a train running underneath the theater brought me abruptly out of it. That cold hand of anxiety had found the back of my neck again, keeping a strong grip. Even if it was there for so long that it started to warm up, it never let go.

Meanwhile, our neighborhood was still infiltrated with police cars and armed soldiers, new barricades and street closures. Cars couldn't go through without having clearance. Police checkpoints were everywhere, and the cops were not friendly. They eyed large bags suspiciously, even if kids were the ones carrying them.

At first, I found this insane.

A twelve-year-old with a Macy's bag? Really?

Then I started wondering:

What if they actually found a twelve-year-old to walk around with a bomb?

It didn't matter if police were now carrying bigger guns. A gun was not going to keep anyone safe from a plane, or stop a car bomb or an exploding backpack. They could be lurking anywhere, at any time, like bogeymen popping out from a dark corner of a haunted house.

Journal Entry, 10/9

If Afghanistan retaliates, what will happen?

We're on full alert so security is higher.

I live by the bridge, what if a plane from Afghanistan flies into it and it's too late?

Chemical threats are scary (the ocean).

The Pentagon is not as paid attention to.

Bin Laden wants to destruct not negotiate.

We're getting nervous by the sounds of fire jets. We have to tell our minds they're protecting us.

Are any other countries considering hurting us? Why? Which ones? Will bin Laden encourage it? If his only problem is his opinion of our culture, we could've talked

about it because that's what the United Nations is for. I try not to show it, but I'm afraid of another 9/11 happening. It would be worse if I was alone.

We should all just have a conference.

We tried to come back from Pathmark but couldn't get through because there was a lockdown. Maybe something happened on the bridge. Stuyvesant High School is going back tomorrow. I don't want to go back to our building. I just can't. I'm nervous because I saw tapes on the news of Afghanistan burning flags. I'm a nervous wreck; my grandpa just fell and is in the hospital. The day after his birthday.

I have changed my mind about the conference after the burning flags footage.

Journal Entry, 10/10

I gave a blind man on the subway $1. Even if he's not really blind, he must be scared like everyone else but has nobody to make him feel better. Not that money will, but maybe he can buy a sandwich.

Journal Entry, 10/11

I just found out that an Islamic man knew a female friend of ours. He ran away with his bags, and she got a letter from him that said don't go near the World Trade Center on September 11th or any malls on Halloween. Oh my God. Halloween? She sent it to the FBI. I am trying to study for my Spanish test.

* * *

The South Street Seaport had always been the main tourist attraction in our neighborhood. Now, there was Ground Zero.

Tourists started coming downtown, which was technically "open" again, asking for directions to the World Trade Center. *There is no World Trade Center, you fucking idiot.*

People weren't at the site reflecting or crying. They lined up to take pictures in front of the pit, smiling and waving, and when green netting was put up around the fence to block people from seeing what was inside, people poked holes in it so they could stick their cameras in and get the shot anyway. Eventually, some sort of bridge was put up to give people a photo opp. They posed, family members with fanny packs and arms around each other, *one, two, three, cheese*, and it made our experience feel even less real.

"I can't believe they're allowed to do this," Sarah said.

Soon, vendors were popping up on the surrounding streets, selling booklets like the ones my parents bought me at Broadway shows, magnets, cups, playing cards, all showing images of the Towers on fire and the planes crashing into them, of people running and screaming, of the collapse. They were mostly people from Chinatown.

What was more disgusting still was that people *wanted* to have this to take home and look at. People were *buying* them. *Who the fuck would want that as a souvenir? Do you understand what that was like?*

We could hear people say, when they arrived at the site, "That's it? There's just a hole?"

"Like they're disappointed," Sarah fumed in the girl's bathroom one day. "What do they want to be there? What part of 'gone' don't they understand?"

"They're just taking pictures and carrying on with their day," I responded back, layering on red lipstick and wetting my hair to keep it from frizzing up. "They're just spectators. It's our neighborhood. They have no right to be there."

I felt angry, and then I felt something new: pure hatred. I hated them.

Since when do I hate anyone? They ruined my entire day just by being there, stomping all over the remains of my old life.

My urge to jab an elbow into anyone with a map in their hand or a camera around their neck grew stronger with time. I wanted to make them feel what they should have felt, being down there: pain. When it got to the point where my mother and I couldn't even get to where we were going, I became a lit stick of dynamite, angrily pushing myself through them, boiling over with this flood of toxic emotions and feelings I didn't recognize. The mood would stay with me for hours, making me snippy and nasty.

"What the hell's the matter with you?" my mother said in a shrill voice that cut through me like a sharp axe made of ice. "You're like an animal! Knock it off."

For years, tourists excitedly flocked to the site. They wanted to be a part of something they never could, and we would have given anything not to be.

* * *

Whenever "Breaking News" interrupted a television program, my entire body seized up in terror, ready to bolt.

All kinds of triggers were setting me off before I knew what a trigger even was. Suddenly, I was agitated, restless, scared, cringing, and crying, and wringing my hands. There was a churning in the middle of my body; the feeling like I needed to act, quickly, but that there was nothing I could do. It felt like driving a car and having one foot on the accelerator and another on the brake, holding them both down with all of my might while the tires just sputtered in the mud.

I need to do something but I don't know what. I'm going to die. You shouldn't be like this.

The threats, the Orange Alerts, began to pile on. Every single human being in New York City was a potential suicide bomber. They could be standing next to you at the corner, in a store, or a garage. They could follow you into your building. There was no real security on the subway or on a bus. Millions of people were just darting around. Now, the UPS guy was a suspect.

Suspicious Package! Walk the other way!

I began having panic attacks on the subway, shaking whenever the train stopped in the tunnel. My brain was shouting "You have to escape!" but there was no way out.

Then this campaign began:

"If you see something, say something."

You were supposed to call the police (even though cell phones were only first starting to become popular, and nobody had service underground) if you saw a suspicious, everyday object left unattended, like a briefcase or a backpack. All someone had to do was leave a briefcase on a subway platform to turn the entire world upside down. These became the objects we feared, as children: duffle bags, suitcases, backpacks, briefcases, purses, boxes, were all lethal and fatal. Nothing made sense anymore.

Greg got out of the subway to make those calls, which sometimes made him late to class.

I don't have a cell phone.

Noises bellowed up from regular city construction projects, from dumpsters, from trucks, from police cars and ambulances. People screamed, and every scream was as startling as having a gun pointed in my face. Wherever I was standing, I was on the lookout, with my hair on end, charged and raring to go. My mind never let me rest. Logic was being redefined, or perhaps it was collapsing into itself as a concept just when I had started to grasp it. I watched as it slipped through my fingers like sand. It was all gone. Our home was quarantined from the rest of society, and a pervasive feeling spread through my body as though it was being injected with a needle: the underlying sense of danger, that everything wasn't what it seemed.

"What if."

Some of my fear, the lack of control, started twisting and contorting into something else: anger. *Someone has to be blamed.* It would've been much more politically correct if none of us were terrified when we saw dark skinned, bearded men wearing caps, and women in burkas on the train or in a store.

But that wasn't the case.

We were being shown these faces, told to look out for these men, who looked a lot like the guys who operated news stands, rode the subway, drove cabs, owned delis, walked around with luggage, just like everyone else.

* * *

After school every day, I went right upstairs to check on Grandma, but the nature of those visits changed. Now, instead of finding comfort, instead of going to be enveloped in the warmth and the joy and the fun, I was going to make sure she was okay, to watch over her.

No matter what my parents tried to do for me, taking me shopping or for ice cream or to the movies, I hated all of it. On top of it, I was upset that I couldn't feel happy, or anything less than permanently awful. The child-like behavior of other kids, the happiness of people around me, made me even angrier.

In late October, we went to Foxwoods Casino in Connecticut to try to "get away from the smell and have some fun." As always, there was a ton of bumper-to-bumper traffic before the entrance to the Lincoln Tunnel. As our car chugged along, stopping and starting, my pulse began to quicken; I craned my neck to see out of the back window, cars in front, cars behind. *Car bomb.* The droning man delivering the news on 1010 Wins agitated me and I kicked my mom's seat in front of me.

"Can you turn off the news? I hate it!" I said. It wasn't the radio host's fault. It was the sensation of being trapped that made everything else feel too tight on me. It was like someone was yelling in my face and the car doors were closing in, a teakettle was whistling in my ear.

That truck is going to explode. You're going to die. You can't get out.
Get out! You have to run!
Get out!
Get out!!!!!!

"We need to go," I said quickly, which was absurd, given the circumstances. "I need to go. I need to go. I need to go. I need to go. Now. Now."

"What are you, crazy? Stop already, you're annoying me now," my mom said.

"Uggggh," I sighed, clonking my head against the window. I squeezed my eyes closed and shut up.

Journal Entry, 10/20
There was a concert for NYC today. There were six thousand police and firemen there. My mom said, who's watching the streets? Billy crystal made a joke, "This is the first time I've seen rock stars back stage running from white powder." I think they meant anthrax. My mom thought that was hysterical, but then started crying when a dead firefighters' family came on, and then everyone was crying. I brought the tape of the concert to Grandma's so she could watch some of the songs.

"Don't go out on Halloween, there's going to be another terrorist attack," I heard Michael say to Greg back at school.

"How do you know?" I intercepted.

"My friend from Hebrew School said his Middle Eastern babysitter told him to stay away from malls or crowded public places," he said.

After Michael's parents picked him up from P.S. 3 on the eleventh, he lay in bed that night thinking two things.

Someone has to pay for what had happened. And I'm the one who needs to make them pay. Then, *this is the most important thing that will ever happen to me in my lifetime. Don't forget what happened today. Try to remember everything. Someday, somebody is going to want to hear my story.* There were many thoughts absent from his mind over the next couple of weeks, months, years: fearful thoughts, flashbacks, nightmares.

Until he got to high school, he felt like he was "pretty much okay."

Charles, who was still adamant about not letting the terrorists win, attended the children's Halloween party in Southbridge dressed as a rescue worker, wearing his father's hardhat, neon vest, and gas mask.

When I.S. 89 had our own Halloween dance, I went dressed as Columbia from the Rocky Horror Picture Show, but nobody knew who I was supposed to be.

As we danced wildly, trying to ignore the huddles of parents by the door, Christine told me about her friend who would only wear flats.

"Why?" I asked.

"She said she has to be able to run in her shoes."

We danced to "Bootylicious" by Destiny's Child, "Miss Jackson" by Outkast, "Family Affair" by Mary J. Blige, and "I Hope You Dance" by Lee Ann Womack.

The last slow song came on at 9:00 p.m., signaling that the dance was over. It was Enrique Iglesias' "Hero," and I danced with Henry while some of the boys, like Devin, made fun of it all. Too soon, the lights abruptly flickered on to reveal all of our parents waiting by the door. Our little cluster of costumes and swinging elbows was broken up by the blast of those sad florescent bulbs. We slowly trudged toward the door, some of us stalling for time, more than just disappointed that the dance was over: we were trying to avoid going back to the nightmare that was our reality.

The next day, President Bush threw the first pitch at the World Series on October 30.

He later said that that was the most nervous he'd ever been in his entire presidency.

Journal Entry, 11/1

Killing for religion seems like an excuse to me. Islamic religion isn't based on killing, but the terrorists changed it around to fit themselves. How could people who got letters that their homes would be destroyed not warn anyone else? It's like Kitty Genovese, they knew it was happening but didn't want to take any action for anyone but themselves. Why haven't we learned from past history? The civil war should have taught ALL of us to wipe out racism, and should've wiped out such uncivilized behavior.

One day, I decided to "like" Henry back.

I thought a boyfriend was exactly what I needed to take my mind off things, and it didn't seem like there were any other takers.

The only problem was, he was with Becca.

So, during violin class in the storage closet, I passed him a note, and he passed one back, and I made a convincing case. Becca never took it out on me, never got angry. Most likely because they weren't doing much boyfriend-and-girlfriend-ing anyway.

Henry came from a very strict Filipino family, so we weren't allowed to hang out after school. We had brief moments of time together, like grabbing a slice of pepperoni pizza and orange soda before we hopped on our separate trains to head home, kissing each other with garlicky, greasy pizza mouths. He got me a rose one day, I called him one night and his mother told me he had to call me back because he was taking a bath. I remember that night specifically because, the next morning, on November 12, American Airlines Flight 587 crashed into a field in Queens. I had just woken from the first nightmare I'd had in two weeks, of a plane crash and fiery remains of buildings blazing, chasing me and Grandma. I woke up and walked in to the living room and saw it on television, and I thought that I was literally losing my mind.

Journal Entry, 11/19
Oh my God we were on the C train, which was delayed for fifteen minutes because there was a fire, and my nerves are shot and I'm sweating and exhausted. I'm going to collapse.

Journal Entry, 11/21
This really nice lady from Colorado came to our school today, and we had a great conversation as we were going from class to class, about everything related to the WTC. It was hard to talk with all the chaos in the hallway. I'm sorry she only came for one day. I thought a lot more people would have opened up to her if they got the chance to talk, and I found it really upsetting that some people made fun of her accent.

I remember that day, because it was the day Thomas told he returned to his Gateway Plaza home in Battery Park City for the first time in November, and waited outside with his aunt by the entrance to World Financial Center while his parents entered, then passed, the checkpoint. He told me there were giant mounds of rubble everywhere. When the first plane hit, it blew out windows and tore at his building.

"The side of it was clean wiped away," he told me at lunch.

The guts of the building were exposed, as if torn open for an architectural autopsy.

"I could count the floors and see into peoples' apartments. Pieces of metal were stuck into the sides of the building."

He was not allowed into the apartment with his mother, who found a leg inside, underneath six inches of dust. In fact, she later told him, there were so many random body parts you couldn't even tell what they were. The dust settled high above the floor, the bed, and the couch. The furniture was burnt and singed. His prized Beanie Baby collection had been destroyed, even the special Princess Diana Bear. His collection of McDonalds toys and little cars were all gone. Nothing in the apartment was salvageable.

He waited, watching people roaming around in gas masks, looking at the skeletal outline of the outline of the World Trade Center yards away and thinking, like he did every day, about what he had seen there two months earlier.

I didn't find out the magnitude of what Thomas had been through until nearly a decade later.

* * *

Jorge the Spanish teacher had circulated through first period Spanish class with a microphone around his neck, winding in and out of desks, teaching the kids a song that they never finished.

Vrooooooooom.

Jorge didn't stop the kids from rushing to the window, but soon Debra, the eighth grade literacy teacher, came in and whispered in his ear.

"We're going to evacuate," Jorge announced.

The kids lined up and mocked fainting, laughing, saying "We're all going to die!"

Thomas laughed nervously and fell in line with the others. His father had just finished parking their car in front of the World Financial Center and appeared in the hallway before the class went down to the cafeteria. Thomas caught Ellen's eye, and the look in it caused his stomach to turn. Her eyes were wide open and searching for something that her frozen stance signified she could not find. *She has no idea what to do.*

As Thomas and his father left the school building, a strange woman ran up to them, took in a sharp breath in, swallowed quickly, and warned them, "Don't go that way! People are falling!" His father ignored her, and they kept walking toward the Towers, toward home.

As they approached the Winter Garden of the World Financial Center, Thomas saw an old lady kneeling on the floor, covered in blood. It was at that moment that the two of them broke into a sprint, surfacing on the other side by the boat basin and watching as one person after the other jumped and fell from the building like dominoes.

Thomas turned around to see a woman melted by jet fuel lying in a pool of blood on the sidewalk.

As they hurried into 600 Gateway Plaza to grab their one-year-old miniature poodle, Eddie, Thomas glanced sideways out of the window facing the Tower, feeling as though he was just inches away.

That would be the last time he saw his apartment for six months.

They were riding in the elevator when the lights began to flicker and the elevator floor began to shake. Eddie whimpered in his carrying case. The power was beginning to cut out.

The elevator eventually reached the lobby, and the doors opened to reveal police with gas masks on barking at them all to get out of the building and over to "the tip of the island."

"Manhattan is going to explode. The jet fuel and gas lines are going to destroy everything!"

Thomas clutched Eddie's carrying case as he and his father were stopped by police putting up barricades and positioning their cars to keep everyone contained in one area.

For twenty minutes, they were corralled in front of Gateway Plaza, watching people jump and land on the pavement in front of them.

A woman in a blue dress.

A man in a white shirt.

A woman with blond hair.

Scream.

Splat.

Crunch.

Scream.

Splat.

Crunch.

Eventually, the cops allowed them to take the back entrance out of Gateway Plaza, so they hurried South toward the water, further downtown, to the edge of Battery Park. Nearing Bowling Green park, Thomas's heart nearly stopped as he heard another *vrooming* noise, like a motorcycle speeding up. It sounded exactly the same as the first noise. Before he could register the next thought, he heard screams everywhere and they ran toward the park, behind the Museum of Jewish Heritage. He suddenly felt dizzy; he was having visions of the woman splattering on the pavement in front of him, limbs flying everywhere.

"This wouldn't happen in Florida. I want to move to Florida," he kept repeating.

"That's not going to help us now, stop saying that," his father barked through a coughing fit.

They sat on a park bench behind the museum to catch their breath, his father silent and stone faced, Thomas with Eddie's cage in his lap.

The woman sitting on the bench next to them suddenly screamed, clutching her poodles to her chest. "Oh my God! Oh my God!" she shouted, over and over. Thomas did not immediately register what he saw as he turned around, nor did he think the cloud of smoke was so close that it could come toward them. But in a millisecond, the cloud wrapped around Liberty Court, pushing the fastest moving crowd he had ever seen further toward the water, closer to the boats.

They didn't have time to reach them before the cloud gained on them.

Thomas and his father hit the floor and rolled underneath more nearby park benches as it passed over them. The last thing Thomas saw was a woman jumping over the railing into the river.

And then it was quiet.

Unable to see even his hands right in front of him, the entire world became black like night. He could feel pieces of debris blowing against and past his face in the darkness. Thomas clutched Eddie's cage and stayed this way for what felt like twenty minutes, barely able to breathe.

Once the darkness began to clear, he emerged from underneath the benches of Wagner Park and he and his father felt their way to the bathrooms by his favorite restaurant, Gigino's, where he'd always watched the fireworks on Fourth of July.

The bathroom was full of children, whose cries and screams were deafening. Fifty people were covered head to toe in what looked like gray powder, many of them trying to comfort the children.

"Mommy, the sky is falling, like Chicken Little said it would," Thomas heard one little girl say.

Adults were splashing their faces with water from the toilets. Some people ran into the bathroom, ripped their clothes off, dunked them into the toilet, then ran out again, wrapping them around their faces.

Thomas and his father stood in there for what felt like an infinite amount of time.

Then, he heard another noise.

Boom.

Boom.

Boom . . .

More people were shouting and running by the bathrooms, fanatical screams of strangers crying, "the Sears Tower got hit" and "planes are dropping all over the city!"

Thomas and his father left the bathroom and found themselves standing knee high in singed paper. An ambulance speeding by slowed down for a moment to ask if they needed oxygen. Thomas and his father quickly boarded the back of the ambulance speeding toward the Towers, riding with the back door open. They took two puffs and were promptly told to leave.

"We've got to go," said the medic, barely stopping for them to get off, and leaving them alone again once more.

They stumbled toward Gateway Plaza again, barely able to see, everything still smokey and dark. They found their way into the packed lobby of a building by Liberty Court, where people fruitlessly tried to make phone calls. Almost everyone was covered in gray ash; those who weren't brought phones downstairs and thrust them into their powdery hands, insisting, "Try mine, try mine." But nobody was getting anywhere. *This call cannot be completed.*

Suddenly, cops rushed the building once again, shouting.

"The island is going to blow up!"

"There's too much fuel!"

"We don't know if there are bombs, you have to get out, go toward the boats!"

Thomas didn't bother trying to cover his face as he pushed his way through a shower of papers, knowing that no matter what he'd still be breathing it all in.

At the dock by the boats, it looked like a scene from the movie *Titanic*. Grown men were hopping the fence, people were swarming the boats, fighting and screaming "I'm here, I'm here," into the darkness.

Men were dangling off the railing trying to jump on, people were climbing lampposts, and everyone was pushing each other.

Still carrying Eddie, Thomas and his father stumbled down the ramp leading to the dock, but had to hop the high fence. Thomas looked around scared and confused: what he and his father were being pushed onto wasn't a boat, it was an inflatable raft with a little motor on the back.

It was built for ten and was being swarmed by three times as many people. Thomas was elbowed and slammed into and smacked in the eye as everyone tried to push their way on, like in some sort of stampede. The cops were still shouting the same message to everyone, "The island is going to explode! Everyone has to get out of here!"

They departed, and, barely off of the dock heading to Jersey City, someone suddenly screamed, "There's water! There's water!"

The back of the boat was sinking.

People tried to move to the front as the boat continued sinking lower, the back eventually disappearing entirely. The engine beginning to sputter.

Everyone's feet were wet, and by the time they made it across the river, half of the boat was under water. But they hadn't made it yet. The docks in New Jersey were six feet high, built for bigger ships and ferries like the New York Waterway. It seemed there was no way to get on land. *Who was around that was going to help them?* Thomas thought.

As if materializing through some sort of miracle, five businessmen on land arrived and began pulling their clothes off, their suit jackets and shirts, and dangling them over the railing. They were bringing everyone within arms reach, to the point where they could grab their hands and hoist them up onto land. They hauled up every single person on the boat this way as it sunk further by the minute.

Thomas was smashed into the side of the wall on his way up, and his father looked on silently. Once they made it over, they watched the city burning, waiting for his mother to possibly arrive in a boat, if she wasn't dead. One crowded boat after another arrived, and the same men stayed on the docks for two hours, pulling everyone off of each one. His mother was not on any of them.

Eventually, Thomas and his father wandered into a nearby office building, and a man took them upstairs to use the phone. The offices they passed were practically ransacked; people were hanging out of windows, just staring across the water, gaping at New York.

Thomas and his father tried every number they could think of, aunts and uncles, but every answer was the same. *Your call cannot be completed.* His father's face, by now, had turned to stone.

Busses started to line up by the docks, but, as they tried to board, the driver said, "You can't go on yet, we have to get you decontaminated."

They pushed everyone into a makeshift coral and hosed them down, making Thomas feel as though they were in a concentration camp. They even sprayed Eddie. Just hours after he had narrowly avoided drowning, Thomas was soaked; but instead of washing away, the gray ash, the debris, the dead people, the building, were all caked onto his body.

Thomas boarded the bus and sat next to a man, who in a matter of seconds began screaming, "Get down, get down!" as the sound of planes roared overhead and sent everyone into a panic. Everyone hit the floor of the bus and covered their heads, except one woman, who ran off.

"They're attacking again!" screamed another woman, over and over.

A Chinese lady got down on the ground, hovering over her child as though protecting him from an air raid, just before a man came on the bus and said "It's ok, the planes are full of Americans."

Everyone started clapping; everyone except for an eleven-year-old boy clutching his one-year-old dog, who thought, *so were the other ones.*

After ten minutes, the bus dropped everyone off at something resembling a YMCA. Thomas and his father used a working pay phone to call every number they could think of, but still, no calls placed to New York would go through. They tried to call one of his dad's friends collect. At first, he wouldn't accept the call, but they kept trying, and, eventually, headed to that friend's apartment. Thomas fell asleep after watching Tower 7 fall on the news, thinking about the woman in a puddle of blood, then the woman in the blue dress, and wondering if his mother was alive.

CHAPTER SIX

Children need predictability, a sense of control, after being in a state of alarm and waiting for the next catastrophe every minute.

They need the stability that comes from routine, or they won't know what to do when they have to make the simplest choices. Having been deprived of the basic choices most children get to make as they begin to discover what they like and who they are, these children have no sense of self and turn to others for guidance.

We make memories, but memories make us too; and though its effects may not always be visible to the untrained eye, when you know what trauma can do to children, sadly, you begin to see its aftermath everywhere.

—Dr. Bruce Perry, *The Boy Who Was Raised as a Dog*

On December 22, passengers on Flight 63 complained of a smoke smell coming from somewhere in the cabin shortly after a meal service. A man was sitting alone near a window and attempting to light a match on his shoe. He pushed the flight attendant to the floor when she tried to stop him, and bit another who tried to do the same.

Because he had worn his shoes for an extra day after the flight was delayed, because it had rained, because maybe he had sweaty feet, the fuse was too damp to be ignited. The "Shoe Bomber" was foiled.

That was right around Christine's birthday, and it was tradition for her brother, her mother, and her aunt to join them for a walk over to Police Plaza. They always had elaborate holiday lights set up over there, and even though it was just a short walk from home, they treated it like an event. She hoped, one day, to be able to take her own kids to see it, even though police headquarters seemed like an odd destination for something like that. That year, Police Plaza was closed off. The stunning decorations and light displays that brightened up an otherwise drab, concrete street, were nowhere to be seen. So, they turned around and walked back home.

Reena spent the night before Christmas in her Gateway Plaza apartment, even though they weren't supposed to go back yet. They had snuck in to have Christmas at home. *This might be our last Christmas here. It might be our last Christmas anywhere.*

As for me, the night before Christmas Eve, I went with my mother to Toys 'R' Us in Times Square, which was packed. My mother must have thought that the setting would be festive: the candy, the miles of toys, the Ferris wheel.

When we got to the back of the store, joining mobs of other people cradling Barbie boxes and holding stuffed tigers, something shifted. I became seized with the certainty that bombs would fall on us and the mob would trample us. We would watch everyone screaming and sobbing and dying, since we were in the back, and Grandma would die of grief after my mother and I died, and who knows what would happen to my dad.

I suddenly thought about a day back in first grade when, during some ball game, everyone dog piled on me, and I couldn't breathe. There were ten kids on top of me, I was gasping for breath and crying, and none of the outdoor "aids" tried to help me. I just stood there, alone, in shock, gasping for breath, thinking I was going to die.

"Mom, we have to go," I said, pulling her toward the door.

"What are you talking about? We didn't pay yet."

"I don't care. Let's go," I said, starting to pull her by the arm.

Something washed over me, this warm feeling, and I started to lose my breath.

"We have to go! We have to go!" I said, starting to cry. "Please!"

I was practically yanking her, trying to get her to move toward the revolving doors that would release us back into the chaos of Times Square, stifling the screams that were trying to push their way out.

I don't remember what happened after that.

Journal Entry, 12/31/01

We went to St. Vincent's today.

We visited a social therapist and he just stared at me. He was bald and dressed very unprofessionally.

The waiting room was empty. The magazines were ripped.

He took us to his office and slumped in his chair and said he was confused by the Red Cross papers. There were weird drawings around his room. We talked about our new guidance counselor Wendy who is from St. Vincent's.

My mom started talking about the fires in 5 WTC and how we were in constant lockdown, and how I was in intensive care when I was a baby for a week projectile vomiting and screaming and disturbing the other babies, so they sent me to another room by myself, and my mom thought I was dead when they got there because I wasn't there. The only things that could put me to sleep were car rides and my grandma. I get nervous and anxious.

We think I have PTSD. I'm more jumpy with sounds and have panic attacks in crowds, and I'm nervous about planes, and my mom gets nervous when other people are nervous. We still can't really open the windows.

My teacher wrote this on a post it:

It's a very tough time and you probably do have PTSD. It's a completely normal reaction. Now they are saying that 40 percent of people downtown have it. You will feel better, but it takes time.

* * *

The waiting room in the hospital was dank and reminded me of my old elementary school. It felt germy and dirty and small, with pale yellow walls that had marks all over them and floors covered in scuffs from peoples' shoes.

I saw a therapist named Donna for a few months. I liked Donna well enough.

She was middle-aged, I guessed, with white, pasty skin and bright red, shiny hair. There were crinkles around her eyes, which had been rubbed with a copper colored shadow.

We'd fill out some paperwork in the lobby, and then we'd get called upstairs.

My mom would wait outside while Donna asked me what I was scared of, what was going in my life, what was stressing me out.

I liked having someone to talk to, but after a few weeks, I got kind of annoyed. I didn't want to talk about it all the time if she wasn't going to be able to change what I seemed unable to change, or control, myself.

What are we going to do about it?

As I would later learn, I was the only patient Donna was seeing. She mainly did intake, giving extensive evaluations to children coming in so they could get assigned to a therapist.

We were going to be taking a trip to Disney World, my mother had announced, so I had to try and get ready.

I told her I was afraid to get on the plane, and Donna asked me what I was afraid of. She listened, and she nodded, and told me to take a book with me. The book would help change my thoughts, she said. She also said I should wear a rubber band and snap it to stop a bad thought when it came.

As an exercise, she told me to come up with a safe place.

"My safe place is a beach, with waves, and warm sand. What's your safe place?"

"Grandma's house," I said.

"Where in your grandmother's house? Is she next to you? What does she smell like? What are you doing together? Watching TV? What are you watching?"

I answered the questions, and she said, "When you're on the plane, go to that place."

I was only covered for twelve weeks of therapy, and so we stopped, right before we left for Florida.

Even with our talk behind us, I doubted that she could ensure my plane wouldn't be hijacked. She didn't have any control over the situation at the airport. If something happened, she'd be alive, wrong, but alive, and I would be dead.

Journey Entry, 3/31/02
4:00 p.m.: Going to Disney. We're getting out of the rental car into American Airlines. I am extremely on edge and nervous.

4:02 p.m.: Outside getting luggage tagged. I have to keep telling myself Floridians aren't murderers.

4:08 p.m.: We're checking our luggage and I've been ok, but after he starting asking us questions about our luggage I got anxious again.

4:14 p.m.: We're at the security checkpoint and it's a long line moving fast. There's tons of security but I don't mind. I know we're ok, but what about others. My dad has to say "yes sir, no sir," because Joe made a wise remark in Arabic and they cavity searched him. I'm lashing out and being nasty to them.

Aside from getting sick after eating French food at Epcot, we had a great time. It was my third trip to Disney World, but it never got old, and I didn't remember much from the time I was seven, anyway.

They had this new thing, "pin" trading—you bought a bunch of pins in the gift shop, and you could trade pins with other staff and kids, so it was like you were always on the hunt for something, the thrill of the pin-chase, which was exciting.

In the back of my mind, the stubborn thought that Disney was a target buzzed around like a mosquito, but there was enough to do and see, enough distraction, to keep swatting it away.

The nightmares followed me there, too.

Journal Entry, 4/5/02

I had a dream that ten planes were circling and two crashed into Pace University down the block, one crashed into my angel on top of the Municipal Building. Aunt Fran was at Grandma's but disappeared, so me and Dad and Grandma were trying to escape. All these buildings were on fire so we got on a train and went by I.S. 89, which turned into the Brooklyn Botanical Gardens, and nobody acted like anything was wrong. I can't believe I have to go back to my stupid life. It would be easier to go home if I didn't live by Ground Zero.

As we boarded the return flight, sad to go back to reality but excited to see Grandma, I saw a man with dark skin board in first class that made me nervous.

He looks like a terrorist.

What's he doing with his shoe?

Oh, he's tying it.

Then, a group of college guys, some student athletes, sat scattered all around us back in coach, whooping and shouting.

"We have to tell the flight attendant to throw them off of the plane for being too rowdy," I told my mom. "And that other guy up front has to go, too."

I clutched the armrest of the seat, saying "Mom, Mom, Mom" over and over through gritted teeth. My parents couldn't calm me down, because—well, they just couldn't. Parents were supposed to be able to walk into your room and explain that thunder is nothing to be scared of, that it's just a change in weather and pressure, open your closet door, and show you that there are no monsters inside. But there was no way for them to disprove the fears I had now.

My dad leaned over and started talking to one of the rowdy college guys, asking them to keep it down because loud noises made me nervous, explaining why it made me nervous. He did it in this cool, friendly way, and they actually listened—well, some of them, anyway.

We landed in one piece, and when we arrived at the baggage claim, people started crowding around the man with the dark skin from first class, holding out their boarding passes and pens. They were asking him to pose for photos.

It turned out to be Ramiro Mendoza, a pitcher for the New York Yankees.

* * *

Allison and I kept that magic of Disney going through our shared love of princess movies, and we would have sleepovers to watch them.

At lunch, we made friends with the bagel guys at Chelsea Market on Ninth Avenue and gave them silly cards we made for them. We would do childish things, like the time I "washed her hair" with leave-in-conditioner while she lay in her bed, and we laughed until our sides hurt. We had bonded, most of all, over our shared desire *not* to go back to I.S. 89, minorities in a majority of kids who demanded we go back to our school so we could have our end-of-the-year dance there.

I wrote a couple of op-eds for a local newspaper, the *Downtown Express*, about how I felt about returning to the school. I looked at the pros and cons of both sides, and ended both on the notion of "holding our heads high," a gag-inducing cliché among adults, but a new phrase for me, at the time, and one that I rather liked.

There would be more reports about the air quality on the news and in the local papers, and mixed reports that my dad brought home from the Community Board 1 meetings he attended.

"It's safe to go back, the air quality is fine."

"New results show that we need to delay the return, as it's still not safe."

We had all formed opinions about going back, something teachers decided to initiate multiple heated discussions about.

Greg said it made him feel safer—understandably so, since he didn't do very well at the O'Henry Learning Center.

I said that I did not feel safer.

Thomas said nothing.

We all saw those discussions as ultimately pointless, though, because it wasn't up to us, anyway.

* * *

Ultimately, we returned to I.S. 89 with a couple of months left in the year, and were welcomed by a few camera crews—fewer than I was expecting.

I was once again pretty annoyed with Paige, because I did not like the interview she gave to the local news station, New York 1, about going to back to I.S. 89. She sat there and talked about how excited she was to go back, how unafraid she was, like a kid who was totally fine. I was sure Ellen, the school principal, picked her out for that reason. I was angry because I felt that her reaction did not represent the rest of us.

So, this time, we were all dying to get on the news.

We only had a half-day that first day back.

Debra, the eighth grade literacy teacher, announced we'd each be given thirty seconds to go through a giant pile of all the stuff that had been left in lockers on September 11th, to find what belonged to us. She stood there with her finger on a stop-watch she must have gotten from the gym teacher, and actually counted down.

I instantly saw my backpack, the black one with the band of colorful daises across it; my notebook, with the big bumper sticker across the front; and a couple of binders full of blank loose leaf paper.

Back in our science classroom, we were given some "gift boxes" that contained sparkly magic markers, a drawing pad, and a CD from either Jewel or some rapper.

"What is this?" Becca asked. "A prize for surviving?"

It was business as usual for the two months that finished out the rest of the year.

Devin used AOL Instant Messenger to get me to admit that I had a crush on Kyle, promising not to tell him, even though, I should have known, Kyle was there with him.

I tried *everything* to get Kyle's attention, but he had a crush on the tall, skinny Japanese girl who wore thongs and a lot of eyeliner, so I went to the Victoria's Secret at the Seaport to buy a black thong as thin as dental floss and some

L'Oreal liquid eyeliner from the drug store and scrawled it on way too thick during class, staring into a compact mirror. My favorite shirt was a red tank top that hugged my B-cup boobs, one that Allison commented, "My mom said when there are those fabric lines across the front of a girl's shirt, it means it's too tight."

The guidance counselor, Emily, sometimes called me, Kyle, Marianne, and Jesse into her office for a therapy session because our parents had all indicated they thought it would be good for us.

"So," Emily would say, uncapping her pen and tossing her blonde dyed ringlets over her shoulder. "Who wants to start?"

I always wanted to start. I was right there with all of my fears, thoughts, and feelings. The problem was, nobody else was.

Kyle would never talk, not a single word. Jesse would kind of agree with me, with an emphatic "yeah!" and Marianne would usually question whatever the guidance counselor said, like, "Is that really supposed to make us feel better? Nothing you can say or do will make us feel better."

* * *

In May, Peter, my summer camp crush, told the *New York Times* that he was afraid to go through tunnels, which he used to think were really cool. Now, he just thought about it being blown up, water flooding in, and dying a slow death. Nikki told them she was suddenly, months later, afraid Osama bin Laden would show up in her room, and she has disturbing dreams about him. She was checking through the window for the source of loud noises.

Some of the elementary school kids from P.S. 234, the *Times* reported, were regressing to earlier childhood behavior, like hitting, kicking, calling names, even wetting the bed. Others hid in their closets every day, or ducked under desks whenever they heard noises.

We also learned through this article that the Board of Education had concluded that about 200,000 of the 712,000 kids in public schools in grades four through twelve were candidates for "some sort of intervention" due to lingering trauma from 9/11.

That's what they did. They "concluded."

* * *

Christine became attached to Mary, who encouraged her—all of us, in fact—to be aware of what was going on in the world, to learn about different types of people instead of believing in "propaganda." We were always excited on the days that the TV and VCR were waiting in her classroom. Mary showed us documentaries like *Four Little Girls* about the Alabama bombings, and she showed us an episode of *Boston Public*, a show that my family and I watched together every week, about the use of the "N" word.

They covered very real and dark topics that felt important. Bra protests, dead teachers, student's parents locking them in the basement and sexually abusing them, a teacher so stressed out that she begins bashing her car when it breaks down, only to be interrupted by a student who came to find her to tell her she changed his life. We were all fans of that show, and its abrupt cancellation was something I did not take well.

Christine also liked Mr. H, who had taken a special interest in her one day after looking over her shoulder and read the poem she was writing. He asked her if she needed to talk. She did. She usually didn't let herself get close to adults, because they tended to leave.

Mr. H announced, in June, that he would not be coming back.

Mary announced that she was fired.

The following September, they were both gone.

***

"I don't know why I stopped seeing you," Donna said.

Fourteen years later to the day that I had that episode in Toys R Us, I'd found her, the woman who helped me get ready to board a plane to Disney World, who I stopped seeing after twelve weeks.

"I think it was because the Red Cross or Crime Victims said I was only covered for twelve sessions."

"That must have been it," she said.

"But twelve weeks doesn't seem like enough time to make sure a kid is okay after something like that," I said.

She shook her head.

"No, it's definitely not. You know, they sent me downtown into another school in the Lower East Side. I stayed with those children for up to six years at a time, and was able to stay consistent with them over those years because we got a grant for trauma and a wellness center."

"Wow," I said. "I could have really used that."

"We worked from this manual," she said, holding up a white binder full of printed pages labeled *Cognitive Behavioral Training for Children.*

"What were the kids coming to you with? What sort of issues?"

"They were afraid, mostly. That more planes were going to go into buildings. They were afraid to go to sleep. They had headaches and stomachaches, they were worried all the time. And I wanted to help them feel safe, so we did specific exercises."

"What were the exercises?"

"Deep breathing, thought-stopping, meditation, mindfulness. I would ask them to tell their narrative, when it began, what happened, telling them not to blame themselves or feel guilty. Some of the kids had 9/11 issues, but others were dealing with different trauma, like the death of a parent."

"What was the end goal?"

"To help them realize the difference between feelings and thoughts."

"That's a big one," I said.

"Yes. For example, let's say there's someone who you think hates you. You may go to say 'Hi' and that someone doesn't say 'Hi' back. Then, you think she's ignoring you, and she hates you, then you feel bad, and you think that nobody likes you."

I nodded, understanding completely.

"But then, I introduce this idea, 'What if they're shy? Maybe it's not about you.' Kids often end up with these self-fulfilling prophecies. The thought is, you're going to do bad on a test. The feeling is that you're stupid. So, the behavior is that you're not going to study, and there you have it. It becomes a reality. It's about navigating this cognitive triangle of thought, feeling, and behavior."

So many years later, the concepts were more than familiar to me; but then, we never understood them. Back then, I was given to Donna as a one-off patient who was given twelve sessions through which to recover.

"These children had reactions to things for a long, long time," she continued. "I would explain, 'You need to learn to talk to yourself, because reactivity starts in the body.' You have to learn to say, 'This is happening right now, but I'm not going to die.' It's called positive self-talk. Otherwise, it becomes explosive."

"What about parents? What do you typically tell parents, in terms of how to help their kid through something like this?"

"First you'd have to see where they are. If the parents doesn't feel safe, they'll impart that on the child."

"My mom was very nervous," I said. "Do you think you gave her any advice?"

"If I did, it would have been to assure her that you were safe."

"I think I was beyond a place where anyone could tell me I was safe," I said. "It was a lot bigger than my parents, bigger than all of our parents."

"That's why I try to get children to a place where they can soothe themselves. We're never taught how to help ourselves when we're anxious. As a teenager or child with trauma, you become hyperactive, hypervigilant, or the opposite, withdrawn. You get overstimulated and that becomes different in different people. Some teenagers cut themselves or feel suicidal. Others develop addictions. Some turn to sexually acting out."

"That sounds about right," I said. "That's what I heard from the other kids."

"You spoke to other children?" she asked.

"The ones who were the most involved in that day had the most severe responses. A lot like mine. Of course, I didn't know it until I spoke to them ten years later. We had mostly lost touch."

She nodded, then asked, "So what did happen to you after our sessions ended?"

* * *

In early September 2002, right before school started, my parents and I traveled to Italy, an eight-hour plane ride that was as unpleasant as you could imagine, while I tried to distract myself by reading *Gossip Girl* books and playing card games with my dad. Walking around in Rome, I was so embarrassed to be seen with my parents that I walked either in front of them or behind them and gave them dirty looks when they held hands.

Two moments stand out strongly in my memory from that trip.

The first is eating at a restaurant where the food just wasn't good, the bald waiter asking us if we wanted something else, and then charging us for the something else, to our surprise— and leaving that restaurant to see a Church, one of the more famous ones. My eyes locked on a small family of Gypsies, a girl, a small boy, their mother, and a dog. I looked at my father, who was already going in his pockets for money.

I handed the mother the gold coin and smiled, and I went in the church, where my own mother explained to me that you were supposed to write down a prayer and put it in the bucket, and then light a candle.

"Please let that family and that dog have enough to eat. Please don't let them go hungry." I said it over and over, squeezing my eyes shut, feeling very aware and very uncomfortable that my mother was watching me.

Back outside the church, the little girl was eating an apple, and the mother was feeding the dog some chopped up carrots.

At the time, I thought it was a miracle.

It could have been that because they found some more money, and they felt comfortable eating what they had.

Either way, that moment banked itself somewhere deep in my subconscious, a sign that I could make some sort of difference to someone who needed help, and that something bigger really was listening to what I put into the universe.

The second thing I remember was going for Gelato at some famous Piazza and catching the eyes of a stray dog. People were petting it, feeding it ice cream, and my dad said, "Poor baby," petting its head.

"Can we take him home with us?" I asked, knowing on some level how crazy that sounded, taking a giant retriever from Rome back on a plane to New York. At the same time, I felt that if I didn't take the dog with us, I was never going to be able to live with myself; I would always be thinking about that dog.

"He'll be okay, honey," my dad said. "People will take care of him."

Shortly after we got back, haunted still, as predicted, by the memory of that dog, I reminded my parents that I was now thirteen years old, which was *definitely* old enough to walk a dog. After years of carrying on, the clouds parted slightly that day, and I got a tentative, "We can start looking."

I was beyond excited to drive to the North Shore Animal League, but I wasn't prepared for what I would see when we got there.

All of those sad, lonely dogs, who used to have love—or worse, maybe they hadn't—were just laying there, abandoned in cold cages, or pawing at them, begging to be let out. Tears rushed to my eyes, coming from a deep, painful place. I imagined all of them must have gathering around, with all the people saying "Aw, how cute" and moving on, probably so many times that the animals had given up hope. Some were so dejected that they didn't even bother to move toward anyone.

The puppies were kept in this giant stacked wall of cages in one isolated section. I locked eyes with a black and white dog who was shaking, scared of people, but nervously licking their fingers, almost frantically.

"Hey you," I whispered to him. "I promise, I am going to save you. I'll be right back."

"Mommy, this one," I said confidently as the pup went back to cowering in the back of the cage.

"How big will he get?" My dad asked the shelter worker.

"About forty to fifty pounds," the worker said.

"Oh, forget it," my mom said, like she was dismissing my request for a pony instead of throwing my soul off of a cliff.

I had become attached to him in those short moments, and abandoning him there tore something inside of me apart, prompting me to cry hysterically all the way home in a way I had never cried before. It wasn't because I didn't get my way. It was because I was supposed to save that dog. I told him he would be safe, and I left him, alone, scared, surrounded by noise and chaos.

The sobs deepened with each thought of another animal I couldn't save.

How many more shelters are full of these dogs?

How many aren't in shelters, but suffering somewhere else?

How can humans abandon such helpless, loving creatures can't take care of themselves?

I was starting to really, really hate people, even if I didn't know them.

The following weekend, we tried a store in Brooklyn, a place we saw advertised in the back of the *New York Daily News*. The shop was located under the tracks of an outside train—something we didn't have in Manhattan—in a damp, dark looking part of town.

The puppies were kept in pens full of crinkly white paper, and the owner, as my dad would describe him, was like fast-talking used-car salesmen, grabbing their jaws and saying, "Look at that face, isn't it precious?"

For some reason, a Mexican woman brought five more puppies up from downstairs.

One of them, a tiny, champagne-colored toy poodle, was so starved for affection that she kept climbing toward my face, almost swimming in place, even after she was already in my arms. She kissed my face emphatically, like her life depended on it. Again, I fell in love.

"This is her. I want her," I said; but my parents were skeptical because they didn't like the sales guy.

"I don't think so Helaina, let's think about it."

Again, I was devastated. I sighed loudly, muttering, "We better come back for her."

"We can just go home, missy," my dad said. "We don't have to try this next place."

I zipped it, because I didn't want to hurt my chances of taking a puppy home.

We drove to a shop in the West Village that my father's friend had told him about, where they groomed dogs and boarded them when people went away. Of course, they also sold puppies.

When we entered, ringing the tiny bell attached to the door, a man with white hair, glasses, and a plaid flannel shirt was yelling at someone picking up their dog.

"Her fur is all matted and something is wrong with her eye! You should be arrested! You shouldn't even be allowed to have a pet. Get out of here before I call the police," he barked.

I was too distracted to get upset over that myself. I looked longingly into a bin of playful puppies wriggling around on top of one another, kicking those same little squiggly scraps of white paper up everywhere. I asked to see the Shih Tzu and the Scottish Terrier.

"Sure thing, sweetheart" the man said in a much different tone than the one he'd just been using. "Let's take them down-stairs so you can get to know them."

They mostly walked around on their own, sniffing, frolicking, but when I said, "Come here boy!" the Shih Tzu came teetering over. The Scottish Terrier wasn't as interested. My mother proceeded to bend down and scoop the Shih Tzu up, and he lay quietly in my mother's arms.

"Can we get him?" I asked, sensing a win.

We got rung up at the register—$1,100, but we could have him for $900—with a leash and some food thrown in.

"His name is Gucci," I proclaimed, inspired by our recent Roman holiday.

We took him home, and for weeks, I could barely concentrate on anything else: the puppy was everything. I knew Grandma loved him too. When she came to watch me—she was still my "babysitter," which was fine, I loved spending time with her even though I was too old to *need* to be watched—she would give him enthusiastic tummy rubs and coo at him in her high-pitched, sweet-as-syrup voice.

About a month later, when we had to start touring high schools, I had a very hard time leaving Gucci behind in his puppy gate, stuck in the kitchen. His cries could be heard into the hallway, all the way by the elevators, and I reasoned that maybe we didn't have to go after all.

"We're going," my mom said as she ushered me onto the elevator and pressed 1.

I could barely concentrate on anything else the whole night, worried that Gucci might die of grief while we were gone, or that I might die of grief being separated from him.

As he got older, Gucci decided he didn't want to sleep in my bed, or give kisses, or learn tricks. He decided he just wanted to lie around, and teetered away and sat under the table when I tried to play with him. He did not sense when I was sad, or scared, and needed to cuddle. In fact, he wanted nothing to do with cuddling. He was supposed to by my best buddy, my sleepover pal, my source of love and affection. Despite the fact that it did not work out that way, I loved him anyway. He couldn't help how he was, and he was still mine to love.

Around this time, a weird "splitting" of thoughts began to occur. I would feed Gucci and instantly think upsetting thoughts at the same time about someone torturing a dog by not feeding it.

Or, I would smile at a baby on the street and think about someone abusing a baby somewhere else.

If I got cold, I immediately thought about homeless people freezing. When I was hungry, I thought about starving children in Africa.

I still stayed up all night, unable to sleep, watching three hundred disturbing images I couldn't turn off flicker across the backdrop of my closed eyes. Attempting to sleep at all was like surrendering into a black pit of quicksand, just waiting to be swallowed up by ominous visions.

* * *

Sarah sat in her advisory at Baruch College Campus High School during the one-year anniversary of 9/11 pressing her pen down so hard that a blue puddle was forming on her notebook.

Everyone had been instructed to write "about that day," what went on, how they felt about it. The first people to share said that they were in a school on Eightieth Street and heard the announcement over the loudspeaker. Sarah shared honestly, and angrily, practically spitting her story at them because they had no idea what suffering meant. They had no idea what it was to be scared that day.

She was immediately sent to the guidance counselor.

"How can I help you?" she asked.

"You can't," Sarah said. "Can you go in my mind and erase everything I saw?"

This was the first time somebody asked her to confront her experience of that day, and Sarah startled even herself with this response. She'd never been rude to a teacher or an adult before.

Still, her voice grew even louder.

"What are you going to do for me? I don't want to talk about it, especially not with you. I want to forget about it."

She ran out of the guidance counselor's office and called her mother from the bathroom.

"Call the school right now and tell them I don't ever want to do that again," she sobbed. Heading back into the hallway, she was completely broken down. Her friends rushed to her side.

"She just made me feel worse," she sniffed. "She singled me out and completely belittled the whole the situation. She made it seem like it was an 'easy problem.'"

But her friends didn't seem to understand what got her so upset either.

"Oh . . . she meant well, though," they said, shooting each other looks.

Nobody could understand. *My own friends think I'm crazy.* Soon, they were no longer her friends. She felt like a freak, and longed to be downtown again with people who "understood."

When I got there, a year later, I didn't even know Baruch had a guidance counselor.

* * *

My year wasn't shaping up to be too hot, either. A girl named Lily told me I had saggy tits and a big Jew nose and fought with me over Henry (AXE body spray was working wonders for this kid). We went on a mandatory eighth grade trip where I got no sleep, as I expected I wouldn't, and where I got seasick on the boat ride we took on the last day. On the bus ride back to the city right after, I fell asleep on Christine's chest.

I was touring and applying to high schools that I hated even more than the middle schools I had toured three years earlier, I still hadn't had my first real kiss, and my period was taking forever to arrive.

Thomas, who was still mostly a quiet kid, didn't respond to me in person much, even though we were in the same class. But he made me mix-tapes on CDs because he knew how to download the songs and burn them for free. I'd use AOL Instant Messenger to send him my requests, and he'd deliver them later that week, with a playlist printed right on the cover of the case and everything. I had no idea that his father was going completely off the deep end, transforming from a fun and outgoing guy into a man who had emotional outbursts, spewing anger and aggression, then retracting quietly into himself for days. Thomas and his mother never knew when he would snap, and lived in constant fear of his moods and reactions.

The police were still doing ID checks, even in 2003, on people who lived in Gateway Plaza, and there were notices on the bulletin boards that proclaimed warnings of bomb threats for Lower Manhattan residential buildings. A man in Thomas's building went door-to-door selling parachutes, so if they had to escape the building, they could "get out when the elevators broke down and the stairs were on fire."

"Did you hear that a man in Columbus, Ohio, was arrested for allegedly feeding information to al-Qaeda about how they might go about bombing the Brooklyn Bridge?" he asked me one day in March. "You should pack a bag."

Rose had become my best friend, replacing Allison, and we took ridiculous pictures with my new digital camera and had sleepovers at her apartment on Ocean Avenue. We prank-called Henry and Lily using her computer's voice converter, this guy named Microsoft Sam. We would type stuff about penises and poop and have him say it in a robotic voice, trying not to laugh too loudly as it happened. We were fans of Clay Aiken on Season 2 of *American Idol*, and were devastated when he lost to Ruben Studdard.

Christine and I became friendlier, too, sharing a love of a show called *Degrassi*, which later became well-known for producing stars like Aubrey "Drake" Graham who played Jimmy, and Nina Dobrev, who later went on to star in the *Vampire Diaries*. But while they were still at Degrassi Jr. High, these kids melodramatically got their periods, came out of the closet, and suffered through teen pregnancy while simultaneously discovering their parents' devastating financial troubles and flirtations with other parents.

When one character named Terri found herself in an abusive relationship with a kid named Rick (the kid who would later bring a gun to school and paralyze Jimmy, aka Drake, and put him in a wheelchair), I shook my head and thought that it was so obvious she needed to break up with him. How lame was it that she couldn't see what a psycho he was?

"What do you mean he loves you and he just gets mad?" I'd shout at the TV. "Get out of there!"

The year carried on like any other year might; rumors circulated about the gym teacher being a secret child pornographer, I accepted Trevor's invitation to go to the dance with him, then took it back because I couldn't get past his severe acne, and

Devin and some other boys ran around with sanitary pads stuck to their foreheads after a particularly riveting science presentation on the subject of female menstruation.

My mother will tell you that by the end of eighth grade, I had cut everyone off. Somebody was talking to Lily, and I didn't want them to. Somebody else couldn't be trusted. I left with about two friends that I'd stay in touch with for a little while, and eventually, I'd lose both of them too.

My mother took me to an expensive hair salon that specialized in curly hair to do my hair for graduation, and bought me a new dress from Express. I made and memorized a speech at the ceremony that was a real crowd-pleaser, and while I couldn't prove it, I knew that bitch Lily broke the star cookie with my name on it at the reception before I could get to it. Afterward, I left to take a walk and sit on the swings of Hudson River Park with Trevor's cute older brother. I thought he was so cool, wearing a baseball cap with his suit, and so sweet, too. I waited for him to kiss me, which he didn't.

Eager to get it over with already, I ended up having my first kiss with another guy, Isaac, who was a "man whore" as both Gina and Jasmine described him. He was a sure thing.

I chose a group movie for the big moment, which was a mistake, because right after I smeared on my cupcake-flavored lip gloss and let him shove his tongue literally down my throat, the other kids started throwing ticket stubs at us.

We left and went back to his apartment on Murray Street, where he kept trying to put his hands up my shirt. I kept stopping him.

"All the other girls let me," he said.

Well, that was too bad.

I left, disappointed once again that I hadn't found the boyfriend I'd always wanted, but maybe I could find one at Downtown Day Camp that summer. It would be my first year working as a counselor, not a camper, and Trevor was one of my co-counselors.

I loved being around the kids. We had a group of first graders, who were just the best.

For one, they were adorable and sweet and funny. But more importantly, they had the ability to pull me into their world with them, which was a much simpler place. Those summer days were full of the sound of bare, wet feet slapping against the tiles around the swimming pool, the smell of pretzel rods wafting off of them as they spoke, crumbs falling off of their lips, the piles of pictures that they drew "of me" where my stick-figure body sported two big, round circles up top, a mass of curly hair with a giant bow, and a big purse that said *Coach* on it.

On a day that it poured, Trevor and I decided, at the end of the day, to just go frolicking through the empty schoolyard while the kids all stayed in their rooms watching movies. For five minutes, we just laughed and kicked at giant puddles. It would have been incredibly romantic if I felt the same way about Trevor that he felt about me.

It was a sticky afternoon a couple of days later, in mid-August, when, suddenly, the lights shut off and the video games and the air hockey table all shut down in the room known as "Fantasy Land." An announcement over the PA system told us to take our groups to our classrooms and stay there.

Oh my God. Not again. Not again.

Trevor and I looked at each other in a way that no other counselors were.

We walked with the kids back to our room, and I asked to use another counselor's phone, because I still didn't have my own.

If it's happening again, I have to stay until all the children are picked up, like Alex did.

"The power's knocked out all along the East Coast," another counselor said as I called my mom's cell. I began to cry.

"Mommy? What's going on? Are you coming home?"

"What? No. Nobody's saying anything on the news, it's probably fine," she said. "Just walk home. It's okay. I'll be there soon. Daddy's home."

Eventually, we were allowed into the yard for pick-up time.

Trevor and looked at each other in "that way" again as we took in all of the cars stopped in the streets, the people rushing to P.S.234 in confusion. I looked outside the gates, at the corner where Ann, Charles, and I had stood two years earlier, looking up at the burning Towers.

"Go ahead," our head counselor said, interrupting my thoughts.

Trevor offered to walk me home, through stalled cars, honking like crazy, through gangs of teenagers in tank tops shouting and cursing and running, through babysitters hurrying along with small children, and mothers pushing strollers a little too quickly. He made sure I got there safely.

It turned out to just be a blackout after all, according to our battery-operated radio, but still, I wasn't so sure.

My mother and I walked over to the Seaport that night, where restaurant bars opened up their coolers and sold drinks at half price.

PART TWO

CHAPTER SEVEN

When you feel that you aren't like everyone else or feel tainted by what has happened to you, it's hard to be optimistic about the future. In fact, for many survivors, it's nearly impossible to imagine the future at all. Many of us are caught in a state where we're still just trying to survive, our sole focus during trauma, and can't think much beyond that.

—Dr. Jasmin Lee Cori, *Healing From Trauma*

S addam Hussein was captured on my grandmother's eighty-seventh birthday, December 13, 2003.

Before that news broke, I had been busy losing myself in the process of mixing, measuring, and baking brownies for Grandma. I loved baking, loved the smell and the way the heat of the oven *whooshed* over me when I checked and checked again to see if they were done, impatient to get upstairs already.

I rang the doorbell, balancing the tray of brownies in my other hand, a shopping bag with a card, flowers, and a gift box dangling from my wrist.

"Oh my goodness, you shouldn't have done this!" she cooed as she opened the door. She looked so surprised, so shocked and delighted, you would have thought I'd just delivered the winning lottery numbers. She had lipstick on, as always, a shade of dark mauve. Her light blond hair was colored and perfectly coiffed as always, and, that day, she was wearing a floral print housedress, the one with the large tropical flowers.

"You are so thoughtful," she said. "Let's share."

As soon as we sat down at the table, she began chewing in a dainty but meaningful way, going "*Mmmm!*" in an exaggerated tone meant to make me feel like the world's best brownie chef.

I took in the slightly musky scent of her feet in pantyhose and slippers mixed with her perfume. I felt calm, in the gentle warmth of the room. Nobody could ever get between the two of us, at that table, at our special place underneath the chandelier that shimmered with smiles and shouts of "I love *you* more!" This was still my safe place, even if it had been modified to "as safe as any place could ever be."

When she finished her brownie, I shouted, "Happy Birthday!" presenting her with a card and a present, the blouse my mom had picked out for me to give her. If anyone could receive a present and make you feel that you'd done right, it was her. I also showed her an article I wrote in the school newspaper.

"Oh my God, I am so proud of you," she said. "You are going to be something special one day."

Grandpa hadn't bothered to come out of the small bedroom, where he was sitting in the blue plush recliner that propelled his legs forward, watching the OTB channel.

Some daytime talk show was on in the living room, and we barely paid attention as Grandma went on to tell me some of the same stories about my mom, how that one time she tricked the teacher in Catholic school, making her think she wasn't paying attention by looking out the window, but she was. Some of these stories, I later learned, were actually not entirely true.

But our focus shifted when the program was interrupted by a photo of Saddam on the screen in front of us, followed by footage of a bunch of men in army gear, looking just like they had two years before, right outside the window, in front of the hospital; was almost like someone had lifted them up from the street outside and plunked them into the TV.

"Saddam Hussein was captured like a rat," said a news anchor.

Grandma seemed hopeful, at first.

"Now that we caught him, maybe it will all be over," she said. The same way she had said, "This means war" two years ago, she seemed almost certain that this, somehow, might change things.

I felt a bit hopeful too. Maybe this would be a new start—not only for the country, but for me.

"But maybe, they're going to get us back for this," she added.

I tried to push the thought out of my mind as we play poker for pennies, which I got to keep. I was old enough to know it couldn't buy me much, but I accepted graciously.

She always made dinner on Saturdays, and I wondered if we'd make pizza like when I was little, when I impatiently waited for the crust to cook so we could spread the sauce around, put it back, cook it more, then do my favorite part, sprinkling the mozzarella cheese over every centimeter, which we shredded ourselves.

Maybe she was making London Broil the way I liked, with the salty gravy and milky, creamy mashed potatoes.

I let my thoughts wander to all of those years sitting on her kitchen counter, watching her dip veal cutlets into egg yolks, bread them, and somehow fit them all in to the pan of bubbling oil when I thought there was no way she could possibly fit one more. I would shriek when the oil popped and a drop landed on her arm, which she didn't even seem to feel.

In a year or so, when Grandma no longer had the strength to make pizza, my mom would start using store-bought Boboli pizza crust, and I would protest, sometimes stopping at Burger King first and using my lunch money so I didn't have to eat it.

That night, it was London Broil.

"Can I help?" I'd asked.

"Go sit down!" she said, gesturing with a hot pan in both hands.

She didn't take any for herself, no matter how many times I said, "Eat, sit with me." I ate everything on my plate, which impressed her even more, and told her that I loved her cooking, and I *hated* Mommy's cooking.

"You mustn't say that," she said, but really, I knew she loved to hear it.

Finally, only after I had finished, she sat down and had just a tiny bit. We watched TV, seated side by side, as close as we could get. I was always dragging my chair closer to hers, even when it couldn't possibly be any closer. The *Golden Girls* was on, and we laughed out loud and commented on everything, especially when Sophia, the old lady, said something funny. "She is too much," Grandma said, shaking her head.

She peeled an apple from the yellow bowl of fruit she left out, and we ate apple slices, and *then*, we got to have ice cream. We sometimes used that yellow bowl to hold green beans in after carefully snapping off the ends and placing them in the red plastic grocery bag. It was a simple task, of course, but I would constantly check in on my handiwork when we did it, because I wanted to see her smile and go, "Yes, my little angel, just like that."

My grandpa finally emerged from the bedroom, wearing his signature white T-shirt—no matter how many shirts my mother or my aunt bought him, he would only where those same, smelly ones with the holes in them—and began picking up pieces of lint off of the carpet. My grandma looked over at him and did a double take, saying, in harsher tones than I was used to hearing, "Charlie, you're soiling yourself!" He didn't say anything, just continued picking up lint.

She told him to get into the bathroom and take his pants off, and in the meantime, filled a white bucket with soap and water and got down on her hands and knees to clean the carpet while he continued to roam around.

When Grandpa started to get lost and fall down, I started going upstairs more often. For the time being, I took it as my queue to go.

I went downstairs, feeling a bit sad and a bit startled, and got started on my homework. My dad had always told me to get it over with the first chance I got, so I didn't have to think about it over the weekend. I didn't mind homework, though, because taking notes out of a textbook and answering questions gave me something to concentrate on.

I watched an episode of *Degrassi* before starting the ritual of tossing and turning that had become more manic each night, until at some point, somehow, I drifted off after screaming with frustration into my pillow.

My mother continued to be my best—and practically only—friend, even though our sharp tongues and opposing views on me and my behavior continued to drive a wedge between us.

We navigated around it, shopping, going out for dinner as a family, alternating between snippy comments and laughter.

I still called Gina and we spoke on the phone, but she lived in Jersey and was never able to hang out after school and was rarely around on weekends, for some reason. Rose was becoming less responsive to me as well, and I had no desire to hang out with Charles or Nadine anymore. Nadine had found her own group of friends at Baruch College Campus High School, where the three of us had ended up together, and it was clear that I was not welcome among them.

The next day, Sunday, the Sephora on Broadway was especially crowded. They had taken away the little containers left out to take samples with, most likely because people like Rose and I had abused the privilege, scooping out eye shadow and squeezing out ten tubes of lip gloss while ducking behind the shiny black panels like giggly criminals.

As I tried to look for the eyeliner I was going for, someone bumped into me, sending a warm surge of adrenaline coursing through me. Someone else did it again, and suddenly, I was grinding my teeth.

By the time I met my mom at the end of the long line to the register, every minute felt excruciating, not just tedious. The longer I waited, the more worked up I got, watching every move that the cashiers made. Standing still was suddenly intolerable. *Too close. Everyone is too close.*

I don't know where this urgency came from—I wasn't in a hurry to go back home and sit in my room and stew, think about how it was Sunday night, *the worst,* how I'd have to endure another week where the clock hands almost moved backward— but it felt like I had to get out of Sephora as fast as possible. I sighed loudly, and the woman on line in front of me turned around and said, "Excuse me, are you having a bad day?"

Not in a nasty way, but in a way that was almost sincere.

"No," I sneered back.

A battle suddenly struck up inside me: drop the stuff and run away, *flight,* or, tell her to go fuck herself and get into an altercation, *fight.*

My mom gave me a warning look, tightening her jaw.

"You're becoming such an embarrassment," she whispered. "I don't want to go anywhere with you anymore."

We sat on the 6 train at Bleecker Street waiting for the doors to close, but they didn't. With every growing second, my heart beat faster. My breath quickened and all of my hairs stood on end.

Something's wrong. Something bad is happening. We're not moving like we're supposed to. We're going to die.

"Mom, we have to go," I said quickly.

She didn't look up from her magazine.

"Mom, we have to go," I said louder, standing up.

"Helaina," she said, annoyed. "Sit down, it's fine."

Two NYPD cops in police vests walked by, talking into their hand radios, a sight that knocked all the wind out of me. I started to tremble, feeling it in my shoulders and in the bowels of my stomach, everything tightening, my neck suddenly feeling tingly and naked, the train car suddenly losing all of its air.

"Mom!" I shouted. A few of the bored passengers who had been reading newspapers or sleeping looked up at me.

We're doomed, we're going to die if we stay here. We're going to die if we don't run, said the invisible little girl who lived in my brain. She had parked herself right in the center of my frontal cortex, sending down serpent-like tentacles of panic through the rest of my body.

"Let's go!" I said. "We have to get out and take a cab!"

My mother ignored me.

"What are we going to do?" I asked, my eyes darting from her to the platform, sticking my head out of the car to try to see what was happening. "How do we know what's going on?"

I was talking quickly, getting up, sitting down.

"I'm leaving! I'm going!" I said, my voice cracking.

Of course, I wasn't going to go. I was too terrified of separating from her.

"You're annoying me now," she said shrilly. "Sit down!"

I sat down, legs shaking, for another three eternal minutes before the train doors closed. The train chugged down past Spring Street, past Canal Street, and finally, down to the Brooklyn Bridge station, which was deserted and quiet.

Monday morning, I sat on the couch, forcing a granola bar down my throat as I watched the MTV music video countdown. I switched the channel to the news during a commercial . . .

then another station, and another, and all seemed to say the same thing.

"How will they retaliate to Saddam Hussein's capture?"

Oh my God. They're going to get us back.

Or are they?

President Bush said, "A dark and painful era is over. A hopeful day has arrived."

Is this good?

Is this bad?

I couldn't keep up.

I flipped back to MTV, and as I watched the video for Outkast's "Hey Ya," I wondered, for the first time, if I should just stay home and crawl back under the covers instead of walking out the door at 8:00 a.m. My mom was inside her bedroom getting ready, spritzing on perfume and making last-minute decisions about accessories. The dish that held her breakfast, half a bran muffin with butter, and the knife, thick with butter and crumbs, was still on the table.

I sat down and finished it, knowing she wouldn't, looking down at the open newspaper; more headlines about the threat of suicide bombers in department stores on Christmas. I pictured them all pressing down on their red trigger buttons, setting themselves off in a perfectly orchestrated line, like the Radio City Rockettes.

On the days I didn't flip through the paper myself, my mom made sure to tell me the headlines, whether it was about a rapist or a homeless person throwing a brick at someone's head.

"Be careful," she'd say, as if there was some way to actually be careful enough to prevent someone from attacking me.

I stomped into my shoes, yanked my jacket off of a hanger, and forced myself out the door, despite the fact that my body felt was heavy and bruised, like I had run the marathon and went nowhere at all.

Before the first day of school four months earlier, I had specifically told my orthodontist that my braces had to come off. No more little kid stuff. I had to be ready for that magical time where I would finally flirt with mature boys and belong to clubs like drama and newspaper. I would finally be a *real* teenager, no more sitting on the floor in a circle like in middle school. I was going to be out of the neighborhood for at least part of the day, a physical distance that I hoped would bring some relief. *Out of sight, out of mind.* I was going to meet new people and make great girlfriends and hang out on the weekends and we were all going to study together in the library and run bake sales, and it would be just like in the movies.

I was going to, but I couldn't, because none of those opportunities were there.

Well, except for the newspaper.

As I walked to the 6 train, everything around me was smoking: rusty metal grates where men chopped meat and then flung it to the side of the grill, people puffing on cigarettes and joints and cigars, smoking street carts filled with nuts that smelled like heaven but tasted like badly burnt candy. Fog billowed up from potholes and long orange construction pillars, and hot, bitter exhaust emanated from the tailpipes of cars. I was caught up in every specific movement of people around me, of the wind, of cars stopping and starting, the roar of plane engines overhead, and the booming noise of trucks going over speed bumps.

The most neutral of looks from fellow subway riders were ominous, and the budding journalist in me was skeptical of everything.

What are they looking at?

What are they saying?

What's in that backpack?

When I arrived at the school building on 23rd and Lexington Avenue, there was a crowd waiting for the elevator, as usual. A few minutes passed before we could all cram inside to get to our classes. The elevator slowed at the tenth floor, and when the doors didn't open immediately, my body surged with adrenaline, falling while standing still. It was like one of my feet was on the gas, the other, on the brake, sputtering and sputtering and going nowhere.

Eventually, the elevator doors opened and spewed us out, a shuffling procession of clunking backpacks and squeaking sneakers. I tried to walk with the other kids, my throat dry as I attempted to blend in and look as bored as everyone else did. My first class was Global Studies with Mr. Schwartz, my favorite teacher. As he talked about Africa's geography, I zoned out, picturing things that pushed their way in with more force whenever I tried to shut the door. Someone on the floor above us moved a piece of furniture, and I flinched.

How strong could a building be, really, to take all of that weight and wear and tear every day without eventually crumbling down?

I felt like I knew something everyone else didn't, and I wasn't being paranoid because I knew firsthand how realistic any sort of threat was.

I saw myself trapped under desks and choking on sawdust, the last to be rescued if I was rescued at all, but just kept scribbling with my pen, taking notes on whatever he was saying about Somalia, which, on a quiz later that week, I would remember incorrectly as "Jumalia" (perhaps a combination of Jordan and Somalia, but in any case, not a real place). Later, in biology class, I took notes on the different stages of cell meiosis and mitosis at a hundred miles an hour, my pencil breaking, then breaking again. There was this weird pressure I couldn't figure out that made my thoughts quicken, made me unable to focus on actually taking in what I was copying down.

"Any questions?" the teacher asked.

I raised my hand and formulated one. Since participation was a big part of our grade, I always participated, and that made the other girls suck their teeth, roll their eyes, and hate me even more. I don't know why they didn't like me in the first place; maybe it was because I wore a short skirt on one of the coldest days of the year, or maybe it was just this vibe I gave off, like they could sense how I felt inside. Maybe it was just because someone had to be "that girl" that nobody liked.

Whatever it was, usually, everyone's classes ran over, so I had to wait awkwardly in front of classrooms, hoping to God that someone didn't come up and ask me a weird question with a smirk, then walk away laughing, relaying the whole thing to someone else. Girls turned briefly to look at each other and whisper in that cruel, obvious way teenage girls do, which made me hope for things like a long line at the cafeteria's vending machine, giving me something to do that didn't require socialization.

That day, like most days, was bleak and painfully lonely.

Only a few more days until Christmas break, I told myself.

At lunchtime, we were given a ridiculous twenty-two minutes to go out onto Twenty-Third Street buy food, come back, and eat it, a time constraint that made the entire ordeal a nail-biting nightmare.

With two minutes left to go before class and barely digesting the sandwich I'd scarfed down, I waited for an Asian girl named Sisi—a large majority of students at Baruch were Asian—to finish shuffling through "our locker."

Because of limited space, everyone had to share lockers. This created all sorts of anxiety, whether it was the prospect of someone's iced tea spilling everywhere because they didn't screw it on tightly enough, or your locker buddy giving someone else the combination.

Charles was the only kid who never used a locker, because he was unwilling to risk having to leave all of his stuff in case of an emergency.

Therefore, everyone wanted to be his "locker partner," but not everyone wanted to be his friend. There were a few people who were friendly toward him, but he was hesitant about how "close to let them get," as he put it.

Charles was still obsessed with current events and politics, overly concerned with the future and researching conspiracy theories. He was more interested in being the school's "town crier" when it came to global, breaking news than he was in discussing everyone's weekend plans.

For the most part, New York City public school students are anti-war; they demonstrate, petition, write papers, write letters, enter, guns blazing, into heated lunchroom discussions. At fourteen, Charles suddenly became pro-Iraq war, professing assertions like "We should take over the world and blow up all our enemies." His new stance was more of a coping mechanism than an actual "thirst for revenge," but as far as the school bullies that inevitably found him, Charles was now biting back. If someone shouted something cruel at him, he'd yell back louder. If they touched him, he'd shove them back harder.

He didn't start any confrontations, but he reacted to them. While many students found themselves, especially with the new outlet of the Internet, bullied to the point of wanting to take their own life, Charles never considered it. He was too afraid of death to think about suicide, and preferred instead to think about the future. He just bounced from group to group in the lunchroom but rarely hung out with anyone after school, and when he did, it was with Sarah and other kids from the neighborhood, because they understood each other in a way other people couldn't.

At the end of the day, I was handed a report card full of scores in the 90s and letter grades in some variation of the letter A in my backpack, the greatest gift I could give Grandma. Armed with this report card, it was like I had a gold bar in my pocket.

Trying desperately to go through the motions, I decided to join a few kids I had become friendly with, and we walked to Union Square Park, a mixed bag of crackheads and wayward businessmen. We smoked cigarettes and they took well-concealed swigs from a rotating bottle of Peach Schnapps as we splayed out on the sprawling steps that opened up onto Fourth Avenue, watching the skateboarders fall off of their boards. Some rally was under way, or maybe it was a protest, and we took whatever pamphlets were handed out to us.

I was actually afraid to drink, at that point, and figured it wouldn't matter anyway.

No matter how many people I was around, I felt disconnected from all of them, like they were all made up of a different substance than I was. This group, in particular, made me nervous.

They drank in the bathroom during school, and one of them talked back to the teachers, and I didn't *want* to get into trouble with them, or do illegal things, or skip class, or be late from lunch. I think they knew that I wasn't quite one of them, but they were all I had, and they were the only ones who didn't seem to think anything was wrong with me. They even brought me to the occasional party, where I would stand, afraid, jumpy, like a nervous dog during a fireworks display until I couldn't take it anymore and found some reason to leave.

Devin, also, seemed to still have a soft spot for me. That soft spot was in his loft bed, in the walkup apartment he shared with his mom on an infamous strip of West Eighth Street. The building, with its white columns and marked-up door, was tucked away between a hat store, a sneaker store, and an Army/ Navy shop with studded belts hanging in the window. Across the street was a sex fetish shop, a dumpling restaurant, and some other confusing place whose only window display was a manne-quin wearing a rainbow afro wig, red feather boa, and nipple tassels. Sets of steps leading down to cellar basements were scat-tered along the sidewalk and left wide open, beckoning anyone who wasn't looking down to fall in and break their neck.

We had settled into a routine: smoking weed, which I discov-ered I found kind of relaxing, making out, and scooping sloppy handfuls of peanut butter and chocolate syrup out of the jar while watching *Dora the Explorer* or one of the *Nightmare on Elm Street* movies. Alone in his room, listening to the dull roar of heavy metal songs crackling through the speakers of his computer, I was able to blur myself into a prickly delusion that everything was going to be okay. We "touched" each other, but never more than that. Even underneath his sheets, inside that dank pot cloud, there was something heavy lingering over me, screaming that the worst was yet to come— and I was somehow smart enough to know that having sex wasn't going to push that feeling any further away.

* * *

When I told my mother I was seriously depressed, she found me an old Jewish therapist on Eighth Street and Fifth Avenue by Washington Square Park, not far from Devin's house.

The long winding hallways of the building, the numerous musty staircases, and unmarked black doors felt ominous.

"I don't want to wake up in the morning," I told Dr. F. "And I can't sleep at night. I'm up for hours playing things over and over. I don't enjoy anything anymore. I don't feel happy. Nobody likes me for some reason. Everyone in school is looking at me like they're going to hurt me."

Dr. F closed his eyes, made grumbling noises, asked me "why" or "when" and then sent me on my way. He didn't tell me that there's a science behind how trauma changes the brain, that neurotransmitters become like short-circuiting wires, sparking wildly from the ends. He didn't tell me that the body remembers its experience with fear so strongly that it begins to respond to other stressful situations in the same extreme way, and sometimes, it responds to things that most people would never respond to or notice. He didn't tell me that depression is often a symptom of post-traumatic stress, or that the past can become the present, years later, simply at the sound of a siren, or the feeling of someone grabbing your arm and startling you. He didn't tell me that what had happened to me had to potential to change the entire direction of my life, causing me to do things and feel things and make decisions that maybe I wouldn't have, and so maybe we should take a closer look at it and figure out how to go from there.

He just said, "See you next week."

So, by the time the thin winter sunlight gave way to the more soothing, golden aura of May, nothing felt different, but I needed to feel different, somehow.

I decided to take my first drink.

It was on a Friday, and I remember that day because I had actually been feeling pretty good about myself for once.

The art teacher had given us a quiz and told us, "Make sure you read all the instructions first before you start." She had repeated it a few times, and a light bulb went off in my head.

My dad once told me the story of how, at Brooklyn College, he was given a final exam with the same instructions. People were getting up after a few minutes, and he sat there watching them, for hours, wondering, *how could they be done?* As it turned out, the final instruction, when you read it all the way through, was simply to write your name and the date, and not answer any of the other questions. So, that day, that's what I did: the last question, number thirty-six, said to simply write your name, the date, and draw a star. I sat there, done, looking at everyone else and smiling at the teacher.

"How is she done?" one girl said, looking at me like I was ridiculous.

For once, knowing something that everyone else didn't wasn't a scary thing.

That night Becca, her older boyfriend, Harry, and his friend, Ron, took us to Pier 25 along the West Side Highway and filled red plastic cups with a small amount of brown liquid that smelled like lighter fluid. They both went to School of the Future, the high school across the street from Baruch. I looked out over the sandy volleyball courts where we'd played at Downtown Day Camp, then looked back down at the inside of my cup. I knew this was wrong, but everyone had to try drinking sometime, right? *Maybe this will help*, the invisible little girl whispered. I didn't know what it meant, that Bacardi 151 was "151 proof." But from the way they talked about it, I figured it was strong.

I took a sip and grimaced, but refused to cough like Becca had.

The boys laughed.

"Wow, she's tough, huh?"

That stuck with me like a badge of honor, and was all the motivation I needed to take another shot, and another. That would be the beginning of feeling that the more I could impress these guys by downing alcohol, the more worthy I was of . . . something.

The next thing I knew, we were on the roof of Harry's building somewhere in Tribeca, and I was sitting between Ron's legs.

The sky was just starting to darken into a deep lavender, thin clouds spreading across it like someone had tried to wipe them away, leaving streaks on the surface. When I looked up and suddenly it all started spinning faster and faster, I didn't feel afraid. When the next thing I saw was Ron, sitting with me a couch, trying to get his belt buckle off, I didn't feel afraid then, either. And when he began pushing my head down, then up, then down. I didn't feel afraid, because I couldn't feel much of anything.

The next morning, Becca and I went to Hudson River Park behind I.S. 89 to "tan." I couldn't put my finger on what exactly I felt or why, but it was a very low-grade nausea and it made lying in the grass, in the sun, very uncomfortable. The food at

McDonald's on Chambers Street tasted weird—I was hungry, but, at the time, it was hard to swallow.

My next drink was two weeks later, and it was Peach Schnapps with a Puerto Rican guy named Matt from School of the Future. He had been adopted by two gay dads and wore a huge white T-shirt to complement his shaggy hair. After school one day, a group of us filed into a limo with a drug dealer named Mike who had to be in his twenties.

We parked the limo somewhere along Sixth Avenue and Twentieth Street, and the other guys, wearing hats tilted to the left and low-slinging jeans, left to "give us some time alone." The limo driver sat up front, and Matt pushed a button to make him disappear. He undid his belt and slid down his jeans while saying, "You don't have to."

"I want to," I said.

I don't know how I knew how to do what I did, and how to look sexy doing it, but I did the same thing to Matt that I did to Ron, hoping, somehow, it would get me closer to this greater thing I couldn't seem to have, some feeling of being a normal teenager.

Inside, I felt like a parent who needed a break from watching over the invisible little girl inside me, the one who was always afraid of something and had access to weapons that could cause me to make some very adult mistakes.

* * *

After that day, things would begin to go really wrong.

I would earn a reputation, and people would threaten me, leaving notes in my locker or confronting me in person.

They'd shout "What!?" randomly in the halls, daring me to say anything.

I had become, to a specific set of girls, a "slut." They did, or didn't, know about that day in the limo, or that later, I'd gone off with Mike the drug dealer, parking somewhere on the cusp of Chinatown underneath the FDR Drive and letting him play with my panty lines, which he thought was "sexy."

I walked those two long avenues from school to the subway like I was trying to avoid stepping on a landmine after being told I should "watch my back."

Suddenly, one of my only friends wasn't talking to me, then, she was dating Matt, then, she started a rumor among two of the older girls in the school—girls who had gone to I.S. 89— that I called *them* sluts.

"You'd better watch your back," they cornered me one day in front of my homeroom class.

Mr. Schwartz appeared just in time, saying, "Helaina, it's time to come inside."

The next day, I was paired with a girl named Gemma for a Spanish project, and it turned out we had gone the entire year without realizing we both lived in Southbridge. She was half Italian, half Chinese, wore long-sleeve black T-shirts, and did not seem to feel the need to wax her massive uni-brow. We decided to translate our own short interpretation of *Beauty and the Beast* into Spanish, enlist Charles to play the beast, and film it in small increments over the course of a week after school. Making that video was the highlight of my year, the cause of so many giggles, belly laughs, sometimes even howling.

When the day came to present our masterpiece to the class, the videocassette failed to work, refusing to play clearly in the classroom's TV/VCR. As the snowy, choppy picture went in and out, Gemma and I laughed until we cried, busting at the seams, knowing exactly just what was so hilarious, not caring that everyone was looking at us with their eyebrows raised like we had all gone off the deep end.

Gemma, Charles, and I continued the movie-making fun for months after that, improvising nonsense and silliness with no real plotline, testing which one of us was willing to be more ridiculous than the next, in what costume, singing which song.

One day, in the midst of making one of these movies, I ran into Christine at the Seaport. We exchanged hellos and pleasantries, and I invited her to come over to my place to watch the movie *Thirteen*, which I had gotten from the library on Murray Street.

I had no idea that she had become someone who didn't want to be touched or even spoken to, who wanted to be alone, who was depressed, with moods changing seemingly on their own for no real reason. I had no idea that she was scared of her own mind, that she couldn't seem to make friends, that she didn't give anyone the chance to know her. I had no idea, because neither of us talked about anything other than the movie, or music, or what was going on with other kids from I.S. 89 who went to Millennium High School with her.

She told me everyone was good, but they were not good, because they didn't tell her much, either.

Michael stayed locked in his West Village bedroom most days after school and on weekends, conducting independent research projects on cultures of resistance and conspiracy theories. Soon, he began to have dreams that he was carrying out school shootings and started making plans to drop out and run away. Eventually, he thought about what it would be like to possibly plan a dramatic suicide attempt that entailed jumping off of a bridge or making a bomb threat, then going out via suicide by cop. But they were just thoughts.

Then, there was Greg, who still often left the subway to call the police, plagued by the *If you see something, say something* signs all over the city. He was having thoughts that were scaring him too. When he tried to open up to his friends, telling them "It's like I'm fighting hard just to suffer. I'm around people but still feel alone. I can't sleep, I just lay in bed and can't turn off these bad thoughts, which just race," he quickly regretted it. Based on the way they reacted, he decided that sharing his innermost feelings with other teenage boys was clearly a mistake. Instead, he began to quell the violent thoughts that emerged with alcohol and weed, which gave him some relief.

His parents tried sending him to a therapist, but, as Greg will tell you, "She was whack as fuck." He went through three different high schools, a natural introvert who, with each transfer, became more paranoid about what people thought of him. He went in and out of outpatient rehab until his parents sent him away to boarding school.

* * *

With the threat of another school year looming overhead and the lighter days of summer vacation as a counselor at Downtown Day Camp slipping away, I sulked out of my room and announced, "If I have to go back to Baruch, I'm going to kill myself. People are threatening me, and telling me to watch my back. I only have one friend. I hate it there."

All of that was true.

My mother was sitting at the computer, which was usually my dad's seat, but my dad was off at a Community Board meeting.

"Well, I'm glad you've made that decision with two weeks left for us to find somewhere else," she said, looking at me in exasperation and throwing her hands up in the air. "What are we supposed to do? Who's going to take you on such short notice?"

Getting into any public school in New York City was difficult, which made this a challenge of Olympic-sized proportions. Still, she did the research and found another school that would take me on short notice, a private Jesuit school on the Upper East Side called Loyola. My parents would have to dip into my college fund to afford it, and my father, who had only retired two years earlier, would have to go back to work, but they were willing to do it.

Mom to the rescue.

During the interview, I came across charming, motivated, and bright, qualities I still possessed underneath all of the muck.

Gemma wasn't nearly as thrilled as I was when they called me later that day with the very quick decision that of course, based on my grades, my enthusiasm for learning, and my glowing personality, they would be happy to welcome me for $25,000 a year.

"Thank you for the gift of Helaina," Loyola wrote me in an official acceptance letter, along with instructions on where to start sending in the checks.

That same week, a plan to "destroy" the New York Stock Exchange and other financial institutions was uncovered by authorities, and a second, unrelated set of arrests were also made for an attempted bombing of the New York City Subway system before the 2004 Republican National Convention.

Still, sophomore year started off as an ocean of possibilities.

It rained on my first day, and I had straightened my then long, curly hair, so my mother called me a car service to take me uptown. She wanted it to be special. As we drove up the FDR, that same scared little girl was right there with me, snuggled into the backseat. She was excited, too, but in my attempts to protect her, I would grow into an even bigger monster.

The entire Upper East Side was glamorous, wide open, clean, and full of potential for the life I wanted. The Lincoln Town Car pulled up to Park Avenue and Eighty-Third Street in front of a big, beautiful building with oak wooden doors. The whole place looked like it had been carefully carved from white marble, just like the high schools I'd seen in movies. I had always wanted to wear a school uniform, and now, there I was, in a tight white polo, plaid skirt, and black knee socks.

On the first day, I zeroed in on a guy named Max, who was almost like a "boyfriend referral" from this other guy I had been hooking up with over the summer, CJ.

CJ worked at an exclusive underground sneaker store with a French name on Bleecker Street, and was really not interested in anything serious. A couple of weeks before school started, after I had gone down on him, he begged me to let him go down on me, something he claimed he "loved doing." I thought the idea of a boy doing that to a girl could be nothing short of extremely unpleasant, and so I said no, and changed the subject, telling him I'd be going to Loyola. That's when he mentioned Max, without a hint of jealousy, not seeming to care at all what would happen when I found him.

Two weeks into September, I was in my glory. I had a new school, a new boyfriend, a new start. I felt Max gave me a leg up, with my being the new girl and all, trying to force my way into the notoriously difficult Upper East Side private school cliques.

Look, see? I'm normal. Since one of you wants me, I'm just like one of you.

For field day, we headed to Central Park, just a few avenues from school.

I remember exactly what I wore: a black velour Ecko sweatshirt that zipped in the front, hugging the outer curves of my breasts, round and prominent under a tight, long-sleeved red tee shirt. I was also wearing my favorite new dark jeans and black New Balance sneakers.

The crisp fall air blew my hair (flat-ironed, of course) across my face, where it stuck to my red lipstick. Max sat in between my knees, sprawled out on the grass across from another "couple," Cal and Kathy. Cal was incredibly flamboyant, but didn't understand why people asked him if he was gay all the time. He'd had me over to hang out once, and we watched the Paris Hilton sex tape, *One Night in Paris*, him focusing more on Rick Salomon than Paris, after giving me a tour of his walk-in closet full of Hermes scarves and peach colored Chinos.

Things started to spiral with one question.

"Is she Jewish?" Max's mom had asked him. That was a half-affirmative, which somehow resulted in his being grounded every single day, save for soccer practice after school. That little nugget of information began to buzz around the common area of the cafeteria, and depleted whatever points I felt I had gathered by linking up with Max for acceptance-by-association.

The trouble was, I happened to really like Max. Like, *a lot*. I can't remember if I used the word love or not, but his mother keeping us apart triggered something in me that started to burn

my second new beginning away. The clinginess, the desperation to see him, the neediness, it was all a little much for him.
Suddenly I was this person whose entire realm of happiness and
stability depended on a fifteen-year-old boy with braces who
made fart jokes and quoted *Family Guy* too often. Every little
thing he said or didn't say weighed a ton.

I was always on the lookout for signs of trouble, something or
someone that would take him from me, to make sure he didn't
leave. I didn't know, then, why I felt so fragile and flaky, attached
to him by a single loose hinge. I was starting to make desperate
threats when he didn't pick up my calls. I clung to him as tightly
as I could, at whatever cost, smothering him and at the same
time lashing out because we couldn't see each other outside of
school, successfully making what I most feared happen.

He "left."

Things continued to spiral down from there. I tried to take on
an undefeated attitude, grinding up on an upperclassman at the
Halloween dance, boobs pushed up to my chin, but something
was wrong with me, beyond just the way I handled disappointment, stress, unexpected changes. All of the other teenagers
around me at that dance seemed ready to conquer the world,
free, fearless, spontaneous, alive, and invincible. But no matter
what I did, standing next to them, I was like a vibrating bundle
of nerves, stuck to the ground.

Maybe I withdrew into myself without knowing it, maybe
Peter had told them all how crazy I was, maybe I just lacked
that self-awareness, that easygoingness that young people use to
form camaraderie with one another.

But soon I was wandering the hallways at lunch or trailing
silently by the quiet crowd.

At my locker, I tried to move as slowly as I could to take up time between class breaks, pretending I was looking for something, since I had nobody to talk to. Three years of high school suddenly seemed like an eternity, hundreds of thousands of minutes spent thrashing around in feelings that felt like they would destroy me. Pulling out my earphones, the band Simple Plan abruptly stopped singing the lines that made me think they totally understood me, that maybe I wasn't the only one who felt this way. *Do you ever feel like breaking down? Do you ever feel out of place. . . .*

The smell of the tables and lockers stung my nostrils as I reluctantly gathered my books from my locker and paraded in a very specific way along the outskirts, like we were in some sort of dog show, to get to my assigned seat on the bleachers. I was never sure what to do with my eyes, but I knew I shouldn't hold my head down—that was a sign of surrender and defeat.

Everyone sitting on the bleachers was divided by class and arranged in alphabetical order, turning over their shoulders to laugh or shove each other. Some girls wearing red stringy "Kabbalah" bracelets like Madonna did, which I noticed when we all stood up to say the "Our Father," that school gymnasium smell hovering low and thick over us.

My assigned seat was next to a quiet, androgynous girl who went by "Ted" instead of Theodora, who was also bullied, and whom I later found out, would become "mysteriously" expelled.

* * *

There was a lot that shook my faith in America, but Bush getting re-elected that November eliminated it entirely.

How could this happen after what we all knew he did—and didn't do?

Even worse, all of the kids in Loyola were cheering him on. They made the announcement over the loudspeaker that John Kerry had "seceded," and I groaned and let my head fall onto my desk.

Later that month, I found another boyfriend, through MySpace, the friend of a boy I had worked with at Downtown Day Camp. His name was Ryan, he was eighteen, and he was beautiful, blond, and had serious Obsessive Compulsive Disorder, which he took several medications for. He lived in the most notoriously expensive building that Central Park West had to offer, and his mother owned a few restaurants. After going on several real dates, and not understanding how I had gotten so lucky, we went into his bedroom, turned on the movie *Ghandi* with Ben Kingsley, and crawled into his bed. He did something to me with his hand for a very long time that gave me my first orgasm, and he did it again the next time we were there, and the next.

A few weeks later, he called me and told me, after a session with his therapist, that he wasn't over his ex-girlfriend, Cassandra, who had just texted him *"Who do you love?"*

I took off the heart necklace he bought me at his school fund-raiser the week before and tossed it under my desk.

My attention was turned back to the kid who tripped me, the one who called me by my new name, "Jewish Whore," and the girl who shoved me in the stairway, saying "Sorry!" and laughing to her friend, hand over her mouth, as soon as she turned away. Now, it was all even bigger.

I kept myself going by writing for the newspaper, stories that mattered to me, indicating that deep down, I had understood something about what I had gone through that I could not put words to on my own.

> *Thousands upon thousands of children living in Southeast Asia have lost everything they own; everyone they loved. As they ran for their lives, they watched everything they treasure disappear, swept up by the ocean in a matter of seconds. Some children were placed in shelters, others still wander amongst the rubble, clutching their blankies, not quite sure of what to do. Seven hundred children were found all by themselves in a village in Indonesia: one village out of hundreds. The concept of exploiting children to further profit from their misery may seem an incomprehensible one, but when natural disasters like the Tsunami occur, thousands of people are displaced and therefore vulnerable to trafficking. The children who do manage to find salvation are afraid to leave their tents just to get water because they're scared of being snatched up and sold. There are in fact military personnel involved in the relief operations, but even their presence has not reduced the number of attacks. . . . Officials are concerned that the trauma of the catastrophe is provoking the culprits to commit crimes such as rape and abduction. Coupled with the increasingly cramped conditions of the refugee camps, this promises to act as a gateway for more and more criminals to surface. In the aftermath of this tragedy, the psychological damage may be more of a blow to the women and children of Southeast Asia than the tidal wave itself.*

Random text messages from numbers I didn't know continued to run up my phone bill, both pranks and threats. I didn't tell my parents for the reasons teenagers never tell their parents when they're bullied: I was ashamed. I didn't want my parents to think they had messed up, that this was their fault, that I was like this because they had failed somehow. It caused a weird combination of being depressed and listless, like my body weighed a thousand pounds, coupled with a sensation that I had to be ready to tackle some sort of threat at any second. It was all too exhausting.

I was still seeing Dr. F, who just asked me the same questions, grumbled, closed his eyes, and sent me on my way.

Before long, I started to refuse to get out of bed in the mornings.

"I'm not calling you in sick again!" my mother shouted from the living room as I hid under the covers. "Stop being dramatic and get up!"

She pulled the covers off of me, making me feel exposed, and left the room.

She went to put on her coat—it must have been late November, by then—came back to find me still in bed, and tried to literally shake me out of it by maneuvering the sheets around. She left the room again, put on her shoes, and then tried to physically pull me out of bed by my arms. I turned toward the wall and pulled the covers over my head as she tried to yank me out, making myself heavy.

"You have to go to school. Daddy went back to work so you could go to school! What's wrong with you?"

But I couldn't go. I just couldn't.

"You're an ungrateful brat!" She yelled, frustrated and angry. She relented and called the school. Slamming the phone down, she called over her shoulder, "Something is really wrong with you!"

Banging the door on her way out, the impact slapped me across the face like a cold hand. I began to cry, trembling in bed for most of the morning. This is how it would go for most of December and January.

School had always been a priority, and now that was slipping away too. I was losing the last thing that made me who I was, what would make my parents and Grandma proud, despite everything.

At night, I would cringe as I listened to them arguing about me outside my room, blaming each other, knowing it would only hurt to listen, but unable not to.

"It's your fault she's like this," my mom would say.

"Maybe you should punish her, then, you created this," my dad would snap back.

When my mother tried to come into my room, the anger that had been bubbling below the surface exploded, and I'd throw things out into the foyer, screaming, trying to physically push her out, flying into a rage as she tried to force her way in.

I started spending my lunch periods in the library or in the school guidance counselor's office, the closest thing I could find to a safe place. Of course, it was smack dab at the end of the cafeteria, so everyone saw me coming in and out of her office and smirked. In fact, it felt like whenever I walked into a room, people were snickering.

I told her I hated my parents and wished I was dead, that I didn't want to stay at school or go home. I told her that small things like making a decision flustered me, like which staircase to take or what to eat for lunch, and it felt like my life *depended* on every decision I made.

She nodded, and then I left.

What I really craved more than anything else was a friend, the kind who knew exactly when to reach out and hug me when my eyes were about to spill over with tears, letting me fall into her, safe, protected.

But I was still alone.

It was a cold December morning when I first took a pair of scissors from the art room, the kind with the colorful plastic handle, into the bathroom during lunch. I locked the door behind me and looked in the mirror, wishing my reflection would leave and I could become somebody, anybody else. More than what was there, I saw what was missing. My heart was pounding and all I could think was *I want go home.* I was largely invisible, and the only times I was visible, I wished I wasn't.

I cringed as I pressed the blade against my wrist. It snapped me back to reality right before it actually broke skin, and, at the same time, I was amazed at how much my skin could endure before breaking.

Did I even want it to break?

What if it did?

What if I actually killed myself?

No, not while Grandma's alive.

I wanted a way out, a new life, and it seemed that no matter where I went, what I did, what I said, the darkness followed me.

Things scared me, and I didn't know why.

I wanted to hurt myself, and I didn't know why.

I was sad all the time, and I didn't know why.

I had nightmares every night, and I didn't know why.

All that other old shit was there that I should be over by now, the anxiety, the irritability, the panic on the subway. It had been three years already, why wasn't it going away?

I felt trapped everywhere—trapped at school, trapped in New York, trapped at home in our apartment. There was no feasible escape in sight—I wasn't old enough to get my hands on liquor on my own, and I didn't have cool friends who went to parties.

Nothing will ever get better for you.

Looking from one haphazardly painted, crayon-blue bathroom wall to the next, inhaling the musty smell of brown paper towels and toilet water, my pulse raced. I shook, wondering if I should just get it over with. Even then, something stronger than me was holding me back from pressing down hard enough to attempt to slit my wrists, which made me feel like I had some control over the pain. So, where only I could see it, there were just scratches, which felt awful. I didn't want to hurt myself, but all of this pressure was building inside me faster and faster, and I had read somewhere, in a book, that this made the girl feel better. It made people take her seriously and find her the help she needed to get better.

I wasn't scared about what I'd done, but I was scared about what drove me to do it. So I told Dr. F, who decided that I was suffering from severe clinical depression, and recommended I started seeing a psychiatrist. That meant a visit to my pediatrician for a referral.

I told my doctor, who knew me since I was born, that I felt like throwing myself in front of a train, and she made my mother leave the room.

"I've started to scrape my wrists, but I don't know why. I don't want to live, but I don't actually want to die when I do it," I said.

"Will you show me?" she asked.

"Yes," I said, and started pulling back my long sleeve. "But only if you don't tell my mom."

She agreed. As soon as she saw the marks, she told me to roll up my shirt and called my mother back into the room, telling me, to leave.

I stood outside the door, listening. Of course, she told her. *Fucking adults can't be trusted.*

"She's faking," my mom said. "She's not cutting herself. She just wants attention."

I could sense the doctor giving my mother a disapproving look.

"Mother," she said, "if your child says she is going to cut herself, we don't say she's faking."

Later that night, I found my mom sitting on her bed crying, which was a first.

"What did we do wrong?" she asked me through sobs. "We loved you, we tried to give you everything."

I sat next to her and awkwardly rubbed her back. We never expressed affection, verbally or physically, a lead of hers that I followed. I resented her for being judgmental, dismissive, unavailable to talk about my feelings with, but I also felt ashamed and incredibly guilty. I didn't want to do this to her. I didn't want to do this to anyone.

"It's ok," I said. Closing the door behind me, I felt as though I had just committed murder.

She didn't come out until the morning.

And in the morning I stared with disdain at my reflection in the dark, scratched windows of the train car. As I child, I'd press my face and hands up against the glass and watch excitedly as we moved through the tunnel, in awe of the majestic movement of the silver car through the dark and mysterious tunnel, the occasional flashes of light.

As I walked from Eighty-Sixth Street and Lexington Avenue to Eighty-Third and Park Avenue, past the Best Buy, the closed pizza shops, and the expensive doorman buildings, my backpack chafing my flesh against the cold, I secretly hoped to get hit by a car. I felt too cowardly to step out into traffic and cursed myself for it. I turned on Eighty-Sixth Street and headed down Park like a dead girl walking. Dragging the dripping, tar covered, smoking baggage I seemed to carry everywhere, I was polluted, damaged, a disaster.

Why am I like this? I thought. *What's happening to me?*

I had the sinking realization that no change of location, or hairdo, or uniform, was going to fix me. Therapy wasn't working, and I couldn't talk to my own mother.

What kept me from taking my own life was the same thing that kept me from drawing blood, this tiny, packing peanut-sized bit of hope. That little piece of me refused to give up, despite the therapist, the guidance counselor—and most recently, the school psychiatrist—not getting it. It was a whisper over the shrieking of this little girl inside me that sent the alarm bells going off, and it told me, "*This isn't going to last forever.*"

But standing there on Eighty-Third Street, staring at the school through the moving cars, the wind stinging my eyes, tears began to fall as I admitted to myself that, even if I wasn't going to take my own life, I actually wanted to die.

CHAPTER EIGHT

The more we lose ourselves in someone else, the more we lose ourselves, period. This loss means a reduced connection to personal strengths, desires, opportunities, experiences, values, and priorities. The feeling of this continued loss can lead to sensations of fear, danger, and other emotions that addictions frequently assuage. Clinging is a dangerous coping mechanism; it gives our power to someone or something else and leaves us more vulnerable and unsafe. This is especially true in romantic relationships—clinging opens us to abuse, betrayal, misdirection, and misguidance.
—Michele Rosenthal, *Healing Your PTSD: Dynamic Strategies That Work*

On January 25, 2005, Loyola had a snow day.

I was feeling particularly nervous, staring out the window at the cold concrete of the basketball court outside my window and at the rimmed, barbed wire fence of the rooftop next door, the wheels in my head turning, quickly.

What if the terrorists have been waiting until it snows?

Babies and grandparents will freeze to death.

"They" have Weapons of Mass Destruction.

I ran my finger along the crevice of the window frame, looking up at the golden angel perched atop a castle of white concrete on the Municipal Building.

Is this it?

Is this staleness just life?

I took down some photo albums from the hall closet, which I did from time to time, looking at pictures of myself from when I was little.

There I was at age four or five, standing on a dining room chair, bent over the table, sticking my butt out at the camera as I cleaned up some sort of Play-Doh–related mess I'd made. My lips pursed in a spiteful smile, I wore a pink nightgown that had a blue satin skirt. I was clearly having a grand old time; who knows what I had been doing with that red clay, which was flagged by items like a wrench, a playing card, a plastic toy, and a pile of square, dry paper towels that had clearly been provided for me.

In another photo, I'm three years old and wearing a black jumper with colorful dots all over it, sitting in the middle of a rainbow parachute. It was the kind preschool teachers used to tell you to "grab a handle of," raising it up into the air and bringing it down again. "Run underneath!" they'd shout, or "Time for Suzy to sit in the middle!" as people made the parachute billow all around. That's what I was doing in this particular snapshot, "Helaina in the middle," wearing a pile of tight curls atop my head and a satisfied look on my face that said, "Of course, this is where I belong! Where else would I be?"

I sighed and coaxed a Zoloft out of the orange bottle my new psychiatrist, Dr. V, prescribed me for the depression, swallowing it with Diet Coke.

I closed the photo album and practically fell into the computer chair in the living room, logging into AOL Instant Messenger to see who was on.

Shane was online, so I sent him a message. He responded:

Yo. Wanna smoke?

The message came up in a blue font with a black background. Another pinging sound brought another message:

Jordan will be there.

Jordan was a baby-faced kid with big eyes, blond hair, and very rosy cheeks who I had decided to develop a mild crush on while working as a camp counselor.

Yeah, 3:00 p.m.? Burger King? I wrote back.

I made sure to pick out jeans that hugged me in the right places, accentuating the thin leanness of my legs and rounder part of my bottom. I spritzed on some Coach perfume, laced up my fuzzy boots, wiggled into my North Face jacket, and headed out the door to wait on the corner of Fulton and Gold, on the concrete benches outside of Burger King.

Shane and a few other guys came sauntering down the block in the way that a group of fourteen-year-old boys trying to look tough would, all puffy jackets and caps tilted artfully at all sorts of angles.

I was not expecting to find the person who would change my life among them, but there he was, sitting in a booth while Shane ordered something. His hat brim was positioned so low that I couldn't see his eyes until he looked up at me from underneath it. My heart stopped—they were big and blue, and they were peering right at me. I was standing up, leaning with my hands behind my back, on a table right across from that booth, and when he introduced himself as "Vin." I took the hand he offered and felt a wave of something pulse through me like jelly.

Before we could say much else, Shane came back carrying a grease-stained brown paper bag and announced, "Okay yo, let's roll."

We walked over to the Seaport and boarded the back of the small, free "Connection" bus that did a looped route from the Seaport, to Wall Street, to Bowling Green Park, and to Battery Park City. As we waited for it to leave, Vin and I sat in the back and talked about how much we loved certain rap music, and he was impressed by how much I knew about the genre. I learned, that he was an eighteen-year-old, almost-high-school-dropout who lived with his adoptive single mother, who was Italian, in Gateway Plaza. He had originally been born in Chile. He was overweight, acne-ridden, and wore his clothes about four sizes too big. He was the one with the weed, which he sold. When I spoke, he nodded, his eyes fixed in front of him, too nervous to make eye contact again.

We filed off of the bus and walked a few blocks in the snow over to a building in Independence Plaza, another housing cooperative two blocks from P.S. 234. It must have been Shane's building, or else, it was one of Vin's friends' buildings. He directed us into the staircase, where we all found a seat, as if we were taking our places in a movie theater. I watched as Vin gutted a cigar, ripped it, then licked it, like an artist at work. He sprinkled weed along its hollow shaft like he was doing something as routine as squeezing toothpaste onto a toothbrush, something he did every day (which, actually, he did).

"Do you want to smoke?" he asked me.

"Sure," I shrugged.

Of course I wanted to smoke. When I smoked, I felt protected by this frosted glass bubble that I was all snug inside, protected from the loud roar of my normal thoughts. For those first few minutes that I was high, it felt like everything would be okay, no matter what was going on around me. After we passed the blunt around, in a fit of downplayed coughing and laughing, the other guys, seated in twos and stacked on the steps above us, got up to leave.

"I'm not going to be a cock block," said Jordan.

I leaned into Vin like a bed I finally felt relaxed in, resting my head on his shoulder. We talked a little more, and I learned that he liked the Yankees, the movie *Shawshank Redemption*, and a rap group called "The Diplomats" that also referred to themselves as "Dipset" and sometimes as "Purple City Byrdgang."

Maybe it was the weed, or the new, elating feeling of a mutual connection with a human being, or maybe it was just the alluring scent of fabric softener on his sweatshirt. Whatever it was, I felt at peace for a few heavenly minutes, just resting my head there, adoring the warmth of another person in a way I never had before. As I nuzzled into his neck, I could feel his pulse quicken as he wrapped a big arm around me and held me gently, like I was a fragile teddy bear suddenly in need of protection by a complete stranger.

I don't know how long we stayed like that, but eventually, I lifted my head up, like waking up from a dream, taking in the surroundings of concrete and chipped white paint and smiling at him directly.

"I'd better catch the bus back home in time for dinner," I said.

"I'll come with you," he said, holding out his hand to take mine. "Let me make sure you get home safe."

As we walked, the snowflakes gathered onto his billowing heather-gray sweatpants and dissolved, leaving tiny dark flecks that eventually grew into giant dark patches.

We waited for the bus by the World Financial Center, and, when it came, he gestured toward the steps, saying, "After you."

I climbed on as he said from behind me, "Wherever you want to sit," which I thought might have been a joke, since the bus was totally empty. We went straight to the back, and took an ear bud each from my iPod.

"I like this song," I said, putting on "Jenny was a Friend of Mine" by the Killers.

A couple of days later, I went to see *Movin' Out* on Broadway with my mom. It was a musical based on the songs of Billy Joel that had no real plotline and a lot of emphatic dancing. This foreign, happy feeling came over me that night as I watched it all unfold, imagining that the dancers on stage were Vin and I, acting out our upcoming love story. Every song made me think about him. I was in this happy fog, absorbing the songs, enjoying myself, not wanting the show to be over.

When the show did end, I didn't even mind that someone had accidentally whacked me in the mouth while putting their coat on, or shoved me in the shoulder as everyone did a painfully slow shuffle toward the exit doors. I had whipped out my phone as soon as the last curtain call ended and was actually smiling, prompting my mom to ask, "Who are you texting?"

"Nobody," I said, stuffing my phone and the rolled-up *Playbill* into my coat pocket.

The next day, Vin told me that his grandmother had been admitted to New York Downtown Hospital, and was not doing very well. He visited her every day, and then came to visit me right across the street. I offered to go up to visit her with him, but he told me he didn't want me to see her in that condition.

A week later, he wrote me a long poem on two pages of loose-leaf paper, in perfect penmanship that surprised me. He gave it to me before we parted ways, and said, "Read it when you get home."

I was captivated until the last line, *You don't have to say it back, but I'll wait for you to feel it, too. I love you.*

I called him immediately in the few seconds I had before dinner.

"I love you too."

He began taking the train all the way uptown just to pick me up from school every day. When the train stopped in the tunnel, or there was "police activity," we'd pop in a headphone each, he'd lip sync to me, and the fear would relent into the furthest corners of the subway car.

"I will never let anything happen to you," he promised.

I believed that more than I believed the promise that came with those armed guards with guns, more than I believed in homeland security or the police. I believed that he, with his focused effort on me, would keep me safe. And if he didn't, then at least I wouldn't die alone. We fell in love with the reckless, all-encompassing abandon that teenagers do, able to make life mostly about one another, everything else coming second. For me, that would bring serious consequences. Because when the world changes—which it always does—it's natural to look for something solid, stable to grab on to.

What I wish I knew then was that another human being is the worst possible thing to reach for, because they, too, are always changing.

* * *

My inner world may have been looking up, but things at school did not. I started skipping entire days without my mom knowing. At least, until the school caught on to the fact that it hadn't, actually, been my father calling me in sick after all.

On those days, we briefly met up with Vin's friends, from whom I soon protectively lured him away. They, too, were drug dealers—not the type of crowd Battery Park City or Tribeca is known for, but there they were.

There was a pale guy nicknamed "Bill" for the twenties he used to snort coke with, and a hard-jaw Dominican named Rio who was always smoking a joint, which would cause his beady eyes to become smaller and redder with every puff. Bill would dip his cigarette in cocaine and called it a "freeze," offering it to me as I shook my head, sticking with the "safer" version of my menthol cigarette. Eventually, though, I would start to smoke those "freezes."

I started to dress like Vin, like someone who had grown up on the wrong side of town. I've since destroyed all photographic evidence of this phase of my life, but I remember with crystal clarity the fitted caps I wore, the big hoop earrings, the Nike sneakers I began to favor over black shoes, the jeans that were so tight they looked like they were painted on. I still painted on liquid eyeliner, but less dramatically, because he liked me "natural." I only put on one coat of mascara, and on days I wanted to wear a little more, like black eye shadow, he got angry.

"You don't need that shit," he'd say.

His high school—which I encouraged him to start going back to, to graduate—was right next to Ground Zero, and it was not a good school to begin with. Again, surprising for the neighborhood, based on its current reputation, but cops often stationed themselves outside of the building. On the days that Vin got out later than I did, I went to pick him up, taking the 4/5 train to Wall Street and stood outside, listening to love songs on my iPod as I stared down the revolving doors he'd eventually bound through. We'd walk over this rickety bridge they'd installed over Ground Zero to connect the East Side to Gateway Plaza, and spend a few hours alone in his room, just being together. His mom was in her bedroom, or still at work, and the floor of the living room was lined in paper that had his dog's poop all over it.

I would have been content to spend my life curled up with him in his room, like a dog with literally nothing else to do, nothing else to care about. To me, that was bliss. That was all I wanted. I could barely stand to be away from him and out of contact during the school day, and I started getting my phone taken away during class after unsuccessfully hiding it under my blazer to text him.

Our bliss rubbed up against reality in a very uncomfortable way. I still had to deal with the horrors of the outside world, and the other people in it—and so did he—which meant the threat of his being around people who could "steal him" from me or "poison" his mind, somehow, in some way that was never quite clear to me. Like a kid tugging on the sleeve of my sweater, the invisible girl inside me began pointing out the seemingly real "what ifs?" creating a fearful, clinging obsession in me, the same one that had driven Max away, but stronger. If Vin didn't pick up the phone, I thought he was dead, or cheating on me, or lying bleeding in a gutter, or on a subway car that had been hijacked, or being held hostage at a bank.

Meanwhile, at his encouragement, I had auditioned and landed the role of Lucy in *You're A Good Man Charlie Brown*, Loyola's school musical. My rendition of "Take Me or Leave Me" from the musical *RENT* had blown the teachers away, sending me straight to the top of the running, past a senior who was the "head canter" in choir, and ultimately shocking everyone when the list was posted in Loyola's common area.

When I called Vin to tell him the news, he answered, but I could barely understand him between sobs. His grandmother had died.

* * *

How I experienced New York City outside of Vin depended on my state of mind on any given day.

On a good day, when everything was okay between us, the city was rich with laughter and choices, with warm patches of sunlight that peaked through the tall buildings and shined right on me, just for a sweet, fleeting moment. It was full of more food options than I could count, and quick ways to get from one neighborhood to another. These neighborhoods were like tiny cities in their own right, with their own set of unique smells, architectural elements, groups of people, restaurants, and stores, all of which I suddenly wanted to explore.

In a darker state of mind, the city was chaotic and dank, a place where people almost got hit by cars, where crazy people yelled at everyone and themselves and nobody at all. The landscape looked like one big frown, reflections from orange streetlights splattering violently against car hoods, constantly emitting loud, unsettling sounds that I never knew the source of. It was the same old shit, the grime, the shoving, the traffic jams, the homeless man carrying a knife who'd stab me straight in the eye before I could even see him coming.

I had started to see a new German psychiatrist, Dr. R, who decided that, in addition to depression, I also had ADD, because I couldn't concentrate or focus on anything.

For that, she prescribed me Wellbutrin, which made me almost faint during class, so I stopped taking that.

Then, she prescribed me Ritalin, which didn't do anything to change the way I felt or behaved, just made me feel tired all the time, in fact, so we stopped that too.

All the while, my mother made her opinion very aggressively clear.

"You don't need to take all of these medications."

"We should trust the doctors," my dad would say.

And so would begin another fight between the two of them, over me.

Most of the fights now were about medication, but sometimes they were about Vin.

The first night he came over for dinner, she immediately sized him up.

"Well, that's nice, Helaina."

"What do you mean, that's nice?"

"He's trash, ugly, stupid. Not for you."

She somehow found out that the elementary school he went to had a strong program for kids with disabilities, so she started calling him "a retard," too, which my dad strongly resented.

I was like an appendage to her, one that she was now simultaneously bruising and nursing, constantly attacking me for spending "so much time with him" or any time with him at all. Ironically, the more she tried to reign me in and keep me away from him, the more she pushed me away, and the more I pushed back. Behind her polished appearance my mother was flat out exhausted, always on edge and exasperated; no amount of expensive makeup could conceal the fact that her eyes were rimmed by dark, puffy circles.

My mom tolerated Vin coming over for dinner, because she never liked to turn anyone away, just like she never liked to cancel play dates when I was little, because she didn't want to "punish the other kid."

I was still mean, irritable, jumpy, and reactive to her, she was reactive twice back, her voice growing shriller and sharper by the day. Our apartment was a chorus of slamming doors, me shoving my body hard against it as she tried to force her way in. We were both so fragile, fighting like children who were desperate to communicate what they needed but couldn't find the words. My father often found himself in the middle of these fights, but he was temperamental and reactive himself, and so there was always a war, everyone switching sides, feeling betrayed.

When my dad tried to break up one of these physical fights, he accidentally knocked me into the door. The next day, when my parents were supposed to come in to meet with me and the headmaster, I slipped straight past the office, out the door, and to Vin's school, where we found a couple of cops and said we wanted to file a report for assault.

We got in the cop car, drove to the First Precinct, sat in a room, and filed a report against my dad. Soon, a social worker came to our apartment, asked us a bunch of questions, which I answered with such phrases as,

"I hate them."

"I don't want to live here."

"They're horrible."

My father sat there, cooperating and patiently answering her questions, until, sooner than later, the social worker found that there was no reason not to simply close the case.

When I decided to "run away" one cold day, Vin and I sat under the Manhattan Bridge, just minutes from home, watching snow fall onto the green, murky water of the East River.

My therapist called, and I sighed, looking out at the orange Watchtower in Brooklyn that let us know the time and temperature, in both Fahrenheit and Celsius.

"Your parents want to talk to you," he droned. "They want you to go home."

I don't give a fuck about what they want.

"That's not going to happen," I said, looking at Vin, who nodded. It was like I was speaking with a hostage negotiator.

"They said they're going to call the cops and have Vin arrested for kidnapping if you don't," he explained. "He's eighteen and you're a minor. They can do it."

I stood there, almost literally frozen, not knowing what to do, and at the same time knowing that I could never *really* run away, because I wouldn't be able to survive, and I wouldn't be able to leave Grandma behind.

The echo of the little girl inside me who used to say *I want to go home* was shaking her head. Home was scary, now, too, because everyone was always fighting.

After entertaining the idea of jumping into the East River with Vin and freezing to death together, depicting a more realistic ending to the movie *Titanic*, I looked at him helplessly and he took my little hand in his big, softer one and lead me home.

I remember getting home and dramatically declaring, "I love him! And nothing you do is going to change that!" before going into my room. We were in very close quarters in our apartment, so my mother continued to just shout outside the door.

Later that night, when I emerged for a snack, my dad was perched in his usual place on the couch, the flashing white light of the TV flickering across his face.

"You're her best friend and she's losing you," he said.

That made me feel both angry and guilty, emotions that were usually fighting each other—although they were on the same team, they worked together to rail against everything around me.

* * *

A couple of weeks before the school play's opening night, out of the blue and some time after I completely stopped talking to him, I got an Instant Message from Max's ex-girlfriend, or on-again girlfriend, or whoever she was, telling me that I was a psycho, and that I'd better back off because "he was hers" and she was going to "slap me in the face."

I told the guidance counselor and the "school psychologist" but they sort of just nodded and listened.

"Nothing we can do," they may as well have said in unison, on a split screen.

They didn't seem to think this was cause for alarm, but I sure as fuck did, so I took the matter of protecting myself into my own hands. I encouraged Vin—who didn't need much persuading, when it came to this sort of thing—to bring a couple of friends to school and "address" the problem to Max directly.

I stayed home "sick" that day, and, almost on cue, around 4:00 p.m., the headmaster left a voicemail for my parents telling them to come in the next day for a meeting after school wrapped up. I went about the school day as usual, went to rehearsal for the musical, where we were supposed to be fitted for costumes, and was quickly pulled out of the auditorium and asked to go down to the office.

"We can't have this kind of behavior at our institution," the headmaster explained from his red leather chair. He was joined by the dean of students, who was seated in an identical chair, and who was wearing an identical blue suit.

"We can't have students threatening other students."

"What about the girl who threatened Helaina?" my dad said. "And the boy involved? Are there no repercussions for them?"

This was dismissed with a wave and sealed with the words "expulsion."

"Can't you just let her finish out the year? It's already March. It's just two more months," my mother said.

"No, we simply can't. I'm sorry," he said.

"I would urge you to reconsider," my dad said, looking from one to the other.

"I don't think so."

And with that, we left, a wave of relief passing over me.

I finally made it out of that hellhole.

"These people have no compassion," my mother fumed as we walked to the car. "They constantly write us asking for money. They are such hypocrites. What's going to happen to Max? Nothing."

"It's ok," I said. "I didn't want to be there anyway."

The feeling of relief was short lived, abruptly disappearing as soon as I pulled the car door closed, leaving me to absorb the disappointment and sadness coming from the two front seats.

All I could muster the nerve to say was, "Don't tell Grandma."

By then, I expected that Grandma most likely knew more about what was going on with me than she let on, way more than I would have liked her to know. I kept our visits light and breezy, but she always seemed sad, somehow, though we never talked about why. I wanted to preserve this idea of the good girl who always made Grandma happy and proud, and now that fantasy was disintegrating into charred bits and pieces with whatever my mom was feeding her.

I later found out that my parents lost the $5,000 deposit they put down for the next year at Loyola, something they had taken a personal loan out to pay that was, "Sorry, not refundable."

This expulsion and its timing had another repercussion that I hadn't thought about: all Grandma wanted more than anything was for me to sing on stage, and this had been my big chance.

As soon as I got home, I ran upstairs, hoping to beat my mother to it. But Grandma was there in her housedress holding a tissue, hanging up the white-chorded phone. I could see she was upset.

Look what Mom did to her.

No, look what YOU did to her! Another voice inside of me shouted back.

"I don't know what's happening to the little girl I knew," Grandma said sadly. She wouldn't even look me in the eye.

* * *

My mother may not have been the kind of mother who took my hand and sat next to me on the bed and said, "Let's talk about it. What's going on?" She may not have beet the type to smooth my hair and kiss my forehead and say, "We'll figure it out together." But she also was not the type to ship her kid, who was a nightmare, off to a boarding school or one of those places where they "fix" problem kids to finally get some peace in her life, which I think many parents would have, by then.

After I got kicked out of Loyola, she somehow managed to find somewhere in New York City that would take a fifteen-year-old who had already been to two other high schools within eighteen months.

The Beekman School was intended to be transitional. Translation: for kids who got kicked out of other private schools. The school requested a letter from my new psychiatrist, Dr. C, about why I needed this type of intimate, private-school environment to succeed, and, once again, my parents got to work figuring out how to afford the tuition for me, at this small school that inhabited a converted townhouse in midtown Manhattan.

The lockers were on the "ground floor," near a back door that led to a small garden. The garden may have just been a slab of concrete with some trees and three benches, but it was like paradise to me. There were four floors, total, with two class-rooms on each floor. There were four or five kids in each class, *small, manageable*. All of the kids looked older, down to earth, like they had all *been through* something. *Just like me*. I fell in love with it immediately.

Most New York City schools don't look like the high schools you see on TV and in the movies. There are no pep rallies, big football games, or homecoming queens. There are no house parties where people hang out on the stairs and someone jumps from the roof into the pool. After school and on weekends, you hung out on rooftops, on the waterfront under some sort of highway or bridge, at someone's apartment while their parents are gone, or, if you could somehow get yourself let into a bar, you went there. You went to a movie, or to a pizza joint, wherever else you could hang out for cheap.

I took the same walk to the 6 train that I always did, walking past the hospital, underneath the Brooklyn Bridge, down the steps of the station, through a tunnel, up some more steps, through a turnstile, down some more steps, the same routine over and over again.

Why is that guy looking up?

Why is that fire truck there?

Why is another fire truck pulling up?

Four years later, and I was no closer to being able to shake off the trigger response that came with it all.

The classes at Beekman were challenging, which commanded my attention and active involvement. I was engaged and participating often. My grades began to shoot right back up.

There were a lot of kids like me; this was good and bad. Good, because if I had a meltdown or a problem, I likely wouldn't be made fun of or antagonized. Bad, because we all thought our behavior, the levels of extremes, were "normal."

The teachers didn't ask, "Are you ok?" if you cried during class. Neither did the students. We all had weird marks—the skin around my thumbnails were framed in giant red patches, where I would run ruts into the skin as a nervous tick, even after they started bleeding. Other kids had bruises here, or "slash marks" there.

There were also kids going in and out on rotation, though a fair amount stayed.

When the President—still George Bush—visited the United Nations just blocks away from the school, it was nothing but a pain in the ass and a traffic jam. Unlike Loyola, nobody here liked Bush. There may have been a few Republicans by blood in the school, but they were smart enough to keep quite about it. We were all allowed—actually, encouraged—to go outside and give him the finger as he passed by.

Report Card Comments, April 11, 2005

Advanced Modern World History: I can tell that Helaina is very bright, and even though she has just started a new school, she has jumped right in and has been on top of the material. Helaina's first quiz grade was excellent, and I hope that she continued to stay on task throughout the rest of the semester.

Science Fiction: Helaina has been a wonderful addition to the class. She is an astute and careful reader and already participates comfortably during classroom discussion. Her writing is also quite good, and she excelled at this week's grammar lesson.

English: Helaina has proven to be a great addition to my class. She is interested, upbeat, and knows her abilities and skills. Her writing style is tight, expressive, and it's clear she enjoys the writing process.

I even made a few new friends.

Jordan was an on-and-off cokehead whose mother worked as head of admissions for one of the most coveted universities in New York. Jordan had been kicked out of LaGuardia High School, and was a singer and actress by trade. Then there was Dave, who was smart and goofy. He had a lazy eye but an amazing sense of humor. He lived in Westchester, wore tie-dye shirts, kept his hair nearly shaved, and was outrageous. I also liked Natalya, who always looked like she had come from a 1960s war rally, with her greasy stringy hair and a green khaki jacket whose pockets were deep enough to keep all of her cigarettes and drugs in. Also among this crew was the daughter of an Oscar-winning celebrity, who, with Jordan, jumped a kid in our school for his iPod one day.

We would go to this catch-all deli/pizza place/Taco Bell for lunch, then smoke around the corner, in front of the back entrance to an office building, hiding behind two large pillars in case a teacher came by. Whatever Jordan and Natalya were thinking about when they stared off into space, or quietly ashed their cigarettes onto a sidewalk grate, I was pretty sure it wasn't *Someone's going to manufacture a virus and make us watch each other suffer until we die. We're all going to panic and kill each other for a place in line trying to get the antidote.*

I immediately developed a crush on a Croatian kid named Alex, who my mother probably would have thought was very much "for me." He lived in a very fancy building by the East River. I didn't think twice about cheating on Vin . . . but after

I hopped off the M15 bus to say goodbye to Vin right after I did it—and right before a weekend trip to Washington—I told him. I created a whole new catastrophe where I hadn't needed to, and, on top of that, made my parents an hour late to hit the road because of all the crying and talking we had to do. We spoke on the car ride there, for two hours of it, until my mother threatened to "throw my cell phone out the window."

After that, something major changed between Vin and I. I thought that the constant screaming fights and violent behavior—punching walls, for example—was a sign of unbridled passion and love. I reasoned that of course, now, he always wanted to know where I was going, with who, and even who I spoke to during the day. Before long, we one-upped each other, doing and saying crazy things to get each other's attention, making threats. He didn't trust me, and I didn't trust him, and I didn't trust the world. In controlling him, I was like a teacher desperately trying to arrange thousands of rowdy kids on a stage and get them to stay put, but every time I got one right, another one moved, and so on and so forth. It took up a lot of energy and resulted in a lot of frustration.

When we fought, I'd stand, sobbing, wiping away my snot with my hand and flinging it into the street, fingers squeezing the life out of the filter of the Newport cigarette I furiously sucked on, surrounded by slinking midtown traffic or the occasional odd car moving through Battery Park's South End Avenue. I was so far apart from people who walked by, as if they belonged to a civilization that I didn't, and yet I felt I was smack dab in the center of everything, painfully visible, and visibly in pain.

* * *

"Do you feel that your moods are very up and down?" Dr. C, my new psychiatrist, asked me.

Her office was on the ground floor of a residential building on Park Avenue, and I sat on the couch, looking at her in her big chair as she took notes on a legal pad.

"Yes," I said, because, it was true.

"When you're up, when you're high, do you feel so happy it's like you're on top of the world? And when you're low, do you feel like you're at the lowest point ever?"

"Yes," I said, because that was also true, and because I was desperate to put a name on this thing and have her fix it.

"Tell me what else is going on," she said.

I launched into it with no problem, so used to having to explain the same thing over and over again.

"I'm afraid that people are looking at me like they want to hurt me. In school, on the subway, everywhere," I said. "I'm nervous all the time, and when I get upset, I feel like I'm out of control. I'm scared of things other people my age aren't scared of. I feel like I'm suffocating, half the time. I'm having headaches so often that I've stopped identifying them as headaches. It's like a permanent background feature of my life, changing only in severity. And, I'm always fighting with my boyfriend over things that he thinks aren't a big deal."

"Your mother said that you're throwing a lot of tantrums, hitting and kicking and screaming, in these highly emotional states," she said.

"Yeah," I said, looking down and shrugging. "I guess so."

"Do you feel like you're hyper-talkative?"

I didn't even know what that meant, but I wanted to make sure I wasn't going to say anything that would cause her to *not* fix me.

So I said, "Maybe."

What she didn't account for in her line of questioning was cause and effect, triggers, and reactivity—it all came from somewhere. Yes, I had periods of depression, and yes, I couldn't sleep. I made bad choices, but I did not have inexplicable, manic episodes, and I never had grandiose or delusional ideas. I did not think I was "chosen" for anything, and I did not go on spending sprees, or disappear for days and then remain unable to account for what had driven that decision or what I had even done.

What she didn't account for was that sometimes, "fight or flight" is as simple as a reaction. If someone made me feel threatened, whether it was my parents, or my boyfriend, or someone at school, or someone on the street, I reacted, impulsively, quickly, aggressively. My entire world revolved around a person who I needed so desperately, who was the only thing that could, temporarily, make me feel "okay," that there was no room for him to be flawed, to make mistakes, to upset me in the way all humans accidentally hurt each other, without everything imploding into sudden catastrophe. My mood rose and fell severely with whatever he said or did. I would later learn that she had added something called "potential secondary trauma due to 9/11" to my chart when we first met, just one sentence long.

But Dr. C seemed to think that the reason for all of this behavior was because I was Bipolar, so she started writing me prescriptions for that.

By late spring of 2005, my life was overflowing with orange pill bottles, medication my body rejected, along with the last meal that I ate. After I got sick the first time I tried a drug, she lowered the dose, unless I got so sick that I was too scared to try again. We tried Seroquel, then Lamictal, then Lexapro, then Prozac, then Depakote, to try to tackle some of these symptoms, which, no matter what, continued to get worse. I sat there like a test subject, being analyzed instead of taught how to do anything differently.

She was just a psychiatrist, so I was still ushered in and out of therapists offices, always going in hopeful, unlike most reluctant, brooding teenagers who sat there and grimaced because their parents "made them go." I tried to explain to therapists what was wrong with me over and over and over again, only to find they couldn't help me, either. I did begin to feel more foolish for getting my hopes up, then resentful of the therapist I was talking to. Nothing seemed to be working.

I was always going for blood tests, and I was no longer the "brave" girl that the nurses marveled at. I had become squeamish. I was already charged up from the trip, trying to find an address I couldn't find, another crisis. "I'm not good at this," I would warn the technician as she wrapped a rubber strap around my arm. I'd look the other way, squeezing my eyes shut, trying to sing a song in my head.

But no matter how many blood tests I got, the answer never seemed to be swimming around in those vials.

* * *

It was a warm night in 2006 when I found myself on West Side Highway by Ground Zero, which was still a hole in the ground, trying to catch my breath. Vin was on his knees, blood smeared along the side of his mouth.

"I'm sorry!" he was crying.

We had left the Battery Park City movie theater just moments earlier after seeing *War of the Worlds*, which was a mistake. I had begun pushing myself to do things I wasn't ready for, testing out my mother's "exposure therapy" by doing something I knew would upset me, because I "should be able to just deal with it."

Going to see *United 93*, the movie about the plane the terrorists hijacked and civilians tackled to the ground on September 11, fell into this category, as did going to "street" events where there were mobs of people because I just "needed to get over my fear of crowds." Naturally, *War of the Worlds*, a movie full of explosions, people running and screaming, triggered me even worse. I kept saying, "We have to leave," and Vin kept saying, "No," and I kept getting mad and frustrated at him, whispering loudly, changing seats, leaving the theater, coming back, until some man shouted, "You guys better shut the fuck up or I'm going to kick your ass!"

I went to the bathroom and called 911 to report the threat, but nobody showed up, perhaps because we hung up too soon, perhaps because we didn't wait long enough.

And somehow, we ended up outside, with Vin on the ground.

This had become commonplace, a catastrophe playing out somewhere in the neighborhood, my hand flying out, my body on the floor, watching myself through blurred vision as if I was a robot being remote controlled.

When that new, invisible girl took hold, I lost all ability to think—I just reacted, on impulse.

There were still the good times, hiding from the world in his room and watching HBO—which we didn't get at home— eating cereal out of the box, ordering chicken cutlet sandwiches with lettuce, tomato, and hot sauce, and eating them in bed, some crazy luxury that felt illegal in the world of bedroom rules. He would call his friends with me on the line and act like an absolute idiot, singing stupid songs until they hung up, which made me laugh and laugh until my stomach hurt. Occasionally, one of his friends would throw a party, but parties made me nervous, and I wanted him all to myself.

We went out to eat at Chevy's on his mother's dime, or we sat outside on park benches, or we went to the smaller street fairs that would take up just a few blocks and eat Zeppoles, getting powdered sugar all over ourselves, laughing and spewing white dust at each other, everyone's stares just egging us on more.

To fund these excursions, Vin sold Cutco knives. He made money by getting people to sit down for a demonstration, since the cutlery wasn't sold in stores, and made additional commission if they bought something.

Grandma, who really didn't need knives, sat through the demo and bought the second most expensive set they had, taking out her checkbook and handing him the slip with a smile. Later, when her mind started to go, she would cut herself with one of them, deeply.

There were still subtle things I couldn't put my finger on, like why, during a fireworks show, with all of the crowds and the exploding noises and smoke and that smell of burning and gunpowder against the backdrop of the water and I.S. 89, I seemed to get inexplicably anxious, edgy, jittery, then upset, and eventually picked a fight with Vin and ran down the esplanade before the show was over.

There was this "every day could be your last" mentality that I had picked up as a result of what happened, which made me feel like nothing could wait. If we were fighting past the time I needed to get home, or go to sleep, we could not "let it go" and pick it up in the morning after we cooled down. There might not *be* a morning. We could not "take a break," because then, if the city was bombed, I would regret it instantly, thinking, *Oh no, I loved him, and now I'm going to die alone.* I was holding on with a death grip, to make sure everything was "okay" and I was not letting go.

Neither was my mother. The more she tried to bring her hand down on the doorknob to try and get some control over me, to block me from going out with him, the more intensely I fought back, with, I believed nothing to lose.

"You're not leaving! It's not safe for you to leave!" my mother shouted one day in May, blocking the door.

I need to get out of here.

"Move!" I shrieked in her ear.

"Helaina!" my dad interjected, trying to get us both to stop, his face awash with concern and desperation.

I was being cornered, and that was the final trigger, being crowded in. *Too close. Everyone was too close.* I started screaming at the top of my lungs, just screaming without words, feeling that I was going to die. Suddenly I had darted into the corner and cowered into in a ball, pulling at my hair.

"Helaina!" they were crying desperately. "Helaina please, stop! Calm down! Take a Klonopin!"

Dr. C had begun to prescribe me the Klonopin for when I had these "reactive, panic" episodes. Or rather, the generic, Clonazepam 0.5 milligrams, which was supposed to calm me down. I ran into my room to take the pill, slamming the door on my way in. The full-length mirror on the back of my door crashed to the ground, shattering everywhere. I just kept screaming, screaming, throwing things against the wall, hyper-ventilating. My breath was becoming shorter.

I'm going to die, I'm going to die, I'm going to die. I'm trapped, I'm trapped, I'm going to die. I have to get out, I have to run.

I exploded back out of my bedroom door and made a run through the living room and to the front door, but my mother was able to throw herself back in front of it in time.

"Move! I hate you!" I shouted, physically pulling at her.

"No!" she gripped the doorframe even harder, sprawled across it like she was up on a crucifix. Her skin still smelled like a combination of cotton and unscented body cream, with hints of whatever perfume she had on that day, a smell that intoxicated me when I was little, a smell that meant safety, comfort, famil-iarity. The smell had soothed me so often as the child who clung to her soft, delicate skin, and now I was ripping away at it.

After a final big reach, I was able to pull my mother off of the door and ignored her shouting and ran as fast as I could down the stairwell.

I kept running down the sidewalk, and instantly recognized this behavior, and all of the behavior like it, as insane, wild, monstrous. They were trying to protect me, and I was taking them down with me. It all happened so fast, when that invisible girl grabbed my hand and put it on the steering wheel. I was speeding further and further from where I should have been, unable to stop, soaking in sweat and shame. I don't remember where I went or what I did—only that I always ran west, toward Ground Zero, toward Vin, away from home, and that every direction was the wrong way.

* * *

The day I decided I was ready to lose my virginity was a day I had decided to stay home sick from school. Vin said he'd cut his afternoon classes and come over. My father had gone back to work for the Board of Education, so he wouldn't be home until 3:00 p.m., and my mom didn't get home until about 6:00 p.m.

I remember I had my period that day, and I figured, *If I'm going to bleed anyway, I'm one step ahead. Maybe it'll hurt less.*

He came over with a plastic grocery bag full of rose petals and told me to leave my bedroom so he could scatter them around.

"Are you ready?" he asked.

I nodded, knowing it wasn't going to be some epic, big deal, and doubting it was going to feel good at all.

He put on a condom. He had a scared look in his eyes, his thing in his hand, and then in me, which felt like little more than just inserting a hot dog–shaped block into a hot dog–shaped hole in a wooden box, almost like a preschool toy.

He went in and out, in and out, and obviously, nobody "came." The whole thing was anticlimactic, and we decided to head across town to his house after, crossing the rickety, make-shift bridge over Ground Zero. I ignored my mom's angry voicemails, the ones she left when my dad got home and told her I wasn't there, after they had specifically called me in to school sick.

"I was feeling better," I said later when I came home for dinner.

The next time I went to Dr. C, I told her I would like to go on birth control, but that I was scared to ask my parents. She said we could call them together.

I can't remember now if she made the call for me, or if we put it on speakerphone.

I do remember feeling the hot flush of embarrassment and frustration when my mother said, "No, you're too young," and the hot-headedness of my saying, "Fine, but we're going to do it anyway."

One night, Vin and I took the train out to Park Slope, to a party in a brownstone. It was the usual suspects and a few people I didn't recognize, beer bottles and weed and loud rap music. Doug, the kid whose house it was, was different from the rest of the group. He was a Brooklyn Italian wearing a Yankee cap, a gray wool pullover sweater over a white T-shirt, and a short gold chain.

I was sitting on the couch next to Vin, who kept his arm around me protectively, until someone suggested we all went for a "joy ride" in someone's car.

The roar of the engine, flying down the street, sent my adrenaline rushing again, did something to me that I tried to hide, giggling and whooping with the rest of the people in the car, pretending to be enjoying myself, to be having harmless fun, when I really wanted to cry, like a child. *I want to go home.*

When we got out, I felt sick, I reacted to something Vin said strongly, I reached out and hit him in front of everyone, he stormed out, and I called Uncle John to see if he could come pick me up.

I didn't remember how we got out there, and I certainly wasn't going to try to figure it out by myself, at 11:00 p.m. I didn't want to call my dad, and I hoped that maybe my uncle would come bail me out of trouble without my parents having to know, like uncles did on TV and in the movies. *The cool uncle coming to save the day.*

I walked three doors down and collapsed onto a stranger's stoop as I held the phone to my ear and watched Vin pass around a forty of Coors Light, my own Yankee cap tilted far enough over my eyes to mask tears, although by now he had to have assumed I was crying, because, these days, I was always crying in public.

"I can't come to get you, but what's wrong, are you ok? Put Vin on the phone," he said gruffly.

I walked back over to the stoop where he sat with his friends, but Vin waved me away, refusing to talk to him. That was the beginning of my uncle hating Vin.

I could have called 311, found the number of a car service, and asked Mom to come downstairs to the corner and bring me cash to pay with. The options floated there in the night, right in front of me, but they were choices that felt like they belonged to someone else, a girl who could be stronger, who could feel empowered enough to walk away from something toxic. Another girl, one who had enough going on in her life, more to show up for, confidence in herself, solid enough to be able to go through the motions of a break-up until it felt a little better, would have made those choices.

Instead, I drank three Smirnoff Ices, waited around by myself in another room, stood by his side, silently, and finally, traveled home with Vin.

"I still love you baby," he said, high or drunk and probably both.

That seemed to bring him bliss, the weed, the drinking, where tonight, it only made me see more clearly all of the bad omens hovering around us.

Report Card Comments, May 25, 2005

Chemistry: Helaina is fitting in very well in chemistry. She is working hard on staying current with the material and catching up on old topics.

Spanish: Helaina has made some great efforts in class. She has been working hard to better her grade and overall performance, has been more focused, and is undoubtedly attempting to genuinely understand the concepts introduced in the course. Helaina is an intelligent individual who has great potential. She still does need to better prepare herself for exams.

One night, I found myself running after Vin during a fight, hurling myself at him on Maiden Lane, jumping on his back to try to get him to stop walking down the narrow streets lined with puddles and garbage bags.

A bald man wearing a windbreaker appeared out of thin air, stepping out of the shadows, coming toward us. Vin tossed the knife I got him for his birthday under a car.

"What's going on here?" the man in the windbreaker had asked, flashing his badge.

"Nothing, we're fine," I'd said.

Suddenly, my dad appeared from around the corner. He had followed me.

"They're just having a fight that got out of control. I think we're okay," my dad said. Whatever else my dad said to the officer, it made him go away.

Vin came back to our apartment, and my father got him a heating pad for his back, setting him up on the couch.

Sometimes, my dad had to call Vin himself when I had an episode, asking him to please talk to me, because he was the only one who could help calm me down.

Report Card Comments, June 6, 2005

Chemistry: Helaina did a fantastic job in chemistry this quarter.

Spanish: Helaina has overall made good progress in the course. She needs to better enhance her study skills, but exhibited genuine determination in her efforts to improve her performance in the course.

Adv. Mod. World History: Helaina's only shortcoming is she has not studied comprehensively for her exams and quizzes

Science Fiction: Helaina's work is undoubtedly excellent across the board. She writes beautifully, both creatively and formally. Her formal essay was sophisticated and well originated.

Despite my major fuck-ups, I was still able to end the year on a high note and make Grandma proud.

First, I won second place in an essay contest for Marymount Manhattan College. The essay was about learning from pain and moving forward, something that was very wise beyond my years, probably a little contrived, and good enough to get me noticed.

Then, there was the school newspaper; the school didn't have one, so I started it, and I ran it myself.

What my mother did or didn't tell Grandma, I was never sure, but she didn't seem quite as giddy about my accomplishments. Of course, she was proud, but there was a sadness to her now, and she would sometimes say what she had said when I was expelled from Loyola, now repeating, "I don't know what happened to the little girl I knew," over poker games and Friday night dinners, when we took her out to eat and I sat next to her.

The guilt kept me from visiting as often as I used to, forging a gap in the memories of us—just us in our little world—that year.

My parents threw me a sweet sixteen party on my birthday, June 30, which felt like a disaster, or rather, a disappointment, because for me they were one in the same.

There were about fifteen guests, Charles included. We had hired one of Vin's friends to DJ, paid in cash, and gave him a playlist of songs we liked. I had gotten my hair done, curls done up on top of my head, and I wore a beige dress that looked kind of like Marilyn Monroe's famous white street-vent dress. We had it at T. J. Byrnes, the nearest and most convenient space that could host a DJ and give us food, and not charge us extra for the space.

My mom would tell you that night went like this:

Someone showed up with alcohol. Matt—from P.S. 116—went home drunk, so his mother called my mother and then, Charlotte from I.S. 89 accused us of serving food that gave them food poisoning. I cried because nobody was dancing, which didn't make anybody dance. I felt awkward because my parents, Charles's parents, and my grandma were sitting nearby watching. My aunt showed up drunk, which made my grandmother furious. I felt especially guilty that my parents had gone through so much trouble of throwing me this party, spent all that money, and it felt so somber, despite Vin feeding me cake like it was our wedding, and Jordan and her date reassuring me that it was "so great!"

It was supposed to be happy, and crowded, full of people and dancing, and it felt like one of the saddest nights of my life.

* * *

A couple of months later, my parents and I went on a trip to Montréal and Quebec. We were eating breakfast at some outdoor café, and my dad was drinking coffee, and I didn't want the sweet crepe with chocolate I had ordered, because I couldn't really stomach anything anymore. I had recently begun to see a stomach doctor because I was nauseous, had diarrhea all the time, and had lost much of my appetite, unable to eat more than a few bites of anything. I was told to take Prilosec, which didn't solve the problem. I was almost afraid to go anywhere, to even leave the house, because I would have some sort of horrific bathroom-related emergency.

"What's your name?" My dad asked the waiter, and I sunk lower in my chair, wanting to die, knowing what was coming next.

"Hi Sean, I'm Paul. This is my wife, Denise, and my daughter, Helaina."

Who the fuck cares!

This was the embarrassment equivalent of taking a gross dump at a party, realizing the flush was broken, and having to exit past a long line of people waiting to use the bathroom.

I sighed audibly.

After an uncomfortable, strained lunch, our key had barely touched the door handle of our hotel room when I made a snarky remark about my dad smelling like the salmon he ate. He pushed me out of his way to get to the bathroom, and it was like someone flipped a switch.

I started screaming, blood curdling screams, like I had to fight for my life.

My hand shot out and sent the lamp crashing to the floor.

I grabbed and threw the chair at the small desk across the room, screaming and screaming like I was possessed.

"No!" I was screaming. Just the word, "No!"

My dad left the room, and I stood there sobbing, and my mother stood there doing whatever it was she did when this happened.

A few moments later, there was a knock at the door.

"Everything ok in here?" security asked.

I sat hunched in the corner, trying to hide, panting, like a rabbit hiding from a dog.

My mother had given me a calling card, so I used it to call Vin, getting his voicemail over and over, leaving him voicemails, crying and just about *willing* him to pick up, until my calling card ran out of minutes.

I was furious at him for not answering his phone, when really, he hadn't done anything at all except play basketball. But not being able to reach him was like an extra circle of hell, in that corner next to the broken lamp and the curtain.

When we got back, a second stomach specialist at NYU Medical Center prescribed me Prevacid, since it now felt like barbed wire was churning inside of me, like something was squeezing me from the outside. Heartburn, cramping, nausea: you name it, my stomach was doing it. I began losing a lot of weight, a time my mother still remembers, almost wistfully, as the time I was a size 0.

* * *

During my Junior year, in history class, we read about nuclear war and the Atomic Bomb and Truman. We studied suicide bombers closely, learning that young men were selected and then prepared to be martyrs. They were observed to see if they could be discreet among other people. They were put in these suicide cells for months and months at a time to study religion, reading chapters of the Koran and praying. They prepared wills and video testaments of their last words. We also learned that, according to Mohamed, it is inappropriate and unholy for martyrs to be vengeful.

"According to suicide bombers, where does fear come from?" our teacher asked us one day after reading from a textbook.

"There is a natural fear of not knowing what lies beyond death," I said. "The fear is not in actually committing the act. They want this success so badly that they are more anxious over something going wrong and not pleasing Allah than his fate or the fate of others."

I took an Advanced English class as well, where we studied the philosophies of Sartre and Nietzsche.

"Hit an old lady, eat a puppy, none of it matters!" our teacher declared at the beginning of class.

The last thing I needed was to hear about more ways that people rationalized acting like monsters and hurting each other, but it was the only Advanced Placement English class the school offered, and I needed all of the academic advantage I could get at that point.

The class focused on topics such as the Weatherman terrorist group, the Khmer Rouge, and the Holocaust. My brain was a horrifying enough place before having to worry about people chopping off my clitoris or making me throw up and then eat it, or ripping my teeth out with pliers, or making me watch as they tortured and gagged and killed my parents. But they entered right into the nightmarish narrative.

We had to watch documentaries about the Viet Kong and Vietnam, and as a class, we went to see the documentary "Ghosts of Abu Ghraib," about the military who tortured prisoners, at the Lincoln Center movie theatre. *Great*, I thought. *Now they're really going to kill us. I would want revenge if I were them too.*

We read *No Exit* by Sartre and *Lolita* by Nabokov, we also read plays by Edward Albee like, *The Goat, or Who is Sylvia,* and essays like "Spock's Brain." We read "The Handsomest Drowned Man in the World," about children who play with a dead man's body, thinking he is a whale. We learned that it was Nietzsche who said, "Hope is the worst of all evils, for it prolongs the torment of man," and our midterm and final exams took about seven hours, for no good reason other than that teacher felt like it.

My mom wrote a note to her telling her I was coming home "deeply disturbed," and asking that I be excused from watching certain documentaries.

"Helaina gets upset by these things because of what she's been through," my mother told the teacher one day.

"No, she has to learn to deal with the real world," the teacher said. "She needs to learn that this is how the world is."

CHAPTER NINE

War is a mind-set, and all action that comes out of such a mind-set will either strengthen the enemy, the perceived evil, or, if the war is won, will create a new enemy, a new evil equal to or often worse than the one that was defeated.

You find peace not by rearranging the circumstances of your life, but by realizing who you are at the deepest level.

To recognize one's own insanity is, of course, the arising of sanity, the beginning of healing.

—*Eckhart Tolle, A New Earth*

In January 2006, Dr. C's chart read:

Seen in emergency room in St. Vincent's. Began taking Risperdal.

It was the first time that whatever had upset me, whatever dark thing had happened as a result of fighting with Vin, had made me actually draw blood in two lines over my wrist.

I presented them to my father right after and told him, "I need to go to the hospital. I want to kill myself."

In a painfully slow, awkward, dragged out, and desperate cry for help, we drove to the St. Vincent's Emergency room—the one at New York Downtown Hospital across the street was to be avoided at all costs, no matter how convenient—and I was led into a small, private emergency room, where a curtain was drawn around us.

They kept me in that room for two hours doing nothing but sitting there.

Eventually, a black woman in a charcoal suit entered carrying a clipboard, wearing her glasses on a colorful chain around her neck.

"We can admit you to the children's psych ward for two weeks if you don't think you can keep yourself safe," she said.

"I don't know. Maybe that would be best," I said.

I knew I didn't belong there. I didn't want to actually kill myself, I had no real plan; what I wanted was to not feel how I was feeling, for someone to help me out of it, not to die.

You're not crazy. A crazy person wouldn't be thinking about getting her homework done right now.

But it looked like I was out of options, and so maybe, having an excuse to be away from everything, from Vin, from school, from my parents, from the subway, was the solution. Literally removing myself from the world.

If they think it's serious enough, maybe they'll give me something I haven't tried yet.

Just then, my mother showed up, throwing back the curtain in time to refuse to let them admit me anywhere.

"You want to go with all those crazy people, those degenerates? You'll be all alone surrounded by crazy people and drug addicts. That's not you. You don't belong there. You're not going."

She turned to the woman.

"She's fine. She's just being dramatic."

My mother gathered up my things.

"Now, let's go see your grandfather, someone who is *actually* sick."

I hadn't even realized that Grandpa was on another floor in the same hospital, going in and out of consciousness after having a stroke.

Where the hell is my head at?

My aunt was there, my grandma was there, and I told my mom, "Please don't tell them I was down there." I watched, suddenly becoming everyone's rock, as they all cried while he made moaning noises.

After that, I took Dr. C's recommendation of some sort of Behavioral Therapy. Dr. K had an office near Columbus Circle, a place just like all of the other tall landmarks that I still was not comfortable being in, but faked that I was, ignoring my elevated heartbeat, trying to look like all of the other people going about their business in like they were playing volleyball on the beach, *nothing to worry about here.*

I told Dr. K everything I had told the other doctors, still not at the point where I had an attitude of "why should I tell you, you can't help me," because I refused to go in that way. If you asked for help, you needed people to want to help you.

It was a good thing, too, because Dr. K didn't just sit there and ask me questions and show me the door when our time was up. She had me *do* things, like "chart" my feelings and fears as they pertained to Hailey, my new, loud, very ill-liked school best friend, and Vin, the only two people I had real, close relationships with. I liked having something to do, like an activity. This was where we started: just chart how you're feeling, and in response to what.

Watching the news made me afraid, so that was high on the chart, like an eight.

Vin not picking up his phone made me panic, so that was a ten.

The way Dr. K spoke to me, the way she started to uncover causes and effect, made me feel like something was clicking. She checked in with my parents, and I got the sense that maybe she could help me break free of all of these nasty cycles I found myself in, and possibly, begin to build myself back up.

"You know," she said. "You always have choices. You don't have to participate in any relationship or any activity that doesn't feel good to you."

Theoretically, yes, I could choose to stay home while Vin went out, or I could choose to stand my ground when I felt hurt, but I could also poke my own eyeballs out with a hot steel blade or create a giant pit of fire for myself to jump into too. Those "choices" felt in line with that. Still, week after week, Dr. K patiently peeled back these layers, almost like the way you'd tiptoe around a giant mess the morning after a party, slowly cleaning it up while everyone was still passed out.

"Everything may feel like the end of the world, but it's not, really," she said. "It's not immediately a crisis, unless you make it one."

One morning after I had a huge fight with Vin, she suggested I try an experiment where I put away my phone for a weekend, and spend it with my parents making pizza and going to the movies. During those 48 hours, I felt the twinge of familiarity, of warmth, of life before things got crazy. I started to feel something shift.

Calling him was strange, after that day. I was walking Gucci, and I decided I was ready to talk, and we said, "Hello" formally, like two strangers, asking how the other one was.

In that moment, I felt I was going backward, a backward fall I had to take because I had made that call, and was already moving down toward the ground, with nothing to grab on to.

Report Card Comments January 27, 2006

Modern Politics: In spite of a somewhat prolonged absence toward the end of the past quarter, Helaina did not fall behind one step in this course. Helaina is one of my most contentious, hard-working students, as she is always the first to make up any missed assignments, do extra credit, and bring up new and interesting topics.

April 10, 2006

Advanced English: Helaina has struggled mightily this year, especially during this past quarter. I am touched by her effort and commitment to the course. No matter how hard things get, Helaina always seems to meet expectations and even surpass them. I feel that I am seeing a deeper, more introspective Helaina;

her writing increases to be more thoughtful and searching. I look forward to working with her this spring.

April 10, 2006

Web Design: A+: Helaina approaches this class with a positive and enthusiastic attitude and consistently completes her work in a timely and meticulous manner. She prepares well for quizzes as demonstrated by her grades. Additionally, she has turned in 100 percent of her homework and class assignments. I am extremely impressed with her performance and look forward to her continued success in the fourth quarter.

Advanced US History: Helaina is always lovely to have in class. She completes her homework in a thorough and detailed manner, and it is always on time. Lately, she seems a bit distracted; her usual A and B grades have slipped a little lower than I'm sure she would like. All in all she is always polite, asks important questions, and is an overall pleasure to teach. Her diligent and studious manner will ensure her future success.

2005–2006: Full-year absences: History: 13, Politics: 10, English: 10, Ecology: 9, Algebra: 9

In the two months that rounded out the end of the school year, a lot happened. I cheated on Vin, again, breaking up with him at junior prom, on a boat, no less. My drinking started to become heavier. Friends and boyfriends would learn to lie when they brought me home, saying, "She's not feeling well." My mother continued to make me feel guilty for how I was acting. Accepting that I was indeed not in control of what was going on would have been too scary—it would have meant it was out of both of our realms of control. "Eat by yourself" she would say angrily. I didn't want to sit with them or talk to them anyway, so this was even better. Deep under her anger was hurt, helplessness, but I didn't know it at the time, and I know she wouldn't have let me see it even if I asked.

Right at the end of the year, after just a few months of working together, with tears in her eyes, Dr. K. told me she had to tell me something.

"I'm leaving. I have to go to another program that's full time, and I won't be seeing any of my clients anymore," she said, her voice catching in her throat.

"I don't want you to leave me. We were doing so well. You're the only one who has ever helped me. Please don't go."

She handed me a tissue.

"I know you're going to keep doing well. You've come so far. I believe so much in you."

I blotted my eyes, and, unwilling to continue with the session, wiped my hands on my jeans, and stood up.

"Thank you for everything. Good luck," I said, and I closed the door behind me.

Dr. K had left a referral for someone else in her office. Dr. E, who made me feel like I was right back at square one. Talking and nodding, talking and nodding.

"Well, what we used to do, she had me do these activities. . . ." I tried to explain the difference between how Dr. K spoke to me and how Dr. E was speaking to me, tried to tell her what we were doing with the charts, but it didn't seem to really register.

After five weeks, I decided my parents shouldn't be wasting their money, and I shouldn't be wasting my time, and a man was arrested for attempting to bomb the New York City and New Jersey PATH train subway tunnels and flood the Financial District, and I stopped therapy.

* * *

Over at Millennium High School, Michael had his first panic attack over a bad grade on a test. He was sent to the guidance counselor's office, and they muttered things to each other, looking at a folder, making a connection to his being "down there on 9/11."

He was sent to a hypnotherapist for six months, and saw two additional doctors, a psychotherapist and a psychiatrist, who diagnosed him with depression and prescribed him Zoloft.

He told them what he was feeling: he blew things out of proportion, his reactions were strong, the smallest things sending him into a depression. The future was hopeless. Nothing he did would ever matter. Nothing would turn out right. The world around him was horrible.

"I'm not going to amount to anything, and neither will the world."

He wanted to be home alone all the time, to run away, drop out of school, start a new life, no friends, no family. He was sad, without a good reason to be.

"I'm disappointing my parents. They just want me to be happy. They're good parents. There's nothing I can do about it."

He found a better medication, though: vodka, which he brought to school in a water bottle one day. He announced at the end of class—his favorite class, with his favorite teacher—"I'm so plastered right now."

His favorite teacher told him to go splash his face in the bathroom, then go to the nurse's office, and followed him into the bathroom.

Michael got in his face and yelled, "Teachers are supposed to stay out of the kids' bathrooms!"

It was a fight that he almost made physical. Instead, he ran into the bathroom stall to throw up. He woke up after three hours in the nurse's office. His father was standing over him.

"This is the worst thing you've ever done. I'm really disappointed in you."

After that, he started drinking alone.

* * *

Dr. C had begun putting me on other mediations she thought could help me out, Busbar, Affexor, Propanolol, and I still had the Klonopin with me at all times. With each new prescription, my mother balked, went on a tirade about how all of these pills were making everything worse, that it wasn't helping, that "me and my father just blindly trust doctors," and that we didn't want to listen to her.

The three of them collectively concluded, according to her notes, that I was being "triggered in extreme ways, primarily experiencing depression, feeling isolated, crying, couldn't eat," that I was "aggressive and out of control." Sudden and uncontrolled and raging eruptions "targeted myself and others," which seemed to "indicate that the Prozac didn't work."

That summer before my senior year of high school we took a trip, as a family, to Los Angeles and Las Vegas, which my mom thought would be a ton of fun for me. She was still trying, in the way she knew how to try.

After wandering around Universal Studios and forcing myself, through more my mother's "egging on" to go on the Mummy Roller Coaster, which was terrifying instead of fun, I began suffering from a horrible headache, without knowing, at the time, that it was a migraine. I was nauseous and could barely eat as we sat at Wolfgang Puck's restaurant. *What the hell is this?* The pain was so intense that it made it hard to even sit up.

"Please, can we go?" I asked when we were done, as Mom sat there sipping her cappuccino. She took her time walking through crowds toward the parking lot.

"Denise, why are you being so insensitive? She's in a lot of pain," my dad said.

"She's just a killjoy," my mom said. "Everyone gets headaches."

In the car, we sat in over an hour of LA traffic while I held my searing head, which felt like it was being squeezed in a meat grinder. I was trying my best not to throw up in the rental car. To make matters worse, a bunch of drunk kids in the car next to us were partying in a stretch limo, periodically hanging out of the sunroof or the window to shout "Wooo!!!!" and blow on some sort of horn.

If I had a gun, then, I would have used it on myself.

As we pulled up to the hotel, I ran into the lobby, began gagging, and somehow made it to the bathroom of our room before I threw up.

Vegas, came and went in heat waves, slot machines, and Billboards of showgirls that made me feel nervous about my own body. When I think of my time there, I think about the hour I spent looking for the perfect shirt to get Vin, and my mom complaining that she was "losing her patience." I remember crying by the fountain of the Bellagio, because Vin wasn't picking up his phone. I remember walking around the casino with my dad on our last night, suddenly deciding that I wanted new gold hoop earrings, because all I wore were hoops.

We found a jewelry store easily, and the salesman's hair was spikey, and he reminded me of Henry, from middle school.

He asked me my name, and told me it was beautiful.

"These are the white gold hoops we have, we don't have any yellow," he said.

"Well, I have my heart set on yellow."

"Really? Most girls go for these," he said as he put them back.

"I'm not most girls."

"I could tell that right away."

I said goodnight and walked away with my dad . . . then I stopped in my tracks.

"I think I'm gonna walk around for a little bit, find something to do," I told him.

I went right back to the store, where the salesman was on the phone.

"So what's there to do here after 11:00 p.m.?" I asked.

He muttered, "I have to call you back . . ." as he let the phone close.

"How old are you?" he asked skeptically

"How old do I look?"

"Twenty, twenty-one?"

"Maybe . . . how old are you?"

"Twenty-two," he said.

"I'm eighteen, but nobody believes me when I tell them," I said.

"I have to close up here, but I'll be done in ten minutes," he said. "You want to just wait around and we'll get some drinks or something?"

We smoked cigarettes and walked around the casino, and he brought me a Long Island iced tea. He led me into a garage, and we began to kiss passionately and sloppily, and as I pulled him out of his fly, a garage employee passed through, causing us to freeze in place and then burst out laughing.

"I'll call you tomorrow morning?" he said.

"It's my last day. We have to go to the airport at 2:00 p.m.," I said.

The next morning, he called, and I told my parents I was going to have lunch with some kids I met the night before.

We got in his car, and he drove me over to a mall where he told me to get whatever I wanted at the California Pizza Kitchen. He looked at me across the table and rubbed my hand. After lunch, I told him to take me to a quiet spot. We drove for about half an hour and I got a little nervous, because I had to make it back on time for our flight.

"I really don't look eighteen?" I asked.

"Not at all," he said.

"Well, I shouldn't. I'm seventeen."

He looked at me and just laughed.

"I had a feeling you were anything but eighteen."

We got to his house, went up to his room, and I pulled him onto the bed.

At the airport, screens displayed the news that the British police foiled a terror plot to carry liquid explosives onto nearly ten aircrafts traveling from the United Kingdom to the United States and Canada—and that was the end of bringing water bottles onto airplanes. The plan was similar to bin Laden's 1995 plan to detonate bombs mid-air, after his "alleged" bombing of the World Trade Center in 1993 didn't quite pan out the way he'd hoped. The plot was described as "sophisticated" and was said to potentially have "rivaled 9/11." That was still everyone's reference point: *another 9/11, worse than 9/11, just like 9/11.* When the men were arrested, President Bush plugged the war he created by reminding everyone that these were the "fascists" we were at war with.

I spent the entire plane ride home with my bra still unhooked in the back. I thought about moving somewhere more quiet, like the majority of Vegas—the part that was all desert—knowing full well I didn't have the guts to move anywhere, but fantasizing about what it would be like not to have to worry that the subways didn't have metal detectors to catch a bomb, or that everything was a landmark waiting to be obliterated.

* * *

Shortly after we got back, Grandpa started falling more often, while he was wandering around, to the point where neighbors were finding him and bringing him home.

"He seems very lost and very frustrated," they would say as they dropped him off at our apartment.

We knew it would break Grandma's heart to put him in a nursing home, even if it was one nearby, so we resisted for as long as we could. We couldn't afford to pay for someone to take care of him full time, and though Grandma tried, she was now eighty-eight years old and just couldn't keep up. When he started wandering around, unable to state where he was, or where he was going, barely able to remember his own name, we had to relent.

In August, he had to be permanently moved into the Village Nursing home, a depressing place in need of much more funding and staffing than it had, not unlike many nursing homes in the country.

We went every Sunday—the only family, it seemed, that did.

It was something I dreaded, seeing my grandmother upset, seeing all of these people who could not take care of themselves, just sitting and staring, empty, lonely. Nothing to do but sit around and think of the fact that they were dying. Seeing the other residents at the home—strangers—was almost harder for me, because nobody ever came to see them. They couldn't feed or clothe themselves, they couldn't go to the bathroom, and they couldn't go for a walk or turn on the TV or call someone. They sat there confused, even scared, in pain, staring at the floor or at their hands, nothing to watch, nothing to eat, nothing to do. Everything around them was bleak, eerily silent. It even smelled of death. Nothing was coming for them but the end, and they were going nowhere else until that happened. Things only got worse, and then, they just stopped.

Out of loyalty to Grandma, I went, no matter how upsetting it was. When we arrived, it was clear that part of Grandpa knew he'd seen our familiar faces before.

When he could no longer speak, he just closed his eyes and let out long sounds, like the notes of a song.

Grandma always started with, "What's my name? Who am I?" which he could never answer, which made her cry.

He used to answer with a laugh, and then could barely even make a gesture. He made sounds that sounded like gibberish, trying to communicate like an infant.

He reached out to touch her face, and she kissed his fingers.

Grandma tried to feed him like she was on a mission, like somehow making sure he ate everything in front of him was going to help, so we always went around lunchtime.

She would also try to get him to talk, a cause that became fruitless.

We took him out for Chinese food across the street from the nursing home, a place with a Lazy Susan that had room for his wheelchair and had the kind of American Chinese food that he liked, until he began choking and could no longer eat solid food.

My father would wheel Grandpa right up to the piano and play for everyone at the home, assume his position near the window, and sing for an hour like he had at my preschool.

"Why Do Fools Fall in Love" was a fan favorite. Some people would tap the table and mouth the words or nod their heads, which were bent toward their chins. "Unchained Melody" and "Will You Still Love Me Tomorrow" were also popular.

While my dad sang, I could read the fear on Grandma's face like a book. She always told us that she wanted to die before anything like this ever happened to her.

She's scared that she's going to be next.

"I'd do anything to help him," Grandma said through tears. Turning to him, she said, "You've got to get better so you can come home. Why are you getting worse?"

He just continued playing with his bib.

"It's ok," I would tell her. "He's doing good. He's ok."

We all knew he wasn't coming home, and that this would go on for several more years, every Sunday, until it stopped.

* * *

The last time I ever saw Vin, I was sitting with my father and two NYPD officers in the lobby of his Gateway Plaza building.

The fight had been a whirlwind. I opened the unlocked apartment door the same way I had every day for the past year and a half, letting myself in just as I had all the times I brought him his juice and muffin when he was sick.

He was still angry from whatever we had been fighting about the night before, so, the second I put my brown Coach purse down on the exercise bike, he pushed me out. I tried to push my way back in, and he kept pushing me out. He threw me into the wall of the hallway so hard that my heel instantly turned purple. I could barely put weight on it.

My bag was still in his apartment so I didn't have my phone, keys, wallet, or anything I could use to get help. I had to keep knocking on the door and ringing the doorbell, but there was no answer on the other end.

I went down to the lobby and asked the doorman, Angel, if he could please open the door with the spare key so I could get my things.

"What are you talking about?" he said from behind the security desk. "No. I should call the cops on you for trespassing."

Angel didn't like me very much.

At that moment, I saw Reena walking though the courtyard. She let me use her cell phone to call my father, who was there within ten minutes.

"What the hell is wrong with you?" Dad shouted at Angel.

"If you don't give me the phone, I'll have you arrested too for obstruction of justice."

The doorman immediately handed the phone over with a shrug. I was in a daze, trying not to let it all register.

The police got the spare key from the doorman, and we found that nobody was inside. They saw the holes Vin had punched through his bedroom door.

"He's not a violent guy at all, is he?" they joked, sarcastic. They handed me my purse, and I had to recount what happened word for word. I heard my voice but didn't know who was speaking; it was all too unreal.

As we filled out that report, Vin came walking through the lobby with his mother: after pushing me out, he had actually climbed out of his bedroom window to exit the building and go to a doctor's appointment.

The policemen told me to stay away from him, and of course, this would be how it had to end; in a tragedy so severe that I literally could not turn back. Still, I refused to press charges.

The next day, Vin still called, texted, and e-mailed as if it was just another fight.

I sat at my desk at work—I was working as an administrative assistant in the office of the company that ran Downtown Day Camp—and waited as my father called Vin and told him not to contact me again. I made myself a cup of rosehip tea, which I hated, but nobody in the office "believed in coffee." I sipped it, limping around on my purple heel, trying to figure out what the hell I was going to do next.

I messaged Gemma, asking her to de-friend Vin on MySpace. By then, Gemma became someone I only called while crying, asking her to steal packs of Parliament cigarettes from one of her mother's many cartons and meet me with it. "Why don't you just break up with him?" she'd ask.

Now, she said: *No, I'm not going to de-friend him.*

Before I could blink an eye, Vin had taken to his MySpace page to write this long explanation of what he believed happened, tracking everyone I talked to that was a mutual friend. He wrote on their pages that I was a slut, a lying bitch, a psycho who cut herself, a whore. He threatened to send naked pictures of me around the city with my address written on the back, spread details about our sex life, tell all of my secrets.

He posted that the cops checked me for bruises and told him that "Nothing was there, that they looked like mosquito bites," that he should be careful, because, they told him, "I could hit myself over the head with a frying pan and say he did it."

It felt like all of New York City was watching me, laughing at me, saying awful and embarrassing things, conspiring against me.

One week later, I was interviewed by My9 news for the five-year anniversary of 9/11. I remember the reporter, a middle-aged blond woman, kept asking me the same questions over and over, not liking my answers, because they weren't dramatic enough.

"But how did you *feel*," she kept pushing.

She got the answers she wanted, syncing them up with footage from that day.

At the end of the segment, the reporter stood in the cafeteria of I.S. 89, where a community meeting was being held.

"Her mother says that Crime Victims is only paying for a short portion of Helaina's long-term therapy."

Days later, my mother and I were eating at an empty, dark diner that felt hollow, somewhere on University Place.

"Please eat," my mom said.

I stared at my sandwich like it was ten feet tall and made of mud.

"I cant. I really can't," I said.

It didn't matter that I hadn't eaten all day. I just wasn't hungry.

I picked up the turkey BLT and took a slow and painful bite. I don't know who it was more painful more, me or my mother. Even when I could force food down, I couldn't even taste it, and I ate so quickly that I only knew the taste from the smell.

I went to a new stomach doctor in Murray Hill, who stuck a camera down my throat and showed me a disgusting picture, explaining the reason I couldn't keep anything down and barely ate was because I had developed ministomach ulcers, and Irritable Bowel Syndrome.

He prescribed several medications that were supposed to help it go away.

I was entering my senior year of high school, and Dr. C took me off of the medication that was supposed to "even me out." I clearly wasn't Bipolar. The source of that up-and-down hysteria was gone.

She also, finally, prescribed me sleeping pills, after my mother relented from her tirade that "seventeen is too young."

* * *

Thomas, by this time, was settling in to his new high school in Florida. His mother had moved him there because they just couldn't take the stress of living in Lower Manhattan anymore, or the danger that living with his father presented.

Things were quiet in Boca Raton, with enough promise of safety to support his decision to repeat the ninth grade, since that would mean free college tuition at a state university when the time came. He didn't have to worry about anyone attacking them in Florida, but he did have to worry about his mother, who would cry despite herself, saying, "I don't know how I'm going to do this alone."

He blended in with the other kids at his new school, who were almost entirely white, suburban kids who acted decades younger than Thomas felt. They had no idea why the 9/11 anniversary would be anything to care about. It wasn't a part of their lives at all, as far as he could see.

But it was part of his, which was why, on one seemingly ordinary day, when a teacher came in and said, "There's been an incident, everyone needs to head into the gymnasium," he felt the blood drain from his face and his body surge with fear.

Everyone else half-cheered, or said, "Oh no, we're all going to die!" and laughed.

It was why Thomas stayed far away from the windows.

It was why he sat by himself on the bleachers, heart pounding, sweating, immediately taking out his phone and texting his mom, *what's happening?* As the other kids made overblown speculations and had fun doing it. *You're all stupid.*

He sat there, on the bleachers, for a full hour and forty-five minutes with the rest of the school. No teachers had information, his mother wasn't answering, and there were no smartphones for Googling.

When they were released at 2:45 p.m., his mother came straight from her office, an interior design firm, to pick him up.

"It was nothing," she explained. "The store across the street was held up at gunpoint, and they haven't caught the guy yet."

* * *

Dad parked the car somewhere near the West Side Highway, and the four of us got out to head to Lilly's, the "fancy-ish" Chinese restaurant next to the movie theater we liked to go to on Vesey Street.

We started to feel the drip drops of rain as we made our way from the car to the restaurant's entrance a hundred feet away.

Mom and Dad were walking ahead, and I was walking with Grandma, holding her arm tightly in mine.

"Uh oh, we'd better hurry," I said, knowing she wouldn't want to get her hair wet.

That had been the running joke of our lifetime—my grandmother never wore a hat, or a scarf over her hair, and you weren't supposed to touch it. She wouldn't even go out in the rain, most of the time, because she didn't want to mess up her hair.

I started to move faster, and she tried, but then she stopped.

"Helaina," she said my name with a gentle warning.

I saw a subtle struggle in her face.

"What's wrong?" I said.

"I can't catch my breath. Hold on," she said, and we stood still.

The drops began to fall quicker from the sky, and I knew something was wrong. My parents were too far ahead, already through the glass doors, assuming that we were right behind them.

"Okay," she said. "Let's go."

But we had to stop again after a few steps.

"I can't breathe," she said.

"Let's get you inside so you can sit down," I said, opening the heavy glass doors.

We went to our table, and she sat there, uncomfortable, trying not to show that she was struggling.

"I can't breathe," she said again.

My dad immediately got up from the table and asked the hostess to call ambulance. I sat there, frozen, not knowing what to do.

"I just peed myself," she said quietly.

The EMTs came in, and everyone else eating their soup dumplings turned to look at us.

The men put her on some sort of weird contraption, the kind you'd carry your luggage on at the airport, and rolled her, upright, outside to an ambulance. I stood with one foot up on the wall as she went inside the vehicle with my mother, watching as a young neighbor of mine walked by but didn't say anything.

"They're going to have to take her to the hospital," my mom said.

"I'm going with her," I said, getting into the ambulance and sitting down next to where Grandma was laying with an oxygen mask over her face.

"Okay," my mom said. "I'll go in the car with Daddy."

* * *

They told Grandma she needed a heart valve replacement, or she would only have a few months to live.

I ran my nails along the foot of my white wooden daybed from IKEA, staring down at the floor, the small blue rug, the desk with all sorts of trinkets and baubles on it. The things I knew other less fortunate kids would be grateful for, but left a sour taste in my mouth, a reminder that this was still the holding cell for the same life I wanted to somehow disintegrate out of. The TV was on for background noise, as it usually was twenty-four hours a day, an attempt to drown out the echoes of everything that had happened over the past five years, which reverberated off of the walls.

Being alone was like watching a scary movie, going to change the channel when something too gruesome or disturbing came on, and realizing the batteries didn't work. It was like getting up to try and change the channel on the cable box, bringing myself even closer to those sounds and images, and realizing that also doesn't work. It was like trying to turn the TV off, seeing that it won't go off, and trying to leave the room, then realizing the door wouldn't open.

So you can understand why, living like this, I needed a distraction from the movies playing in my own head. Nobody else really wanted to spend time with me, except for Hailey, at lunch, and Jordan, but Jordan didn't like Hailey, so there was that, and besides, Jordan was always with her boyfriend.

I switched my MySpace profile picture to a photo of me in a gray button up sweater, chest pushed up slightly, six-pack abs on display, wet, curly hair held up in one hand, elbow propped toward the sky, a vacant stare into the camera.

I started "friending" male friends' of existing friends I had on MySpace, justifying that because they were not total strangers, it didn't count as "meeting strangers online."

Want to meet? they'd message me.

Yeah, do you have a car? I'd write back.

There was a thrill that came along with going off with an older guy, a tough looking guy, getting drunk, and living to tell about it. Or, maybe I'd get lucky, and I wouldn't.

For a few hours, I could try to escape my family, my neighborhood, my life, through whatever physical distance that a used car with empty bottles rattling around under the seats could provide. I tried to find ways to just keep myself going, just get to college, that was my new goal. Just get through it.

I thought about how Grandma used to run me though a repeated ritual of saying "no!" to strangers who tried various attempts at luring me into their cars with them. I was very adamant about the emphatic "no!" I gave her each time, feeling proud that I had somehow "outsmarted" her in every scenario of candy and ice cream promises.

On this particular September day in 2006, darkness followed me into a beaten up white Chevy with a guy named Q who picked me up in his car and brought me out to Queens. We stopped at a liquor store under one of the bridges somewhere. I was wearing a pleather jacket, one with a snap on a strap around the neck. I had never seen a liquor store like that one. You didn't actually go inside; someone sat behind glass window, and you told them what you wanted. You slid the money through a slot and they passed your bottle through an opening. We got a $10 bottle of something way bigger than we would have gotten for that price at a liquor store in Manhattan.

Back in the car, I stared out the window at the metal pull-down gates that protected storefronts that were closed, lighting up the cigarette hanging out of the side of my mouth by tilting my head toward the flame.

After he parked, we went up to his apartment, and I was taken aback by how empty it was: the living room only had a metal desk with a computer on top and a couch. No photos, no armchairs with blankets draped over them, no end tables or magazines or any sign that someone lived there.

"I'll be right back," he said, ducking into another room.

I wandered over to the computer, clicking the mouse to bring the dark screen to life. I searched through an iTunes library and scrolled down until I found a song I recognized. I sat on the couch and waited for him to come back with the bottle cracked open. He poured me a cup of something that tasted like poisonous fruit, something that could have been named after Snow White's Apple. I lit up another cigarette and chugged what was in the plastic cup, and when he got up to refill my glass, I put a hand up to stop him. I walked over to the kitchen island, picked up the bottle by the neck, and chugged the vodka straight from there, trying not to wince as it went down and "chasing" the triple shot with the drag of my cigarette.

"Wow, you are not playing games, little girl," he said.

Another song I knew came on, and I started to sing it, quietly.

"Damn girl, you can sing? Sing!" he prompted me.

So I did, facing the window, not him, looking over an industrial landscape of buildings and trucks and bridges, of trucks and parked cars and garages. I belted out that song, the vodka loosening up the block that lived inside me when I was sober, too ashamed of how I had "blown it" when my singing teacher told my grandma she shouldn't bother with the singing lessons anymore, because, at nine years old, I just wasn't practicing enough and wasn't taking it seriously.

After I finished, he clapped, scooped me up, and brought me down onto a bed in another room, shirt over my head. Suddenly, I was staring down the lens of a camera.

"What are you doing?" I asked, putting my hand up in front of the lens.

He still had all of his clothes on, which was a plus, but I didn't understand where the camera had come from and why he was taking pictures of me.

"Stop," I said. "Just stop. If you want to have sex, I'll have sex with you. But get the fucking camera out of here."

He tossed the camera into a closet and pulled out an aluminum foil pouch. He unfolded its corners to reveal a bunch of pills with strange markings on them.

"Want one?" he asked. "Ecstasy?" I guessed.

He nodded.

"No thanks," I said. "And I'd appreciate it if you didn't, either. You have to drive me home."

Then, my memory goes black. I wish I could remember if we had sex. Part of me believes that I was strong enough to say no, the same way I said no to the photos, which I'm sure he still has somewhere. Another part of me knows that it could very well have happened, because I could have just lost consciousness and not been able to do anything but let my body go through the motions, a body that was craving attention and warmth and wasn't very discerning.

Whatever happened, the next thing I remember is being back in Q's car as he explained that we had to make a detour on the way home.

"This guy who's buying from me, he's a big Reggaeton producer," he said, referencing the latest Latin crossover song that I might know, which I did know, very well.

We went up to the apartment, and he introduced me, like a gentleman. The producer looked me up and down.

I'm sure I was something to look at—long, straight jet black hair, the tight jeans that held my legs together so they didn't buckle in fear underneath me, the tank top that was nearly bursting at the seams under my swollen chest, the painted, sad eyes glazed over with defeat.

Behind that defeat, which I hoped he couldn't see, was fear about what was going to happen next.

"You want some?" the producer offered me.

"No, thank you," I shook my head. "I have to get going. My parents are waiting for me. I have school tomorrow."

The point got across, and in the hallway, as we waited for the elevators that had no numbered lights to indicate whether they were on their way, I asked Q, "You good to drive?"

"Ma, of course I am. I got you."

On the way home Nelly Furtado's "Promiscuous Girl" came on the radio, and I moved my shoulders to the beat, lighting up another cigarette and hating myself for it, imagining the tar and the smoke blackening my lungs.

I don't know what sort of lies I devised to my parents, but I continued to go off with boys, and I never came home "trashed." Or, if I did, I hid it, or I thought I did. When my dad finally said, "I think you should ask your friend to come up and say hello," I was relieved that it was an art student from Pratt who was downstairs, not someone like Q. If my parents knew I was meeting strange guys online and taking the L train from Brooklyn at one in the morning, they would have put me under house arrest.

* * *

They say you date at a level of your self-esteem, which would explain why everyone I met was so tough on the outside, and dead, empty on the inside The boys I met all had something in common—they had real problems. They seemed older. Ideally, they had a car, and they could take me somewhere else. *Just get me out of here. I need to get out of here.* I was attracted to the sad, the difficult, the complicated. I liked guys who seemed like they had been through shit. On some level, through the sex, the booze, the weed, I was actually making real connections. Whoever I was with, there was always a brief moment in our time together that I believed I could "save" them, but my rescue van was always low on gas, so I'd pick up this hitchhiker and then strand us both off in the mountains somewhere.

Not all of them were dangerous bad boys I met online. There would be more like Q, but sometimes I met people while drinking and smoking with other people, having long talks, going with one bad boy to a party and meeting a girl who would introduce me to another. There were musicians, athletes, college art students, and I could keep up with all of them, quick-witted and smart, able to figure out what each of them wanted from a girl, from a conversation, and, more importantly, what they didn't want. I was malleable, because I was barely anything, or anyone, myself.

The players changed, but the plot was always the same: we'd be sitting on some bench, staring out at either body of water around the island, the East River or the Hudson River, from Queens, Brooklyn, New Jersey, Randall's Island, downtown or midtown or uptown, to the east or to the west, lighting up a joint, or a cigarette, or swigging from a well-concealed bottle.

I always "gave it up," because I didn't even care. I didn't enjoy sex—usually, I was thinking about something else, or I was too drunk to think. There was some humanity in the deed, some affection, but that wasn't the point. These encounters gave me something to pull me forward, the ghost of girl who wasn't quite dead yet, only a reflection of whoever I happened to be near. I didn't care either way. My body was just there, this thing that I carried around. It wasn't something that I had respect or no respect for. I didn't regard it in that way, because I didn't regard it at all.

I put it out there, and you take the bait. It was comforting, almost, having that kind of power, knowing the outcome.

When the day came that I found out, for no reason that I could ever figure out, my best friend Hailey, who hated Vin, had secretly been *friends* with Vin for two months, the world turned upside down. She had given me access to her MySpace so I could "keep an eye on him," so he knew I was cyber-stalking him. She had listened when I told her I wanted to have him jumped, and relayed the message to him, trying to talk me out of doing it. She had three-way called him when I told her I had gotten my results back, dialing him in just in time for him to hear that I had "gotten gonorrhea and didn't know who from."

After that, Hailey would call Vin during lunch at school, talking to him in front of me, putting other kids on the line with him. While they may not have been intending to "hurt" me, I definitely found enough evidence to support the fact that I was being "plotted against." I linked up with a black guy, who went by the name of "Vivo," whose father never seemed to be at their Upper East Side home, who would call or message Vin every once and a while warning him to stop talking shit about me. I posed with him in pictures and posted them online, throwing up gang signs I had no clue about, trying to look tough, not hurt, normal.

In a particularly dark moment of desperation and desire to be part of the world, I reached back out to Isaac, my first "kiss." We drank with his friends at a spot in the East Village, a bar with an outdoor garden that we sat in even though it was cold. Huddled under heat lamps, wearing our puffiest jackets, we drank something called "Devil's Spring" that's exactly as strong as it sounds. Before moving to another party, we went back to Isaac's apartment, the apartment that, three years earlier, he tried to feel me up in. This time, I let him do whatever he wanted.

We met back up with everyone on the roof of someone's apartment right by the Seaport, where we drank and I clung to Isaac, then let him go when I saw Trevor.

Slurring my words, I said, "Trevor, let's go have sex."

"You just had sex with my best friend," he said, looking at me like I was crazy.

Trevor was in his own special kind of hell, I would later learn—therapists, bottles, drugs, throwing furniture at his parents, blacking out, and wishing for the permanence of that conscious absence.

I smiled. "Okay then."

I felt my phone vibrating; it was the guy I had called to tell I believed it was him who had given me Gonorrhea—he went to Millennium, and I had met him through Christine. I knew it had to be him, because it was right after our "tryst" that I went home and started burning. Fortunately, our biology teacher at Baruch taught us the symptoms of STDs, and I had gone to the gynecologist right away, and it could be cleared up in a day or two with just one pill. Unfortunately, she had left the test results right there on our house phone answering machine for my dad to hear.

But on this call, on the other line, it was a girl.

"Let me tell you something. This is his girlfriend, and if his tests come back positive, we're going to have a problem. I know where to find you," she said, threatening me in a thick Dominican accent.

It must have been the alcohol talking, when, cool as a cucumber, I said, "Listen. I don't do things the way you do. If something happens to me, I will trace it to you, and I will make sure you're arrested. My cousin's a lawyer," I said, throwing in some curse words before hanging up.

I never heard from either of them again.

* * *

"A plane just went into a building uptown."

I whipped my head around to face Jeremy, who had made the announcement.

"What?" leapt out of my throat, along with my heart.

It was October 11, 2006, math class, the last class of the day. There were just four of us there. I just started running. I shot down the stairs . . . then back up the stairs . . . then down the stairs again. *It's happening. It's finally happening again.*

I ran back into the classroom.

"Okay, we have to go. I have to go. I have to go home. Are their subways? What's happening?"

Nobody had any answers.

I took what I needed from my locker and called my mom on the way out.

"I didn't hear anything," she said. "Let me check. . . ."

I waited, standing on the corner of Fifty-First Street, watching people with briefcases zoom by, watching the hot dog guy flip the wieners in the water, watching the homeless man shake his paper cup, all in slow motion. Like a runner before the gun, I was braced and ready to do whatever I had to do to get home.

"It's okay," she said. "It was a small plane. I don't think it's terrorism. You're probably okay to get on the subway."

I got on the subway and, keeping both eyes wide open, thought about my visit with the college counselor who had come in earlier to talk to me about a place called Eugene Lang college. I pulled the catalogue out of my bag and looked over all of their writing courses.

"What is that? I've never heard of it," I'd said.

"It's part of The New School," she said.

"What new school?" I asked.

"It's called The New School. They have a strong writing program. I think you'll like it. Take a look."

The school was right here in the West Village, which was close to home. As much as I wanted to "get away from my parents"—although things had been better with Vin out of the picture—I knew that leaving home wasn't an option for me. For one, I wasn't going to leave Grandma; even if I wanted to, the world was too slippery for me to be able to uproot myself and venture out alone into. If there was an emergency, I wouldn't know what to do. My doctors, my pharmacy, my therapists, my family, my home, my subway system, my taxi routes, everything I knew, was here.

Arriving at my stop, speed-walking home, and heading directly to Grandma's place, I found out that it turned out to be an accident, after all: a Yankees pitcher named Cory Lidle was piloting the plane when it crashed.

* * *

Just to humor my mother, I went with her on the MetroNorth train to visit SUNY Purchase. No way in hell was I going to live in a dorm—especially when proper college campuses, like Virginia Tech, were prone to shootings—but, "Sure, let's take a look."

We took the tour, looking into classrooms and student housing. Along the way, a lesbian couple holding hands looked defiantly at our tour group.

"Oh please," my mom leaned in and said to me, rolling her eyes. "We're from New York. You're not shocking us."

Marymount Manhattan was my second option, and I had a leg up if I wanted it, after winning that essay contest. I got in, and they even offered me a partial scholarship, as did Pace University, which was literally across the street from home.

But something about Marymount smacked of Loyola, and I had a feeling Pace just wasn't for me.

I was accepted to the New School, and they invited me in to sit in on a couple of classes as I made my final decision.

It was one of the first subway trips I took by myself in a neighborhood I had never really navigated before, long before an iPhone with navigation systems came into my life. I finally found it, and sat through a very boring Literacy class on the novel *Frankenstein*. The classes were an hour and forty minutes long, which, for a restless person, is excruciating. As it turned out, I wouldn't need to sit through the entire class: about an hour in, a fire alarm began to sound.

Everyone got up, left their stuff, and headed outside.

The alarm bells were triggering something in me, so while everyone else was talking and laughing on the sidewalk, I was having a silent meltdown.

I didn't even know which way the train was, I didn't recognize anything, and when fire engines started pulling up to the building, I started texting Aaron, my new boyfriend, that I wanted to leave, that I wanted to just go over to his house.

How would it look for me not to finish the tour?

I called a few times, and texted a few times, and finally he responded:

"I'm sleeping."

The invisible girl spun black webs of panic in my mind as time ticked away . . . five minutes . . . fifteen minutes . . . twenty minutes . . . and I was nearly about to pass out when the crowd began filing back in.

I was so anxious that I didn't want to stay for the second class they had me scheduled to sit in on. I decided to head to Aaron's house anyway, even though I wasn't due over there until around 2:00 p.m.

I had met Aaron on Facebook. I'd heard his name thrown around dozens of times but had never met personally. He was tall, lean, with small, beady eyes, black hair he kept cut close, and wore long sleeve shirts like thermals and sweaters that made him stand out, to me, from someone like Vin. His jeans fit, and he wore his fitted hat the right way. He lived in Becca's apartment complex, and because he was a high school drop-out, had gotten his GED and was taking community classes at the Borough of Manhattan Community College.

That day, his mother let me in, and he moved over for me to lay down with him in his twin bed. Obviously, I was more than wide awake.

"Hey, I want to tell you about what happened," I said. He told me to be quiet, but I wouldn't, and before I knew it, he had thrown me across the room, and I started crying and screaming.

His mother knocked on the door, "What's going on in here?" she said.

"I need to leave," I said.

Aaron looked at her.

"Go ahead, get her out of here," he said with a shrug.

I took a long, awkward drive down the West Side Highway with his mother, who didn't seem to think anything out of the ordinary had happened.

"I think you guys both just need time to cool down," she said.

I thanked her and got out.

This wasn't the first time something like this had happened, and of course, I had gone right from bad to worse, finding out that while sweet dispositions were in short supply to begin with, soon, more unsettling changes were under way. He never had a girlfriend before, so to his credit, maybe he didn't know, yet, that when triggered by love, he was a violent psychopath.

* * *

Three days before Christmas, Grandma tried to travel alone on the subway to visit my grandpa in the nursing home on her own. My dad always offered to take her, but she didn't like to rely on anyone or make them feel as though she was inconveniencing them. On the platform of the 2/3 train at Fulton Street, as she tried to board the train, a group of men pushed her out of the way.

She fell, and the conductor closed the doors on her hip and broke it.

There was a doctor with his family on the platform. He stayed with her and told his wife to go call 911.

She was in the hospital on Christmas Eve, and we tried to put on a brave face to open presents in her room, ignoring the beeping of the monitors and the snoring of a stranger in the next bed over. I opened a glittery gold wallet she had gotten me from coach, and we wished her Merry Christmas before we left, although I didn't want to leave, I wanted to stay.

"Will you be ok?" I asked, still holding her hand.

"Of course," she said. "I'll be home soon, that's what matters."

But she wouldn't. She would be transferred to the nursing home, alongside my grandfather, where she had to stay for in-patient rehab to try and walk again. Sometimes, we'd wheel my grandfather into the room to be with her and have them hold hands. I'd bring her flowers, or cookies, and the doctors said, "She should be home in six months."

What if something happens?
How do we transport her with the wheelchair?
How do they transport all of the other patients?
Will vehicles be allowed to leave the city?
Will we be strong enough to carry her?
What about her medications?
What about our medications?
What if my dad has a heart attack?

Grandma, strong, stubborn, and determined, came home in six weeks.

She also began to do less.

She couldn't cook.

She had to use the cane.

She had to use the walker.

She fell again.

She was riding the elevators up and down.

She was wandering in the hallway.

"I don't know what's happening to me," she said. "I wish I would just die."

Report Card Comment, January 26, 2007

Advanced Science: A: Helaina was a joy to have in class. She is a fantastic student. Her project and presentation on eating disorders was fantastic and a big hit with many of the outside judges. She turned in quality work according to scheduled deadlines and turned in several rewrites leading to a well-constructed and nearly perfect science project.

English: A: Helaina did stellar work this quarter her papers were very well written and her homework was excellent as well. She sets a wonderful example for the class in her attention to her work and her focus during discussions.

Creative Writing: A+: Helaina's enthusiasm for writing has gotten stronger, as has her writing. She's especially good at expressing deep emotions, especially anger, which is difficult to do. I've really enjoyed having Helaina in my class these last few semesters. Her hard work and diligence are greatly appreciated.

I knew that something was very wrong with Aaron, but I was also always unhappy. How could it be everyone else and not me?

The truth was, something was very wrong with both of us.

When his hand slipped down to the back of my neck to pinch it, I had to gasp and try not to cry out in the middle of the sidewalk. Nobody else could tell what he was doing. He'd storm off, I'd run down the street after him, and he'd ignore me after I caught up. I didn't care what I looked like, on Sixth Avenue, on Eighth Avenue, running after someone who was literally running up and down subway steps to get away from me. *If you leave me here, I'll die.*

One night I went shot for shot with Aaron's friend, not realizing that Tequila is very different from Bacardi Smirnoff Ice. Aaron let me go home on the 6 train from Bleecker to Brooklyn Bridge alone. I vaguely remember falling in the street before clamoring through my bedroom door with my pants around my ankles.

"Vin hurt me," I kept saying, sticking my finger down my throat, making myself throw up over and over, as my parents helplessly watched, not quite knowing what to do. Frankly, I'm pretty sure there's not much you can do with a half naked teen-ager in this state.

The next day I had such a hangover I could hardly believe that there wasn't another word for it. I still, to this day, will never forget the fierce combination of migraine and nausea that spread through my entire body like wildfire, which stayed for twelve hours, retching, shaking, my head pulsing. *Never again*, I vowed. For the most part, I did stay away from drinking to get drunk, for a while. I was addicted to something, someone, who was worse for me, and I had so little self-worth that I didn't have the ability to "choose" anything that was good for me.

Prom was a week away, and Jordan and I had spent months planning it and coordinating it ourselves.

We told the school most of us didn't want to do "prom on the boat" again, and asked if we could have it at a hotel. They said no, they were doing the boat. So, Jordan and I found a caterer, a DJ (the brother of a very famous actress who was in a movie about New York kids in her early career), and a loft space to use on Thirty-Fifth Street and Eighth Avenue.

Once every kid had bought a ticket to our prom, the school said they'd like to send chaperones. "Nope, sorry," Jordan said. Everybody, except for Hailey came.

A girl who's father owned a chain of restaurants brought handles and handles of vodka, we had too much food, people got drunk and mostly hung out and smoked weed in the staircase. The room, and the dance floor, was mostly empty at any given time. It pretty much looked like any other New York City high school party. One of Aaron's friend worked "security," dressed up in a suit and basically just checked everyone's name off of a list. He was also in charge of putting a junior who drank too much and threw up in the sink into a cab. I didn't enjoy myself even for a second, but then, I didn't enjoy anything anymore.

I received a number of awards at graduation, as I had the year before, with my Uncle John yelling "Wow!", and as the teacher read off the long list of classes I'd excelled at, Aunt Fran, Grandma, and my parents clapping loudly. I made a well-written and recited speech that got more whoops and hollers, looking up at the audience and looking down at perfectly timed intervals. A few other kids made lame, three-line "thank you" speeches that they read off of crumpled piece of paper.

Instead of sitting with my family to snack and relax, I spent the entire reception chasing people down to sign my yearbook or take pictures, not realizing until I got home that while everyone else's names were written perfectly under their picture, mine had a "typo." Under my picture, it read, *Helaina HOvitz* in black and white. I was on a lot of committees, so I was in a lot of pictures: literary journal, yearbook, newspaper, and, upon further inspection, it seemed that in each of my pictures, my eyes had been darkened so that it looked like I had two black eyes.

Hailey, I thought. No, I knew.

On the way home, I sat in the car between Aunt Fran and Grandma.

"Fran was upset because you ignored her," she said. "I wonder how Fran got home."

We had a dinner that felt celebratory but depressing, as everything I did that was supposed to feel celebratory felt depressing. A few days later, on June 3, four men were arrested after it was discovered that they were going to try and bomb the fuel line at John F. Kennedy Airport.

PART THREE

CHAPTER TEN

A heightened awareness of potential threat might make someone prone to fighting, as she would be looking everywhere for signs that someone might be about to attack her again, causing her to overreact to the smallest potential signals.

In one specific case of a teenage girl diagnosed with PTSD, I observed that she tended to view the entire world as a potential threat.

Positive comments from others or neutral remarks were spun into negative exchanges and catastrophic personal attacks. She constantly perceived slights where none were intended, which made the relationships she did have difficult and eliminated many others before they could start.

She "sensed other people could sense she was bad" and projected her self-hate into the world, becoming sensitive to any sign of rejection. Everyone was out to hurt her. She was creating a self-fulfilling prophecy that people didn't like her by giving "leave me alone signals," that got negative responses.

Of course, those reactions further enforced her perception that the world was full of people who didn't like her.
        —Dr. Bruce Perry, *The Child Who Was Raised as a Dog*

I made my entrance at the New School with all of the enthusiasm I could muster.

It was scary, pushing my way through the courtyard that separated the Twelfth Street building of the New School from the Eleventh Street building.

That small enclosure was essentially one big cigarette smoke cloud full of hopelessly emo kids from Alabama or Baltimore; trendy fashion students who were also taking classes at Parsons, the New School of Design; and guys who just pulled out their guitars and started playing. On my first day, I saw one of the actresses from the beloved show of my youth, *Degrassi*, who, as it turned out, was also taking classes there.

In some ways, I made a new start. That first semester, in 2007, my classes were called "The Spiritual Autobiography," "The Girl as Media Image," and "Poet in New York." There was no math, no science, no lectures, just discussion-based classes in a small group setting. I wrote personal essays for "The Spiritual Autobiography" about what I had been through with Vin, penning revelations about what I'd learned about myself and what love was.

"Poet in New York" with Mark Statman was my favorite, even though it wasn't my favorite subject. Mark, who told us to call him Mark, had a ponytail and earrings and tripped over the chair to get to the board because he just *had* to furiously write down this thing a student said. Something about that class—this place, this school—felt very real, and very alive.

I made a couple of new friends, Katie from New Mexico, whose mothers were gay, and Lisa, who was from Los Angeles and wore winged eyeliner the same way I did. We were put in the same awkward circle of people on "accepted students day," who had to discuss their hopes and dreams for college, and we both had the same sarcastic, *why am I here* attitude.

We also had participate in a mandatory weekly advisory class, and I got stuck listening to everyone talk about "adjusting" to New York City, making observations about how people either did or didn't fit "the 'rude' stereotype," or how the food was really expensive and how "great it was to see drag queens and gay couples just walking around." I felt ownership over the city and my place here, and that ownership made me resentful of these who had been dumped here from whatever fucking suburb they came from. I did not share their collective sense of awe and wonderment at how "late" everywhere stayed open until. There was no big "wow" about the number of pizzerias around. I had no desire to "discover" the world above Ninety-Sixth Street, like Harlem, or across the river in DUMBO (the area right under the Brooklyn Bridge on the opposite side of the river), or Williamsburg.

What I did have a desire to do, even though I was still "with" Aaron, was stay close to a guy named Patrick.

Patrick was an Irish, pouty-lipped, guitar-playing, weed-smoking guy from Boston with big biceps whose flirtation with me was kept alive until it came to the throwdown of "Why don't you kiss me" and "Because I have a girlfriend" after a few beers on my friend's roof, where we had been singing *Hey There Delilah* at the top of our lungs along with my iPod.

Patrick told me I had "the soul of the blues," but I didn't know what that meant. When he explained, I half believed him.

I don't know who heard us when we belted out songs with no inhibition, into the sky, high notes rattling up against people's windows. Maybe nobody, maybe everybody.

He taught me how to hold a guitar, and I kept quiet about Aaron and what he was like, for the most part. I didn't want him to see me as this damaged girl who was looking for a savior in the new guy from out of town. As for Aaron, he knew about Patrick, but he didn't act jealous in a way that I hoped would cement his feelings for me, perpetuate the thinly veiled illusion that he actually really needed me, too. Once in a while he would offer, "Why is this dude hanging around you?" but that was it.

In other ways, college felt like one long continuation of high school—all of these kids were starting on this exciting journey on their own, in a new place, and here I was, everything the same—my neighborhood, my situation, my boyfriend, my feelings, my fucked up brain.

The subway was still a house of horrors.

Getting to and from class every day, even six years after 9/11, was like entering a house of horrors.

On the platform, I'd look over my shoulder to make sure that the guy who was standing a little too close wasn't going to whop me over the head with a bat. I'd listen to the haunting soundtrack of announcements about police activity or how the train would no longer be running, causing me to panic in trying to figure out how to get home or get to class on time.

Around this dark turn was a train pulling into the station with a young black man bleeding from the head, screaming, his hands up against the glass of the doors, banging on them before they opened, shoving me to the side and running while two guys followed him. Around that turn, you had a Muslim man clutching a backpack on his lap, muttering something in another language with his eyes closed.

Around the next corner, someone was lighting up a cigarette while sitting on a bench, and people were walking past, looking back at him over their shoulders like that was just the beginning of something else that was about to start smoking. Through the next dark passageway was the startling image of a woman running down the subway platform at Fourteenth Street, and other people running, too, forcing me to decide if I was going to get off of the train or if I was going to stay on, popping a Klonopin to keep from completely losing my shit before class.

Above ground, the world became a caricature of itself.

Girls chattering with nasal voices rubbed me the wrong way, every syllable digging deeper into that fresh bruise, making me want to be the violent one who hit *them* in the back of their heads with a bat.

A homeless man with a dog stayed with me all day, even after I ducked into a deli to buy a can of dog food and a banana for them.

Six nuclear weapons had been accidentally loaded onto the wing of a plane going from North Dakota to Louisiana. Accidentally, because, you know, accidents happen.

Steam pipes were exploding in midtown.

More allegations came of US troops killing innocent people in Baghdad.

The President of Iran was trying to visit Ground Zero, but "we" wouldn't let him, which meant, to me, we would see some sort of retaliation.

* * *

One night, I invited Lisa to come hang out with Aaron and his friends in Brooklyn. The boys played beer pong, blasted rap songs, rolled blunts, and made runs to the deli for more forties. The tables were covered with cartons of Orange Juice, Dutch guts, ashtrays, crumpled brown paper bags, packs of cigarettes. Hats and sneakers were in pristine condition, while the boys who lived in them weren't.

I thought she would think it was all really cool, like I half-did, but the next day, she said, "Helaina, they don't have any ambitions, they're not doing anything with their lives."

For a couple of months, I called her when Aaron and I had fights. She tried to help me, but I was so clearly unwilling to help myself that she finally just threw her hands up and said, "Forget it."

Although, she didn't say "Forget it." She just stopped answering my texts.

I felt abandoned, like for the life of me I couldn't find someone who knew what it was to be a friend. I thought she was mad because I wouldn't listen to her, the same way I, myself, took everything personally. I didn't see that I was treating her like a human life preserver, calling for help, clearly able to make a choice to leave him, then backing out.

I still hadn't gone back to therapy, and the few other friends that I made when I arrived at The New School quickly gave up on me, further proving that I was worthless. I still had these knee-jerk reactions of anger, impatience, feeling slighted. It was not hard to trigger this deep mistrust that sat bubbling like a cauldron of tar, just waiting for something harmless to set it to a boil. Despite how nicely dressed and made-up I was on the outside, I must have emitted an energy that made people think, *Not with a ten-foot pole.* Soon, it became very apparent just how sad I was, because I wasn't able to contain it like I imagine other people did. I was an easy tell, walking into class bleary-eyed, books crumpled from when Aaron ripped them out of my hands and threw them across his bedroom.

On the inside of the girl's two-stall bathroom on the second floor of the Eleventh Street school building, I hyperventilated before class, hiding behind my big black Chanel sunglasses. I'd saved up to buy them with my own money, and it wasn't long before the lenses looked worn out after being smeared with so many tears and streaked with so much mascara. I blotted at my eyes with the unforgiving, rough bathroom paper towels that smelled like mothballs.

Once inside the classroom, I'd slip into a chair around a medium-sized round table, "rewetting" my contact lenses with eye drops so that I had a reason for the redness under my eyes, and probably not fooling anyone because of the redness around my nose.

Focus. This is all you have. Focus.

For a few hours a day, I did focus. Somehow, with that determination, I maintained a 3.8 GPA during that first semester. I turned in papers early for constructive comments, and I shared as often as I could get my hand up or get a word in during class, and I never missed an assignment.

On the outside, I was a pretty girl with a promising college career and a grandmother who would be so crushed by a suicide that God knows what would happen to her. So, I kept going for her, and for my mom and dad, and because my mother had told me, when I was little, that "Only cowards kill themselves and take the easy way out."

On the inside, I was the same girl, crying herself to sleep, sitting alone on my bed and operating a halfway house for intrusive thoughts, disturbing new fears and paranoid delusions, rehashing the past and kicking myself for everything.

Panning out even further, you'd see a girl sitting in the corner at some guy's house, like a kid being punished, while her boyfriend played video games with his friends. You'd see me getting drunk and standing dangerously close to the curb on a moving highway. Or, you'd see me stoned, sitting along the ledge of my friend Syd's roof, the roof that had been a stage for all of those "performances" with Patrick, who was now also out of the picture for the same reason everyone eventually faded away.

Syd, I learned, lived across the street, and, unlike me, had access to the roof of his building. It went from a fun, casual, weed-smoking, movie-watching, beer-drinking friendship to something more. He became my lifeline.

We sat up there, at a green plastic table with diamond-shaped holes, and I would cry for hours. I didn't believe I could choose not having Aaron—abuse I could survive, but being alone, I couldn't. Sometimes, Syd would leave to get water and find me sitting with my legs dangling over the ledge and have to physically pull me back.

It's never going to get better.

Syd often had to drop what he was doing to keep me from doing "something stupid," which resulted in his losing a job or two.

"You told me you were standing on a chair on your terrace," he'd later tell me. "I couldn't go back inside after that. I left when I got those calls."

I started to hold handfuls of pills in my hands, opening and closing my fist around them, then letting them fall to the bathroom tiles underneath me.

It's never going to get better.

I tossed the orange bottle across the room, cursed myself that for not having the courage. I decided it was time to get help. Real help. Help beyond the Celexa I was now taking for anxiety, beyond the Klonopin that wasn't quite doing it, beyond the sleeping pills that quieted the hell out of my waking mind for eight hours. There were still sixteen excruciating hours to get through, and I knew I had to give it one more shot, take one last leap of faith, before I took an actual attempt at something drastic that couldn't be undone.

I reached out to Dr. C for what I resolved would be one last time, and she gave me a referral to another CBT therapist, saying she thought I should give it another try.

I sat down to send therapist number eight an email. I wrote that I was at the end of my rope, that I really didn't know how much longer I was going to last, that I was trying to break up with an abusive boyfriend, and had no friends, and spent most of my time crying and hyperventilating, that, no pressure or anything, but she was my last hope.

She probably won't even write back.

Two hours later, I had a response.

That sounds like a lot. I think I can help. Come to my office. Here's a list of my available days and times.

* * *

I left class that Wednesday afternoon to hop on the 2 train from Fourteenth Street to Seventy-Second street.

I hurried off of the train, up the subway stairs, and crossed a very dangerous four-way intersection of conflicting traffic lights and walk signals.

The avenue was long, with many trees and brownstones. Nothing but homes as far as the eye could see, which was unusual.

I found the door, so tiny that I missed it the first time, and walked through the very narrow hallway of the first floor. I peered at the writing on each person's office door, looking for a name. I finally found Dr. A's room in the back, but her door was closed.

The time was 4:01.

I sat on the folding chair outside of it, flipping nervously through a magazine, tossing one page, then the next, violently to the left, not liking to have to wait for even a minute when I rushed to be on time. The restless energy was whipping around inside me like a hailstorm.

Eventually, she opened the door.

"Helaina?" she asked as she let someone else slip through and waved goodbye.

She looked like she was in her late thirties, was about 5'10", wearing her chestnut hair in a short, low ponytail, a beige

cardigan over a white tank top, and a large diamond engage-
ment ring with matching wedding band.

"Come on in," she said.

I forced a smile, conflicted on whether or not I should show
her that I was annoyed that she had run a few minutes late.

"Okay," she smiled, taking a deep breath. "So, I got your email,
obviously. But why don't you catch me up. Tell me a bit more
about what's going on."

I told her everything, what the past few years had been
like, why I gave up, why I came back, and what my life was
like now.

"I don't even want to be conscious half the time. Aaron wakes
up late on weekends, so I take sleeping pills to go back to sleep
until 1:00 p.m. myself. Then I just have to fill up time, and I have
nothing to do if I've already done schoolwork. The less time I'm
awake and thinking, the better."

"You told me you feel like you want to die, and I want to
make sure I understand," she said. "Do you actually want to die,
or do you want to not feel how you're feeling now?"

Click.

"I don't actually want to kill myself, but my world is just
becoming too small. All I do is count down the time until I
can see Aaron again, and he's horrible. I have nothing in my
life except the memories of bad things that keep pushing their
way into my brain over and over. I can't have a good thought
without a bad thought smashing into it. I can't seem to make
any friends, either."

"Okay. That's a lot. Let's back up a second. First, we need to
change the way you express how you're feeling. Instead of telling

someone you want to kill yourself, can you take a step back and think about how to communicate how you're actually feeling? You're overwhelmed, or you feel so bad you don't want to be here. You want things to get better. You feel like you're not being heard."

"But at the same time, I do feel like I want to die, because it's that bad, in that moment."

"Understandable, but if you say that, people are going to respond to that and call 911 or take you to the emergency room."

"Okay, okay," I said, thinking we had more pressing issues to deal with. "Got it. I'll try."

"How else are you communicating with people? How is your relationship with your dad? Your mom?"

"They're ok with my dad, but my mom is quick to fight with me or criticize me, and I defend myself, and then we start fighting."

"What happens when you try to remove yourself from the fight?"

"She keeps carrying on, she'll push her way into my room, or text me, or email me, or keep talking outside of the door or loud enough for me to hear from the living room."

"Can you tell her how you're feeling when you feel really bad?"

"She wouldn't listen, or care, or stop what she was doing or saying or carrying on about," I said, trying to picture her actually responding to my talking about "how I felt" in the middle of an escalating argument.

The session continued that way, until Dr. A sat back in her chair and put down her legal pad.

"Do you know how strong you are?" she asked, catching me off guard.

"No . . ." I said with a huff.

"I know you don't feel that way. But over the last few years, you've been pushed in so many directions by doctors telling you ways they were going to help you, to fix you, and they were wrong. That can be traumatic too. And still, you're actively asking for help. Something in you is not willing to give up, and by now, I bet you many people probably would have."

Click.

She was actually telling me that what I had been feeling, even if it was bad, was reasonable.

"You were told, 'This is the right way to feel better,' and then, it didn't work. That would make me feel pretty lost and helpless too. But here you are. It's not going to be easy, but if you want to do the work. I think we can make things better."

We didn't talk about 9/11 that day, or on any day, at length. She would, years later, tell me that she was worried I wouldn't be able to revisit it directly without spiraling. She had gotten notes from my psychiatrist, and she was, to the extent she could be caught up, caught up.

We started with one of my biggest hurdles: the train stopping in the tunnel.

"Why panic when the train stops? That won't make the train move."

You think I want to panic, lady?

"I can't help it," I said. "It just happens, without my having any say. And then, I'm all riled up when I get to where I'm going."

"What can you do when you start to worry? Refocus your brain," she said. "Listen for the bass in a song on your iPod. It's subtle, so you really have to concentrate. Or, you can observe your surroundings, narrate what you're doing in the moment, and don't get ahead of yourself."

She sent me home with worksheets.

"When "blank" happens, I feel "blank." I believe it means "blank."

What it "meant" was often something very dramatic, a severe conclusion that, when I matched it against the initial thing that happened, seemed like a long shot, a far cry, a lot of steps ahead. That didn't mean it stopped happening, but I was starting to recognize it, become aware of it, and that was something.

> When someone doesn't answer my texts, it makes me feel like a piece of shit. I believe it means that they're ignoring me, because nobody likes me, because I can never make friends, because I'm fucked up, because people are horrible, and I'm going to be lonely for the rest of my life.

> When I hear a bang outside the window, it makes me feel afraid. I believe it means that there's another attack happening and I'm not going to find out in time to do anything about it, because we'll all just be sitting in class, or it will be in the middle of the night, and we'll all think it's just outside New York City noises, and we'll die a long slow death, and my parents will die, and we won't be able to save Grandma or get her out in time, and the cops will be stopping all the cars from leaving, and we won't have anywhere to go, and they'll bomb the bridges while we try to leave.

> When I see one of Vin's friends around, it makes me feel worried. I believe it means he may be around, and something bad will happen, like that time I was with Aaron and

*we saw him by the Seaport, but I didn't have my glasses on
and I didn't know I needed contacts. So while I was actually running into a store to just go into the store, he thought
I was running away from him, and he was with Gemma,
and he made some comment, and him and Aaron started
shouting. Then there was the time that he was outside
my building waiting for Gemma, and he came up to me
directly, and he pushed his way into the lobby, and I started
screaming and crying and didn't know what to say, and I
called Aaron to leave work early to try and call him out and
fight him, because I thought that would make it stop, and it
didn't work.*

I usually needed to use the back of the worksheet.

I went back to the familiar task of charting my level of
emotion when I felt triggered—panicked, angry, upset, or
anxious—logging the reaction's intensity on a scale from one
to ten in the moment. It was known clinically as the Subjective
Units of Distress Scale for emotions, and I usually rated what
I was feeling as a ten. Sometimes, I'd draw a thermometer and
fill it up to the level I felt. Soon, I realized that I wasn't always
a ten, I just felt overwhelmed and "not empowered" to solve my
problems, as Dr. A said.

In person, she asked me simple questions I'd never thought
about before, checking fact to reality, truth to perception, thought
to fiction. I'd never known there was a difference between any
of them.

I was supposed to stop and write down:

What is it I'm really reacting to?

Is it justified?

What is the worst that could happen?

How likely is it?

"You have to be alert to thoughts that upset you, try to catch them and burst them like bubbles. They're sabotaging you and you don't even know it."

"Everyone is going to try and hurt me," I said. "That's what I have to try to be alert to."

"How?"

"I don't know."

"Will they succeed?"

"Yeah, if I'm not constantly thinking about it, if I'm not looking out for it. Look what happened with Vin and Hailey and Gemma. For example, this guy, Q, won't stop emailing and texting me. I only went out with a couple of times, over a year ago, he knows where I live. He can find me and kill me."

"I don't think anything is going to happen based on whether you think about it or not."

"Yes it is, how am I supposed to keep myself safe if I don't pay attention to what's dangerous?

"You're not going to, because it's out of your control. You have to let it go."

I thought she was nuts, but I took notes on everything she said and took her suggestions. I left the apartment just to go for a walk to the Seaport and back again. I bought satchels of lavender from the Union Square farmer's market and inhaled them, hoping it would calm me down. I held an ice cube in my hand when I felt like I wanted to hurt myself, or I felt myself getting "out of control." In doing that, I very quickly began to realize that substituting pain for more pain wasn't what I wanted after all.

"Feelings pass, you know. They do," she tried to explain. "So even if something is bad at the time, you can keep in mind that you will feel better."

I tried to tell her that I never moved past it. I fell into darkness and never came out on the other side. I stayed swimming in those murky waters; I thrashed around and nearly drowned in them, desperately trying to avoid it.

"I know you've been through a lot of traumatic things, but there are so many levels here because you keep exposing yourself to situations that aren't good for you," she said.

I ate up all of this new information, but we could only do so much at once, so the digestion was slow.

Learn new skills, get stuck.

Skills, stuck.

I tried to break away from Aaron, saying, "I'm not going to call him or text him today," and going at that for fairly long stretches at a time. I took my Grandma to dinner at T. J. Byrnes and to the Chinese restaurant across the street. I went to the gym. I tried to talk to strangers sitting outside at the Seaport just to talk to them, figuring out how to start a conversation, how to connect with someone when I felt I literally didn't have a friend in the world, except for Gina, who was sometimes there on the other end of the phone, but still never seemed to be free to hang out in person.

When my Grandma's birthday rolled around, we went to lunch, then to their favorite store, Loehman's. She was so happy that day, having all of us together. I was closer to being "the little girl" she knew again, and she was slipping further away from being the woman she had been her whole life.

Two months later, in February 2008, a whole new world was opened up to me. It was wild, glamorous, seductive, destructive, and crazy, a world that loved swallowing up and spitting out vulnerable young girls who just wanted to feel like they were special, like they belonged.

* * *

I was walking Gucci when Jordan got in touch with me over Facebook.

"You have to come to this club. This guy from that show *The O.C.* is going to be there, because Carissa's sort of dating him, and it's *the* hottest club right now. Meet me in front of Exchange on Twenty-Sixth and Tenth at 11:30 p.m. We're meeting the promoters there, then going to Suzie Wong."

I didn't know what a "promoter" was, or what a Suzie Wong was, but Jordan emphasized that these were *special* promoters, not just regular club promoters, as if that was supposed to mean something. I couldn't remember the last time I'd been invited anywhere, though, so it meant enough to me to prompt me to pull a low-cut purple satin top out of my drawer, slip on high heels, straighten my hair, do my makeup, and wait five hours until 11:30 p.m., when I hailed a cab and took it to Twenty-Eighth Street and Tenth Avenue. I had Googled Suzie Wong, and apparently, that was where *Page 6* found everyone who was anyone.

In the cab, I tried to shake off the anxiety that came with my excitement. My mother always told me about her days as a dancing queen, how she and my aunt always went out with their girlfriends on the weekends. Now, I could tell her that I was doing the same. I was going out with the girls, and if it killed me, I was going to like it.

If I didn't, that's what drinks were for. I'd learned that when Aaron started making sure I had something to drink, usually a forty of Coors Light that I forced myself to down even though I didn't like the taste, to accompany the weed and amuse myself while he hung out with his friends. Or, he'd fill a glass with Smirnoff Orange Vodka mixed with some sort of fruity Mango Papaya Orange Juice we bought at the store as soon as we got to a party, knowing it would help take the edge off.

When the cab pulled up, I saw Jordan outside, smoking a cigarette. *This isn't Suzie Wong*, I thought. Next to her was an older man smoking an American Spirit cigarette with one hand (the other was tucked in his pocket). He was snapping his gum, eyes darting around, wearing an intense look of concentration at nothing in particular. He looked like an awkward high schooler, constantly moving and spinning around. He wore a hat that said "Rockstar" on it.

"It's been a long time," Jordan said, kissing me on the cheek. I hadn't seen her in at least eight months, and she had put on weight after graduation (and after, I learned, she initially kicked the cocaine habit). With her freckled nose and slightly puffy cheeks, she wasn't exactly a vision in the pink strapless satin dress she was wearing, but she had curves, and passed for alluring with enough makeup. For some reason, Jordan never needed to look classically attractive to be popular.

"Is this it?" I asked.

It looked more like a lounge than the hottest club in town.

Jordan laughed almost condescendingly.

"This is where we're meeting Kate. It's her job to get girls like us into the clubs. This is her husband, Rockstar. Well, Richard. But everyone calls him Rockstar."

Rockstar looked up from under the brim of his hat and nodded.

Jordan told me to just bring my college ID for the night, explaining that she'd get me a better one the following week, with my real name and picture on it for $150. I pulled my New School ID out of my wallet and held my breath as the doorman checked it. I tried not to panic as the thoughts swooped in.

Why is he taking so long to look it over?

If I can't even get in here, none of this is real.

You thought you were going to get your life back? Ha.

You can't even get close to the club. You're going to spend the rest of your nights at home, alone.

The doorman waved me in, and I rolled my eyes at him as if he had offended me by checking it in the first place.

Carissa was inside already, staring at us with her icy blue eyes as we entered. She quickly flashed me a smile and extended her arms.

We'd never been too friendly in high school, but we were friendly enough. Carissa could only hold a conversation for about five minutes before you got bored with her, her voice flat and uninviting. Luckily, she'd never said much to me in our two plus years at Beekman.

After a round of apple martinis, we gathered our coats and headed down the block toward Eleventh Avenue and the West Side Highway.

I heard my mother's neurotic voice in the back of my head as soon as we entered Suzie Wong.

Be careful, don't stay with your friends, and don't leave your drink.

We went right by the lines of people on either side of the massive set of wooden doors, waiting to get in. Walking through the entrance was like being sucked into a whole other underground world.

I was instantly smacked in the face with the bass of whatever the DJ was playing, pulsing purple lights, the floor vibrating underneath my feet. People were bumping into me, sipping drinks, laughing, and kissing each other on the cheek. We were led to a table, one that I later learned cost thousands of dollars. I learned a lot of things that night, like what a "CFO" was (the guy who bought the table was the Chief Financial Officer of a huge internet company), what "bottle service" was (the agreement to pay ten to fifteen times what a bottle of alcohol is worth, plus gratuity, for a tiny table the size of a cardboard box and permission to sit or stand near it), and that if you make eye contact with a man at a club twice, not once, he will come over and offer to buy you another drink, and/or dance with you.

I stood around the table with everyone else and watched as waitresses in short, black, crushed velvet dresses and stilettos brought over this tower of glasses and multitiered tray of strawberries, chocolate, and lemon wedges, two buckets full of ice, one with champagne, another with vodka, and four carafes filled with seltzer, cranberry juice, orange juice, and water.

This is all for us?

The scene constantly changed with the song or the people passing through, and there was a lot of shouting even if we were standing right next to each other. There was very little actual dancing before 1:00 a.m., and when 1:00 a.m. came around, there was so much happening it was hard not to get lost in it.

Individual drinks at the bar were about $20 a pop, and all of the girls standing around it looked like clones that had been shipped from the same factory. They either had short black hair or long blonde highlighted hair that had been curled with an iron, then tussled. The uniform was a black dress or skin-tight red, white, or black tube skirt with some sort of shiny top that was either low cut or backless. Shiny red lips matched the shiny red nails that held glowing cell phone screens, all perched atop four-inch heels that looked incredibly painful just to stand in, and flagged by a tiny purse that cost a small fortune tucked under an armpit.

There was a certain way to hold your glass, a certain way to dance in place, a certain way to subtly size other girls up.

I didn't get drunk that night, I just danced with my friends, and when Kate put my number in her phone, I felt like I was "in." For the first time in my life, I had earned my place somewhere, all because I was "hot."

I went home, and I thought, *this is going to fix everything.* If I went back there the next night, or the next week, I could finally have something that resembled a life. I was finally going to be normal; no, *better* than normal, and everyone would be jealous when they knew. Somewhere in Wisconsin or Boston, girls in dorm rooms were drinking beer in their pajamas and sneakers with stupid boys in fleece pullovers who took shots and quoted Adam Sandler movies. This . . . this was something else. This was where everyone really wanted to be, and for the first time, I was on the other side.

The next night I showed up was a Thursday night. I didn't have class on Friday, just work at P.S. 150 (formerly known as the Early Childhood Center, where I had gone to kindergarten, first, and second grade, which had morphed into a full-fledged K-5 elementary school), where I was now an after-school counselor, and I didn't have to be there until 3:00 p.m.

We had all made it successfully to the front doors of Marquee, the "next hot club," but Rockstar had needed to make a bit of a scene first.

I didn't have my fake ID yet, and a couple of the other girls were definitely not twenty-one, either, and we were holding up the line at the front. Rockstar felt it necessary to yell, "C'mon, I've got six hot girls here!" as if he was scalping tickets. I fiddled around in my bag to avoid making eye contact with anyone when this happened.

This isn't you, my conscience whispered. So I drowned her, as soon as we walked right through the velvet ropes and were led to a table in the center of the club.

I started drinking because strawberries and pink lemonade and chocolate were brought with every bottle, and it was fucking awesome. I kept drinking so I could lose all inhibition and hit the dance floor. I drank some more because the alcohol silenced the fear of their judgment, the envy I had of other people, the anxiety I carried inside me at all times. I had always dreamed of rolling with the "in crowd," and there we were, dancing among celebrities and the Manhattan elite. With every sip I expected to feel lighter, sillier, out of my head, and into the reckless abandon of the music. The alcohol drowned out the anxious voices in my head and made me feel calm, confident, more connected to the people around me, including my new well-connected "friends" who weren't really my friends, but I wanted them to be.

And, because I drank, I was able to shrug off Rockstar's hand when it went up my dress as he hoisted me up onto a club couch, which you weren't supposed to dance on, but we could, all eyes on me, or on us, wiggling around in the middle of thousands of people, lights flashing, the song's bass punching me in the face in the best way, sweating and pulsing and glasses clanking, because we were special.

On those nights, I usually went home with someone I didn't know and woke up slapping my forehead: *Oh God, not again.* Or even worse, on rare occasion, I didn't hook up with anyone, and I felt like such a failure. *So worthless, all wrong.*

All the while, I was trying to break free of Aaron, who I was more addicted to than any of it, still feeling that without him, I had nothing.

I went home with the beefy banker who, at his apartment near The Beekman School, took hits from a big bong and had some fancy Apple-powered music system connected to the TV that I could play around with.

I went home with a red-haired high school teacher named Adam who lived in a Bleecker Street walk up and only kept beer and bread in his fridge. I remember him, specifically, because he warned me not to try and make him do it "doggy style" because it would be over quick, which was exactly what I wanted, anyway.

I went home with stock-broker Jim, who I met at the table next to us at Guest House one night. He was thirty-nine, worked twenty hours a day, seven days a week, and took something called Yin Yang to keep him going. He had a Puggle named Nigel who pooped next to the bed because he was jealous of us. While walking Nigel around Central Park's Great Lawn the next morning (Jim just sat in a folding chair reading the *Wall*

Street Journal), I got to meet other guys, like the thirty-seven-year-old gym teacher who took me to a comedy club.

I remember the gym teacher (but not his name) because I got so drunk and so sick to my stomach that night that I told him he needed to call 911. I walked to the ambulance with just my tank top on, as if it were a dress, and after waiting for two hours in the emergency room, simply went home in a cab and found myself trying to explain the ambulance bill to my parents a month later.

The more men I slept with, the more distance I put between me and reality. Until the very moment I got drunk, I lived in and cringed at the past and was terrified of the future. The slight nausea that came like clockwork after four drinks temporarily blotted it all out and was easily remedied by a cigarette and some fresh air. I mixed vodka with pink lemonade, threw it back, gagged. I hated the way alcohol tasted. But I loved what it did to me.

I wouldn't like what it did the next day, but that didn't matter.

It was the closest to being unconscious as I could get, even though I could never quite get drunk enough not to worry about what happened when the drunkenness faded.

* * *

Back on the Upper West Side, a particularly difficult session with Dr. A was starting to bring up the old instinct to cut someone off.

Her.

First, she told me that I was getting in the way of my own progress.

"Meeting all of these guys and making unhealthy friends and bad choices is making you feel even worse."

She said I was blurring any ability to look back and see my actual progress, waking up to "what I did last night" like a bag of rocks whopped across my face.

"Why do you have to keep getting drunk and going home with strange guys? Can you not drink? Or if you do, can you go home alone?"

"Yeah, great idea! Because when I'm alone, I want to die, and I'm alone almost all of the time."

What did she want me to do? Nothing? Nothing at all, except schoolwork? With the semester ending, that would leave me pretty barren.

"What about meditating?" she offered.

"Sure, let's throw gasoline on the dynamite. I'll just let all these psycho thoughts have free reign to take over and make me dizzy."

I had an attitude for a reason, but we hadn't talked about it yet.

Over the weekend, I had called her during a time when I felt very triggered. She told me I could start calling her when I felt it was an emergency, and that she would get back to me when she could. I had called three times, actually, and I could tell that on the fourth time, she sent me straight to voicemail. So, I left a message that probably reflected the initial distress that prompted the call, coupled with the feelings of rejection and even betrayal at the fact that she hadn't answered.

It was Thursday, and she had not gotten back to me.

Obviously, I was going to have to be the one to bring this up.

So I sighed, and asked, "Oh hey, did you get my voicemail?" my voice dripping in resentment.

"Yes, and I'm not going to answer a message like that."

"Excuse me? A message like what?"

"Do you realize how you sounded? It was incredibly rude."

"No, didn't realize, because I was too busy feeling like I was going to have a complete meltdown," I snapped. "Why don't you enlighten me?"

"You sounded angry with me for not answering, but that's not any way to get what you're asking for."

"Now you're *judging* me? You're telling me to be comfortable asking you for help, and you're kicking me while I'm down because I didn't 'do it right?'" I fumed.

She held her clipboard rather tightly, the only barrier she had between the twelve inches of space between my couch and her chair, and stood her ground.

"When my boys do this, I don't respond to them. If they throw a tantrum, I tell them that when they're ready to be nice, I'll listen and try to get them what they need. But they have to tell me calmly."

I started to shake, I was so angry.

"I'm holding you to a higher standard because I'm treating you like any other adult I respect. If you're going to get anywhere with people, you have to try and be skillful, even when you're on edge."

I took a sip of water, sniffling and trying not to completely fall apart.

"You have to learn to say, 'I understand you're busy, but I want help.' You have to get past this desperation for another person and learn to talk yourself off of a ledge."

This was part of the larger social struggle I was having with the way I communicated. I must have picked up some of it from my parents, or at the very least, my mom, who blamed and attacked when she felt hurt or worried, instead of making an appeal.

I left the session feeling a whirlwind of different things, almost shell-shocked from how much I had to absorb.

* * *

The next morning, my mother woke me up at 8:00 a.m., saying, "Grandma fell again. We don't know how long she's been on the floor."

I ran upstairs with her in my pajamas to find her on the floor between the small bedroom and the bathroom, just laying there, looking in front of her.

"Hi, Grandma," I said, crouching down, then letting my legs fall to the side so I was as close to eye level with her as I could get. My mom called 911.

"What are you doing down here, silly goose? We should get up soon, but let's stay down here for a few more minutes. I like it down here." I knew we would have to wait for the EMTs to arrive and move her, in case she had hit her head or broken something.

From then on, the hospital became a revolving door.

Grandma's insurance would not cover twenty-four-hour home care, and we couldn't afford it out of pocket. So, we tried everything, taking turns sleeping upstairs, my mother, Aunt Fran, and me, trying to honor her wish of keeping her out of a nursing home.

She came down to eat dinner with us every Friday night, and my father cut up her pizza into teeny tiny pieces night after night so that she could eat them.

I went upstairs to spend time with her several times a week and on weekends, and my mom checked on her most evenings.

We tried to play cards, and she tried not to show that she didn't understand the rules anymore.

Whenever she was at the hospital, my dad "gently" stalked the staff to make sure she was being given the attention she deserved. I stroked her forehead, which she felt was soothing, and tried to ignore the scared look in her eye, a look that defied her attempted bravery, a look that only someone who knew those eyes so well could discern from the simple composition of pupil and retina.

* * *

Syd, like me, was close to his grandmother, who lived about ten minutes away in another apartment complex closer to Chinatown. We learned all sorts of things about one another, though he was mostly silent and I was pretty chatty.

But in all of that time sitting on the roof together, we never talked about what happened on 9/11. We didn't bring it up, because it was so far behind us, not a topic of conversation you brought up like what movie you'd seen lately or the silly thing you did the last time you were drunk.

It wasn't until years later that we talked about how, on that day, he had surfaced from the subway, leaving a subway car so packed he couldn't move an inch, into madness. It had taken him hours to get home by subway, as close as he could get. By the time he surfaced, there were no cops to stop him.

He could have gone to his grandmother's apartment, which was farther from the Towers than his own apartment was, but instead, he went home.

Stepping onto his terrace, he collected a handful of debris in his hand. *Who am I holding?* he thought. A couple of years my senior, he had the intuition to immediately know that there were people in those ashes.

The next few hours disappeared, and when time returned, he was helping doctors and nurses at the neighboring New York Downtown Hospital up and down the slippery, ash-covered stairs of his building with a flashlight. Many of the medical staff lived in his building.

"Mom, I want to go down there to help," he told his mom, a nurse at the hospital.

"You're not going over there, it's too dangerous," she insisted.

"Okay, can I at least give blood?" he asked.

"No, you're fourteen, you can't give blood."

Two days later, he did manage to get close to the site, closer than most, with his video camera. He watched people with no masks or protective gear sifting through the debris, bare-handed.

"They were mobilizing, flushing their eyes with water then going back in. They had to be looking for survivors. Desperately. Why else would you expose yourself to that?"

Not only did he not tell me all of this until years later, but he didn't talk about it with anyone at all.

"Whenever I left the state and people knew I was from Lower Manhattan, I lied about being here to avoid their intrusive questions. My counselors at school tried to talk to me about it, but I was 'unresponsive' as they'd say. In eighth grade, I was a happy kid. I'd go to friend's houses after school at St. Joseph's, we'd play video games like Golden Eye, or we'd play at Cherry Street Park, or at least we'd try to—it wasn't conducive to football because of all the concrete, and the assholes in the grade above us tried to clothesline us by sticking their arms out."

The talkative kid who worked the room on his first day of high school fell silent. He began getting into fights and acting recklessly. He became an angry, irritable shell of what he used to be, and began to constantly put himself in danger. The lines between reality and fantasy were blurred.

"I didn't understand the way I thought and acted, but I knew I was prone to emotional outbursts," he said. "My friends were always telling me to chill out. I only slept for a few hours every few days. My parents saw how pale I was. I looked sickly. But the nightmares were so bad that I avoided sleep. The thoughts that came when I tried to lie down were morbid."

He began speeding down highways at insane speeds at 6:30 a.m., one time, "Holding a plastic bag out the window and watching it disintegrate," then getting back to the city in time for class.

"I was in a Mustang, because I ran with kids who made a business of buying Mustangs online and flipping them," he explained.

"Have you ever thought about suicide?" I asked, thinking about all the time he'd spent trying to stop me.

"I'm not sure. Would you say that taking a harmful drug excessively is a form of attempted suicide?"

"I don't know," I said, thinking about the ways I put myself in situations I almost hoped I wouldn't make it out of.

Desperate for an escape from the torture of simply being, he began binge drinking day and night, which continued throughout college. He unsuccessfully attended four different colleges attempting to earn a nursing degree. He began working odd jobs, which he could never hold. Most of those reasons were his own, and that one time, it was because of me.

"What do you want to do with your life, though? You can't just keep picking up all of these random gigs."

"I'd want to join the Coast Guard to help rescue people in disaster zones, but . . ."

"But what?"

"I have psychological issues that they'll find out. They'll get in my way. They won't let me in."

* * *

For a while, I kept going to the clubs, bopping around in this bubble of celebrities and ignoring texts from my mom that read *"Another girl was abducted from a club and killed."* I wore nice clothes, my makeup was always perfectly done, but I left lipstick all over countless collars, waistbands, and martini glasses. One sip started a fire: *what's next, what's next, what's next.* This restlessness grew inside me, a desire to chase the feeling, keep it going, even though drinking more always made more of a mess. I was the same girl on the inside that I had always been, and I was still unable to completely let Aaron go.

I kept it up until the bubble burst one Saturday night, the "off-night" of the week. The club we were supposed to go to had been shut down by cops on a drug raid, so we were stuck at

Marquee, where the magic was somehow lost, because *nobody* went to Marquee on a Saturday. No crowds, no glamour, practically empty save for a few sailors in town for Fleet Week. Rockstar and I picked a random table to sit at with our drinks. Nobody even cared that we hadn't paid for the table, because all of them were empty. It was like someone had flipped on the lights during a Broadway spectacular, removed the scenery, stripped away the costumes, and left this hollow, sad skeleton in its wake.

When it became apparent that I was not going to go home with Rockstar, he left to find someone who would.

On Sunday, Rockstar emceed a karaoke night at Kenny's Castaway that took a tragic turn and ended in a public fight between the two of us out on Bleecker Street, so my exit from the club world turned out to be abrupt as my entrance.

I still went out with the guys who I'd kept in touch with, because I needed a reason to drink, even if—*especially* if—I didn't like the person I was sitting across from.

I went to the expensive steakhouse in the Time Warner Building and drank lychee martinis with my broiled three-pound lobster. I went to an expensive sushi restaurant on the Lower East Side and drank lychee martinis and ate shrimp tempura rolls. I went to that expensive lounge in the Meatpacking District and nibbled on empanadas and drank—you guessed it—lychee martinis.

I let the liquor loosen the hold life had on me, going home with one guy, getting three hours of sleep, going out with another guy, resolving to do a quick dinner and drinking too much, throwing that plan to hell, taking a cab ride to his place, showing up slightly hung over to work at P.S. 150, and repeating the next night, never feeling good about a single moment of those nights I lost control.

But no matter how much work I did in therapy, this was still the only social outlet I had, the only chance for fun. Often, it was fun, at least, for most of the night.

* * *

After one violent fight with Aaron too many, I came home totally broken on the inside and only slightly bruised on the outside.

After he'd put his hands around my neck and flung me across the room, and I had made my escape by darting past him, past his parents, who were rolling on some sort of drug, out the door, down eighteen flights of stairs into the subway and home. He called me that night, from his roof, saying he was going to kill himself.

"I'm such a monster, I can't stop doing this to you. I don't want to live."

I wandered into the living room and just handed the phone to my dad. I wasn't about to have his blood on my hands.

"Can you talk him down?" I said. "He wants to die."

I'd never let on to my parents about how things really were between Aaron and me. He showed up a perfect gentleman on holidays, and whenever I cried, or came home crying, I just quickly hustled into my room, or tried to cry quietly, hoping nobody would notice.

The next morning, I could hear my mom and dad talking over coffee, sitting at the dining room table. My father was nodding, and smiled when he saw me.

"How you doing, baby?"

I sighed.

"I've been better."

"Listen, I know your mother and I are supposed to be going to Amsterdam and Brussels next week, but I was thinking, would you want to take my ticket? I bet you guys could have a great time," Dad said.

"No, I don't want to do that. You deserve a vacation."

"It's okay, honey. I think you can use the break more than I can. I'll have Gucci to keep me company."

So, I wrote to all of my college professors, asking permission, and they said yes, no problem, because I had proven myself someone who could keep up, and it was settled.

After a turbulent plane ride spent digging my nails into my mothers arm, we got into a cab and arrived at a lovely boutique hotel in Brussels, exhausted and in need of a nap. Before that could happen, though, the manager came clacking out in her heels, offering us snacks, and tea, and suggestions of where to take a walk that afternoon.

We did manage to take that nap, then walk around for hours, down cobblestone streets and majestic alleys, looking into this shop and that one, passing fountain after fountain. I wasn't afraid, even though we were two tiny ladies alone in a foreign city. We carried almost nothing with us except our feet and our eyes, curiosity and wonder, adventure and excitement. All of my baggage was literally back in the room.

After a long train ride to Amsterdam, we checked into a hotel next to a shimmering canal—there were shimmering canals everywhere, all of these beautiful arches and waterways, more people and children on bicycles than you could count, and, surprisingly, nobody smoking weed (later, in the Red Light District, we'd find most of the weed smokers—tourists, all of them—shoveling Pommes Frites from a cone into their mouths).

At night, without being carded or having to pay anything, we wandered into a club that smelled like stale beer and cologne. We just took a seat and listened to a cover band. A man wrote in broken English on the back of a coaster that he thought I was pretty, and we joined them at their table. We left and wandered into another bar, a slightly fancier one, and listened to a man with a guitar sing "Sitting on the Dock of the Bay."

On our fourth day, we visited Anne Frank's house. The house, too, was along a canal, with a blink-and-you'll-miss-it entryway that looked like all of the other four-story buildings along the street.

We walked through the house, and this feeling of sadness ran the cold pads of its fingers across my face, tapping my eyes, my temples, my neck, spreading everywhere. The annex, Anne's room, was closed for repairs, but a mirror had been set up at an angle, so that a good portion of the room could be seen in the reflection. Something happened to me at that very moment.

She had no choice. You do.

Anne couldn't go outside.

Yet, she took out her notebook and wrote that the best remedy for people who felt lonely was to go outside.

More importantly, she wrote that all children must look after their own upbringing, and that she had to believe people were good at heart because she simply could not build a foundation for herself consisting of confusion, misery, and death.

***

I finished out my freshman year strong, even though I had made the very poor choice to take an Existential Philosophy class, feeling, initially, that my prior AP class in high school would give me a competitive edge, not realizing that I would still despise the subject itself. I wrote an interesting final paper, entitled "A Socially Acceptable Form of Schizophrenia," which opened with a quote from Sartre's "Consciousness and Action."

It was a paper about how a person's past plays a large part in determining her identity, because she makes future decisions and defines herself based on those experiences. Essentially, my theory was this: if someone can begin to register impulses in a different way, they can begin to change their actions. Sartre profiles a skier, whose purpose is to illustrate how the evidence of one's past never truly leaves him.

> *The tracks are always there, accumulating over time, creating a value system upon which he bases his life. Ideally, these tracks, more readily known as one's memories, would not have a permanent affect on someone's choices. Sartre says that there are always more possible versions of the self, they are just waiting to emerge once we disregard our present perception. A person can alter her way of thinking and let go of this fear by accepting the new ideas that surface. Writing*

is a way for her to see her thoughts enter the real world;
they are existent outside the self, more readily changed with
a simple deletion and replacement. When a person allows
herself to write something new, she is changing her plan
and freeing herself of the constraint of writing what she is
comfortable with, what is expected of her.

That summer, I woke up at 6:00 a.m. every day to commute up to Harlem to work in the office at a camp for at-risk kids. I felt very much the "other," the only white girl there, except the art teacher, and it was made clear very quickly that people were not a fan, that they didn't really "understand" what I was doing there. To be frank, it was the only summer job I could find that year, not wanting to return to Downtown Day Camp or its offices. It wasn't an enjoyable job, and the only moments of happiness I had were hugs from the kids as they passed the office, but I had to do *something* to get myself out of the house every day.

That gig all the way uptown ended badly, too: a bad fight with a male counselor, a suspension, a relocation even further into Harlem, an exile after asking to be switched to their main office in Central Park.

My mom, who sent me texts from work like *"Slasher at Thirty-Fourth Street, be careful"* or *"Random stabbing in Washington Heights, and don't look at your phone when you're on the subway"* and *"A girl got hit on the head with a hammer on Prince Street, so make sure you pay attention,"* was not sorry to see me out of that neighborhood and back home, even if the grounds over which I was fired were unfair.

I tried to ask her to stop, but she insisted she was just "keeping me safe."

I explained this to Dr. A, who said, "You need to communicate with her in a way that she can understand, and hopefully, treat you the way you wanted to be treated."

"Yeah, except she insists that what she's doing is right, that her opinion is always right, that she knows best."

I was trying to separate from my mom, dissolve what I felt was this toxic glue, this attachment, to be healthier myself and try to improve our relationship. I didn't want a war with her anymore.

"My mother always tells me I'm the problem. She doesn't understand a lot of things, and she doesn't see I'm doing the best I can. She just says, 'There's something wrong with you.'"

The following week, when I showed up for our appointment, I found my mom inside.

What the fuck?

She had become "involved" in my *private* work. I was livid.

I literally screamed "No!" and left the room.

Then, I came back in, slamming the door behind me.

"Actually, no, *she* has to leave," I insisted.

I kept going in and out, slamming the door and shouting, until the doctor in the office next door asked us to "Please keep it down" because she could hear screaming in her office.

I had not yet learned that there was a way to get through a moment like this, when I felt like I was on fire, when things felt painful and difficult and scary, without making it worse.

But I would.

CHAPTER ELEVEN

We are more often frightened than hurt, and we suffer more from imagination than from reality.

—Lucius Annaeus Seneca, philosopher

The year the housing bubble burst, I was dating a very nice, buttoned-up guy who worked for one of the big banks.

John tried to explain to me why we were heading toward a recession, because the way my Intro to Media Studies professor broke it down that morning went in one ear and out the other.

"The stock market is crashing because the big banks really, really fucked up," he'd said over Mexican food. "They gave everyone something called subprime loans, and credit default swaps, and now it looks like millions of people are going to lose their jobs and their homes."

I was rotating my glass, making the coconut martini inside swill around like I was letting a fine wine breathe.

"So basically, we're going to have another great depression?"

"I hope not," he said, spearing a piece of his pork quesadilla.

Despite the rounds of layoffs that would follow, John would manage to keep his job, and the word "recession" would become a permanent part of the landscape in 2008 and 2009.

John and I had been friends for a year before I made the decision to let the guy "be my boyfriend." I knew he had feelings for me, and Dr. A had said, "This could be great for you." His mother was from Ecuador, and his father was an Italian retired military lieutenant. He lived in a three-family house in Sheepshead Bay, Brooklyn, which was a solid hour from the city on a train I'd never taken in my life. I had met him online, and we met up every now and then and caught an independent movie at the Angelika Film Center on Bleecker Street.

I drained my second coconut martini, thinking if I drank it faster, maybe it would hit me harder. I didn't have time for a third, because we had to make the movie.

Besides, if I did have a third, I would have to pee too many times during the movie.

"Don't let me have another one," I'd tell him, because it was becoming clear, then, that if I answered the waiter's question, I was going to say "yes, I would like another one," as automatically and thoughtlessly as if someone was asking me what my name was.

John would say, "No, she's good," and when the time came, I'd scrunch up my face and say, "Well . . . ." like I was making a lighthearted decision about whether to go with the pink nail polish or the blue, "Eh, I'll just have one more."

John would try to stop me, and I'd wave him away dismissively and motion again to the waiter, tapping the rim of my glass and winking at him.

"It's fine," I'd say to John, who'd be raising an eyebrow. "I'm eating."

Unlike in the clubs, now, I was saying, "yes" because I couldn't get the word "no" out of my mouth. Because he saw past my alcohol-related antics and further down into my "good heart" John put up with it, just like he put up with my neediness and my controlling behavior. The dynamic, for me, had shifted: I had gone from being just plain afraid of Aaron to being so terrified of losing John, a great guy, that I absolutely smothered him.

Nothing made me happier than the fact that Grandma liked John.

She was eating dinner with us more often during the week now, slipping Gucci food under the table while my dad asked her to "please not feed the dog at the table." Sometimes, I brought John upstairs with me to visit her, and she would call him "Poor John." Maybe it was deliberate, she was being funny, or maybe the dementia was laying its early groundwork, because she had given that name to my Uncle John when he first asked permission to marry my aunt.

When John had to go to Raleigh, North Carolina, on business for three nights, I reacted like he had just been drafted into battle overseas.

I cried for hours, and texted him incessantly, and I especially missed him cuddling up in bed next to me when I got the migraines.

I was getting them more frequently now, with varying intensity, and John would come over after work and lay down with me, and say, "I feel so bad, I wish there was something I could do," and eventually we'd leave my room and join the rest of the family for dinner.

Because of the college's absence policy, I had to register with the New School's disabilities services department.

Nothing over the counter helped, so my mom suggested I see a specialist.

At first, the doctor suggested several medications that my mother vetoed, explaining that they had made her terribly sick when she tried them (she got migraines, too).

"You'll throw up and dry heave," she said. "The migraine itself is better than that."

So we tried other medications through trial-and-error with minimal results.

That doctor wasn't very responsive, and these migraines were seriously disrupting my life.

But when I called him twice in one week, the next response I got was a letter in the mail, stating that leaving two voicemails in one week was overkill and "I'd damaged the patient doctor relationship." He refused to see me anymore.

I went to another neurologist, who looked over all of my notes, and told me to take something called Nortryptalin every night to prevent them, and to take something called Axert when I got them, which would sometimes take a few hours to kick in. I woke up each morning knowing the day likely would not end well, that by 2:00 p.m., I'd be on my way home to lay in the dark, reeling.

I woke up, knowing I'd have no choice, because I had to wake up.

* * *

Soon, another health crisis surfaced.

After a routine gynecological checkup, I was called back because there were "abnormal results" on my pap smear.

"What does that mean?" I asked the nurse on the phone.

"The doctor can explain it to you when you come in," she said in her Australian accent.

"They say that all the time, it's probably nothing," my mom offered.

Things were a little bit better between she and I. We were trying. She bought us tickets to shows because they were on sale at the Theater Development Fund, and we went to the Borgata Casino in Atlantic City to have dinner at Wolfgang Puck's restaurant and see the comedy show. And, of course, on the weekends we went shopping.

She wasn't working that day, so we went to the doctor together.

When Dr. P. called me into the room, she asked, "Do you want your mom to stay in the room with you?"

"Yes . . ."

Why is she asking me that?

"You have HPV," she said.

"How can I have HPV if I just got the second round of the Gardasil vaccine two weeks ago?"

"It's sexually transmitted," she said.

"Yeah, I know, but my boyfriend was a virgin," I explained. "Mom, can you excuse us for a moment?"

"That's why I asked if you wanted her in the room," Dr. P said, as if I were supposed to have been able to see that coming.

She continued, "If you've had an STD before, it can hang around and cause a strain of the virus. So, here it is. Now, it causes cervical cancer, as you were made aware, which is why you got the vaccine. So, we're going to have to take a culture of the abnormal cells to see if they're high risk or low risk. Then, if they're high risk, we're going to have to take a biopsy to see if we need to freeze that part of your cervix and remove it."

In a daze, I left the examination room and scheduled the follow-up appointments I needed with reception, then turned to see my mother sobbing in the waiting room.

"What's the difference between this and AIDS?" she asked, sniffling as we walked out of the building.

"HPV, Mom," I said with a sigh, patting her on the back. "Not HIV."

The doctor called again to let me know that they were high risk, that I had precancerous cells in my cervix. At this point, I don't need to draw you a picture of the panic that ensued; and I won't draw you a picture of what it felt like to go, every three months, for a painful cervical biopsy, sans numbing agents or anesthesia.

* * *

As part of an assignment for my Intro to Journalism class, we were told to "find and cover a protest." I loved that professor. His name was Sean Elder, he was really tall, and he had snow white hair even though he wasn't very old at all. He was so freaking cool, being in his class was like hanging out with a beat journalist on his coffee break who filled us in on everything we needed to know about old-school and new-school journalism.

We had read an essay from George Saunders called "The Braindead Megaphone," and I had copied a quote from it directly into my notebook:

"In the beginning, there's a blank mind. Then that mind gets an idea in it, and the trouble begins, because the mind mistakes the idea for the world."

I couldn't wait to get out there and find that protest, so, that very afternoon, a brisk one for October, I headed right to where I knew I would definitely find one.

Union Square would always remind me of my time sitting on those steps after school my freshman year at Baruch, watching skateboarders with headphones in their ears try and jump the steps. The park had not quite "cleaned up its act" the way other areas of the city had post-Giuliani. It was still a meeting place for druggies, high school drop outs, Hare Krishnas, radicals, and the homeless, who meandered around well-manicured women walking their expensive Pomeranian puppies and hipster couples shopping at the farmer's market with re-usable hemp bags.

On this one afternoon in particular, some people had stopped to lend an ear to a rugged, red-faced man with a megaphone, ranting on the steps. He had a mane of salt-and-pepper hair and wore a brown bomber jacket. Growing up here, you learned to first be scared of these "street crazies," then to just ignore them, and, then, maybe, you embrace them for what they are: people with enough balls to try to get people to listen in a city where millions of voices weave in and out of blaring car horns and random music blasting.

John was with me that day, wearing a suit, as he always did. He had met me after work, walking fourteen blocks down Park

Avenue South from his office. I told him I was just going to "knock this assignment out" before we headed over to a French restaurant we liked for the French dip sandwiches, frites, and coffee martinis—well, I drank those, and he had a Stella Artois beer.

"Give a man a megaphone and people will stop to listen," was the takeaway from Sean's journalism class that day after we read George Saunders' essay, so this could not have been more perfect. The unique thing about the crowd I'd stumbled upon was its size—I had never seen such a large, captive audience there before. Some "protests" or "rallies" or "talks" were of real political relevance, others were more performances in a concrete, three-ring circus.

I settled in next to John and a pair of smirking, private high school girls in skirted uniforms and watched as a man in a cowboy hat sidled up next to the man with the megaphone, holding a sign that read, *I write for Paris Hilton* that neither John nor I could figure out the significance of.

In just a month, the 2008 presidential election would take place, and the American people were still watching the damage of the recession percolate, largely unsure about where to direct whatever hope they had left.

"People who believe in Obama are being fooled," the man barked into his megaphone. "The candidates should be arrested, not put in office."

When one of the spectators shouted something in response, the man with the megaphone tried to get him to join him up front to say a few words. The spectator nobly refused, repeatedly, while laughing, maybe at himself, maybe out of politeness, maybe at the situation.

I looked closer, and it became clear that the device wasn't just a megaphone, but a contraption made from what looked like a school bus driver's hand microphone *attached* to a megaphone.

Just then, a middle-aged red headed woman with the bulldog-esque mug of a 1940s gangster showed up. Her sweatshirt stated that she was a Yankees fan, and she was, with her cigarette-smoking raspy voice, the anti-American girl, the roughneck. Between two lampposts and pea green trashcans, the three performers set their stage.

She began to talk, and the man with the megaphone began heading for the street.

"I'll be right back," I said to John. I couldn't really follow what this was supposed to be, and I needed more information for my paper.

I ran up to the man with the megaphone and introduced myself.

"Erin Grassi," he said, shaking my hand and explaining that he was just a guy with a goal to create a new political party based on "sound economic ideas." He seemed to come up with its name on the spot, "The Liberty Party."

He asked me to join him as he crossed Union Square East to get a soda, so we walked through the zoo of people and cars and pets that was Fourteenth Street and Fourth Avenue. He smelled of whiskey and cigarettes, which I caught wind of when he removed a bill from his wallet and handed it over to the vendor without looking. He palmed the can of ginger ale, which was wrapped in a thin white napkin to absorb some of the moisture.

John was craning his neck out from over on the steps to make sure the guy wasn't pulling a "walk with me or I'll kill you" move with a gun to my side.

"I belong to a movement that nobody officially needs to belong to. We've been congregating in Union Square for the past few years but have never formally created a group," Grassi explained.

"Is there a website I can go to, to find out more?" I ask.

"No" Grassi quipped. "But what we do have is an understanding of the triple rent levels, of 9/11, and why wage levels are severely stagnant."

Suddenly, a bald man wearing glasses and a stained vintage T-shirt emerged from the sea of cars on Broadway, his nose scrunched up and his mouth open in a weird "O" shape. He was lugging a beat up brown leather bowling bag.

His name was Nathaniel, and Grassi immediately dumped him on me.

"Talk to this guy," he said before he vanished.

Without any prompting, Nathaniel launched into his bit.

"How old are you, nineteen, twenty? Well, 9/11 youngsters were thirteen years old when it happened, and are politically moot in this time. If you're from before this time, one would assume you have more perspective. Democrats were called leftist. This generation is being brainwashed."

What?

I looked to the left, where MTV was setting up their cameras about a hundred feet from the makeshift stage. Those crews had been prowling through Union Square for the past month to interview opinionated and bitter young New Yorkers about the upcoming election, and they were most likely getting some of this for b-roll footage. Grassi was winding through the audience of onlookers, moving in dangerously close to their faces.

"Our generation is full of doubters, of paranoid middle-class workers, of unsure voters and the people who choose ignorance over anxiety," Nathaniel said. "Without access to media, elections are pointless. The only people allowed on TV are the third floor of Goldman Sachs and the fourth floor of Goldman Sachs."

I allowed his voice to fade as I looked down at my notebook and wondered just how willing people were, at this point, to listen to any voice that broadcasted skepticism or confusion when it came to the state of our country.

I concluded my paper:

Only time would tell if we will see "The Liberty Party" on the ballot in our lifetime, or if Nathaniel will be the next president. What I know for sure, now, is that yes, if you give a man a megaphone, people will listen—luckily for people like Grassi and Nathaniel, who, when asked what his role in the rally was, answered simply, "I like to talk," before descending back into the crowd.

* * *

Like every other party girl, I was always in search of the perfect New Year's Eve. I rang in 2009 at a club on the Lower East Side with John; my new friend, Marley; and John's friend Gary. I had met Marley in an English class; she lived at the dorms down on William Street, a few blocks from Southbridge. She answered my texts and met me for coffee and we even went to a movie together once. I would visit her at the dorms, and she understood whenever I'd have to push the time back because I had a migraine.

On December 31, 2008, champagne rained down on all of our heads at midnight as we stood on a dance floor spilling over with clumsy, well-dressed people and vodka. I had always been searching for this feeling of euphoria, and I had reached that beautiful point where I was slightly tipsy but not yet drunk. I vowed to stay there this time.

Marley wasn't having as much luck—I followed her to the bathroom where she hovered over the toilet, but nothing came out. *What a good friend I am.* We put her in a cab—which she later got kicked out of for throwing up in—and John and I got in one ourselves.

Somehow I managed to talk John into hitting up one more bar before we headed back to my apartment (my parents had agreed to let him stay on the couch). And somehow, I managed to down another drink, then another, despite his hand reaching out to stop me. The bartender slipped a bracelet on my wrist which meant I could "drink all night," a gesture that caused John's face to contort in horror.

"Another White Russian!" I cried.

The bartender set it down in front of me, and John moved it away, and the bartender put it back in front of me.

"The lady gets what she wants," the bartender said.

I remember flashes of dancing, and then stumbling home down Gold Street, screaming something about the "golden-haired prince," a waiter I just *knew* was flirting with me.

When I got home, I ran to the bathroom to throw up, and then came back as if nothing had happened. I did this multiple times before passing out, mascara smeared all over my face, one heel on and the other off. I was still wearing my glittery dress.

A week later, when John was stuck underground in the subway, I sat in my room calling, and calling, my panic escalating to intolerable levels every time I got his answering machine. I called Marley and asked if she would call his house because nobody was answering at the house number he gave me.

"Ok, ok, calm down, I'll call," she said.

It turned out John had changed his house number in my phone after all of the crazy drunken threats I'd made on New Year's Eve.

What threats? What the hell did I say?

A few days later, Marley sent me an email telling me:

My therapist said I can't be dragged into other people's crises, so if you want to still be friends, I guess that would be okay, but that can't happen again.

I didn't answer—but I forwarded it to Dr. A, who explained why maybe it would be overwhelming for Marley, and that if I could take a step back, I would likely see it too.

"Well, I'll have to be a better friend and resolve not to do that," I said.

"Actually," said Dr. A. "She's kind of clearly telling you that she doesn't really give a fuck either way."

Excuse me? Here I was trying to hold on to the friends that I could, and she was telling me not to bother.

"So I should say nothing?"

"Not everything needs a response."

Filled with this new sense that time was limited because of the pre-cancerous cells, I quickly shifted gears and presented her with a list of all of the qualities I wanted, of what the girl I wanted to be looked like.

"I want to be calm. I want to be able to get from one place to another like a normal person. I want to be a cool girlfriend who doesn't start fights and worry all the time. I want to be a happy daughter. I want to be someone who's fun in social situations instead of feeling like I'm in a pressure cooker. I want to be able to hear a truck go over a bump outside and not lose my shit."

"I'm going to give you two big suggestions, and we're going to work toward these. Ready? Write these down."

I took out my notebook.

"One, act the opposite of how you feel. Fake it 'til you make it."

"Got it," I said, writing that down.

"Two, learn to be where you are. Not worrying about what happened before, or what will happen tomorrow or next year, or what's happening after hearing a sound or a threat on the news without knowing exactly what's going on. Stay in each moment."

She smiled at me and took a deep breath, like there was more.

"What is it?" I asked.

"Well . . . I'm pregnant," she said.

"Wow, congratulations!" I said automatically.

"I'm going to refer you to someone I think you'll do really well with," she said. "Her name is Jennifer, she's a really cool therapist who's on TV and specializes in young people. She knows CBT and also something called DBT, which is like what we've been doing but with mindfulness skills."

Mindfulness, I wrote down, reminding myself to look up the definition.

"I know you feel like I'm leaving you. But we can always pick it back up, if you want, later on."

"Okay, I understand."

Remember what happened when your last therapist referred you to someone else?

Part of me did think, *not again,* but outside of that worry, I really felt happy for her and her new baby.

"I want you to know that I've really enjoyed working with you," she said. "You've taught me more than any other patient I've worked with."

I must have made a face, like, *yeah, right.*

"I'm serious! You came in willing to embrace change, and to make that happen for yourself, even with no immediate results. You've had faith in something. You were brave enough look at what's not working and try to change that. Some people spend forty years doing what's not working."

I hugged her, and I thanked her, and on the subway ride home, I bit back tears, more afraid than I wanted to be that this next person would not understand me at all, that I was going right back into the dizzying vortex of trying someone new out again, who was just going to leave, or who was going to help me, and then leave.

The paper I had gotten back from Sean on the rally in Union Square was sticking out of my bag, marked up in red pen.

I had begun with one of George Saunders' quotes from his essay, and next to that quote was a grade: A.

> *"No, war will not be stopped. But it is a comfort, in the midst of a war, to read an antiwar book this good, and be reminded that just because something keeps happening, doesn't mean we get to stop regretting it. Massacres are bad, the death of innocents is bad, hate is bad, and there's something cleansing about hearing it said so purely."*

* * *

It was the beginning of junior year, and I had just left my Intermediate Journalism class to head uptown in a downpour. My jeans were five shades darker than they were when I left the school building and getting darker by the minute as I got lost on Twenty-Fifth Street and went back the way I came, all the while fixing my umbrella, which threatened to blow inside out with each small gust of wind. I still had a stupid flip phone, so the way I tried to find addresses was simply by walking in one direction, seeing which way the numbers went for long enough to know, then either continuing that way or doing an about-face. Breathing quickly, I started to panic as time ticked by.

I cursed myself as I ran through a puddle, causing it to splash with even more force than if I were to have stopped for a second to find a way around it, or over it, or gently touched it with my toe.

Finally, I squinted and saw building 226. The lobby smelled musty, like cardboard and mothballs. The elevator was old, with black buttons that did not light up. The door to 3B was unlocked, and I barreled through it, noticeably flustered, trying to cover up the obvious fact that I was panting.

A red headed woman dressed casually in a cute flower top and jeans smiled at me and held out her hand. She had an ease about her that contradicted everything I had ever associated with a "therapist."

"Helaina?" she asked.

"Hi," I said, almost throwing myself down against the back of the green couch.

"Hi there, I'm Jen . . ." she trailed off looking at my expression. "Why so anxious?"

"Well, I couldn't get a cab, so I had to take the train, and I couldn't find the building, and I worried that if I was late, you'd get a bad first impression of me, and that would ruin everything we tried to do after because you wouldn't like me . . ."

She listened as I continued, and calmly began once I finished speaking.

"Let me ask you something. If you moved at the same pace, but inside, you were calm, would it make a difference in the time it took you to get here?"

Click.

"No, I don't think so," I said. "I don't know, I've never known any other way. It just happens. It's not my choice."

"You always have a choice," she said.

Here we go again.

"I never have a choice," I said. "I told that to Dr. A all the time. Everything just happens automatically."

"Whether or not you get worked up, everything is going to happen exactly same way. That's all out of your control."

Her tone was matter-of-fact, but had a certain lightness to it.

"Right now, everything is a reflex, a pattern you've been practicing for years," she said as she unwrapped a Jolly Rancher. "But you can control your reaction, your response to it. It's going to take practice, but you can."

"We'll see," I said. "I mean, I would like that. I would love that. Dr. A said the same thing."

"And have you made any progress at all?" she asked.

"No," I said.

"You sure about that?"

Now that she mentioned it, I didn't want to kill myself anymore, and come to think of it . . . no, there was no time for that. There was a bigger issue at hand.

"My boyfriend, John, broke up with me two nights ago, and I feel like it's literally the end of the world," I began to cry. "My life is over."

"Is it really over?" she asked.

I sighed.

"Well, I'm sitting here, so technically, no, but you know what I mean."

"I think that's more of a feeling, or, maybe, more of a fear. Why does one person get so much power? Why does it feel like your life depends on someone else?"

"I don't know!" I wailed. "He said I was always crying, that I was always panicking, and always getting drunk and causing problems. I never wanted to do any of those things, but it always just happened. It's so intense, all I do is worry and freak out, worry and freak out."

"So, you're not going to love this, but is it possible that you were pushing him away without even realizing it?"

"Why the hell would I do that?" I asked.

"Maybe you've done it with other people too. So they can't hurt or abandon you first."

I just stared down at my fingers, picking off my nail polish.

"The fear of abandonment, the need to control everything and everyone around you, isn't working. It's going to keep you stuck. You need to challenge these conclusions you're jumping to."

Suddenly, she interrupted herself, saying, "Stop picking at your nails. Sit on your hands."

I sat on my hands.

"Let me explain to you what's been going on. You want to be in control of every situation so it feels safe, and when things don't go according to plan, the anxiety kicks up, and it's difficult for friends or boyfriends to handle."

The conversation continued, but it wasn't a standard introductory "tell me everything about your medical history" type session. She didn't take any notes on me, didn't write anything down. As we continued talking, she directed a giant spotlight onto the murky mess that I'd made of my mind, of my inner life, right on the invisible little girl that never left, still causing me to react so strongly, to feel so intensely, to cut everyone off and push them away, and manipulate my tone of voice so that it sounded angry, intimidating.

She knew this invisible girl. She'd worked with her before. She knew how to challenge her. In fact, she knew exactly where that invisible little girl had come from. She even took a guess at her birthday. She told me, in no uncertain terms, why everything had begun, eight years ago, to feel like the end of the world.

* * *

"If we get ourselves angry, we are altering that part of ourselves. Good will is the only intrinsically valuable thing," said Emmanuel Kant.

I started taking an interesting philosophy class that correlated with Dr. J's session. It was an "ethics" class, but it focused more on philosophy, the pursuit of happiness, the way people's minds worked.

I learned that Epicurus observed that anxiety is not inevitable; it is caused by false beliefs.

I learned that Seneca distinguished between what things are up to us and what things aren't, and tried to locate the point at which things are inside of our control.

His structure of our mental lives looked a lot like what I learned with Dr. J.

What is fact and what is judgment or opinion or emotion?

Essentially, said my professor, "Shit happens, how equipped are you to deal with it?"

When Dr. J and I sat down to figure out just what I was so anxious about every week, we continued the groundwork Dr. A laid of trying to figure out what was rooted in reality and what was based on fear of what might happen, combined with some sort of mind-reading and script-writing I was projecting onto other people and situations. While some anxiety kept me safe, as it does for everyone, much of it was noise that needed to be turned down, then eliminated entirely.

"When you allow yourself to be seized by 'what if,' you stay stuck, running and freezing and never going anywhere," she said.

We practiced letting my emotions come—letting the news make me scared, feeling rejected by a classmate—and then redirecting my attention. First, I was supposed to acknowledge it without running from it, and then I was supposed to . . . do nothing.

"If you call it out, it will lose its power. Build your capacity to feel it."

There were things we tried and failed, like pushing a difficult situation out of my mind for a while. "On the shelf, I can think about it later," I was supposed to say.

That usually didn't work very well, until, one day, it did.

That was the beginning of learning to control the intrusive thoughts; because there was a difference between choosing not to think about something and "suppressing" it. I could acknowledge that I saw it and decide to deal with it when I felt more ready, if it was important, rather than obsessively worry about it during the middle of class.

Dr. J gave me her email address and her cell number and told me that I could text her or call her if there was an emergency, and that she responded to email within twenty-four hours. This was the kind of support I had needed all along, when things came up in real-world time.

It was exhausting, a lot of hard work, and a lot of uncomfortable "acting opposite" of how I felt or wanted to act, which wasn't always successful.

This work, though, was an essential part of facing fears I had been avoiding, and uncurling my fingers around things I didn't want to let go.

* * *

I was especially surprised at Dr. J's reaction to Anthony.

I had met Anthony while on a date with someone else, and while we made zero sense on paper, we made sense to each other, at that exact moment in our lives. A long, on and off, three-year moment.

"He's eighteen years older than me," I told her. "He doesn't have money or anything. In fact, he's not doing so great right now. His business was hit hard after 9/11 and again with the recession last year, and now he's waiting for his divorce to be finalized," I explained.

"Do you like spending time with him?" she asked.

"Yes, but people will look at us, and they'll think I'm a gold digger, or that I'm weird," I said.

"Who cares what people think?" she said.

"Yeah, I wish," I huffed.

"No, really. So what? What are those people going to do? Why does the opinion of strangers, which you actually don't know, but are speculating, matter?"

I was pretty surprised at this. I was expecting her, like my mother or any other adult in my life, to discourage me from what was an "iffy" idea at best.

She empowered me to make a choice and to own it, and I spent a few uncomfortable months vetting the stares of people until one day, I didn't notice them at all. Something had finally sunk in: *what other people thought didn't matter.* I had always thought it was an excuse, or a defense, "not caring what other people thought." I felt like people used it as an excuse to behave poorly, as a justification for bad behavior or a bad attitude. *If you aren't hurting anyone, it's okay not to care.*

The glaring difference in our age was most apparent when I took him to see a student Cabaret showcase at the New School and two girls did an interpretive dance that involved crawling around on the floor on their backs, and he made a face that made me laugh so hard I had to go to the bathroom to stifle it. Or, maybe it was most apparent when he first came around to meet my parents, and then, for the holidays, and we all kind of skirted around the uncomfortable notion that he was closer to my mom's age than mine.

He owned a flower business uptown, I worked part-time at a school—and *went* to school.

He had gray hair, and mine was almost jet-black.

Still feeling like an outsider at school, I straightened that hair every single day, not letting my curls show. I'd stare at my reflection in the bathroom mirror of my apartment every morning, my hands shaking with impatience at nothing in particular, my head buzzing with the twenty-four hours of neurotic commentary I still couldn't turn off. I would walk into a classroom and *know* that everyone was thinking about me, and that the thoughts they were forming were bad ones. I still felt I had to be one step ahead of things, making accusations of Anthony or predictions about how a night would play out, trying to figure out all the possible threats to my relationships and academic career that weren't actually threats at all until I turned them into big fat problems.

Simple things, like taking a taxi home from his house to mine without his accompanying me, felt terrifying. Like a child, I needed him to come with me to make sure I was safe. For a twenty-year-old, this sounds ridiculous, but you have to remember that on the inside, I was still a scared twelve-year-old in so many ways. Another difference, one that didn't matter was much, was that Anthony could drink legally, and I still couldn't. He had moved back into his parent's apartment, but they were rarely there, and usually at their second home in Tom's River, and I started to sneak sips of alcohol from his parents' liquor cabinet, then shout into the other room to make sure he had a plan to pick up weed from his cousin.

Then, I drank too much and fell off a bar stool in front of his friends.

I drank too much and fell off my chair at French Roast on the Upper West Side in the middle of dinner and thought it was hilarious.

I drank too much and threw a shot glass at his head when he was trying to tell his cousin to stop talking over my emotional karaoke rendition of Jewel's *Foolish Games* at a local Thai restaurant.

Something about that relationship with Anthony triggered me emotionally in a way that, when I was high or drunk, brought out the terrified fifteen-year-old who screamed, cried, and threw things. I was so freaked out by my own feelings that I just couldn't sit still with them—I had to fight them, or fight someone, something.

John never fought back. He had just given up, when I got like this. But Anthony did fight back.

So I called and texted Dr. J, determined, and freaking out, until I heard back. I left her a voicemail, on one occasion, that was just screaming. No words, just screaming, so she couldn't tell if I had left her the voicemail by accident, or if I wanted her to hear what was going on.

My crises were now almost entirely of the interpersonal nature, so when, on one occasion, I called her, and she texted me that she "needed fifteen minutes" because she was in her friend's jewelry store, and took longer than fifteen minutes, I called again and again.

Then I texted, and I called, and I texted, determined and desperate. I was no longer suicidal, no longer facing actual life or death circumstances, but feeling that I was.

"Do you need to get that?" The woman in the jewelry store had asked her.

"No, she'll be okay," Dr. J said, knowing that I would be.

She was starting to try and get me to make it through these moments on my own, but at the same time, she was challenging me to move through what felt impossible-to-handle triggers. I started turning to alcohol and weed to try and make it all stop, and they just fueled the invisible little girl even worse.

"You can't be mindful when you're high or drunk," Dr. J observed, one day, noting that when "crises" happened, I wasn't sober.

Her words went in one ear and out the other, since the invisible girl protected herself by plugging them up, singing, *la la la la la.*

I only saw Dr. J once a week, and she couldn't always answer my texts. I needed something of an urban Sherpa to help carry my luggage for me. So, I would drink and smoke away the epiphanies we came to, taking two steps forward, one big drunk stumble back.

I didn't want to admit I was unhappy, but I expected things from people that would never happen, and I expected the world and everything else in it to change to make things feel better for me.

And it didn't.

Which is how I ended up calling Dr. J from the Brooklyn Queens Expressway one night not knowing where I was, because I had been drinking and got in a car with some guy and literally had no clue where I was or how to get home.

I was drinking through a relationship that felt wrong, then drinking and cheating, then drinking so much that I landed in the emergency room across the street.

Meanwhile, I took an internship with a local paper, the *Downtown Express,* and I always prayed that on reporting and office days, the migraines would stay away.

They were still excruciating and unpredictable; I would get stuck in traffic in a car for hours on a three-hour trip to see distant family, or it would hit in the middle of work, or while I was at Anthony's parent's house in New Jersey. The most devastating aspect was not being able to predict when they would happen, and being trapped wherever I was, praying that the preventative medication, the acupuncture, the physical therapy, the Axert, would work. Sometimes it did, sometimes it didn't.

But nothing was going to stop me from covering a story. I *loved* covering stories, and I was so thrilled at the chance to have an actual byline that I happily covered an ice rink opening up in Battery Park, a parade in Hudson River Park, some Little League games.

I was content to tackle those small potatoes, until, one day, my editor sent me down to Vin's old high school.

"There's a teacher getting an award, and he's legally blind and only has one arm," he said.

It was November when I headed down there in the middle of the Yankees' victory parade, so it was chaos—they had just won the World Series—and wrote a story called, "Blindness Is No Handicap to Great Teaching."

Homer Panteloglou would pace the room to make sure nobody was on their phones, since he couldn't see to the back.

"His handicap makes him unique because he's the type of person who will always find a way," said one of his students. "Even though it might be difficult for him sometimes, he'll find a way to make things work."

However, she does notice some difficulties because of his vision.

"We see him having to hold the paper really close to his face," she said. *"It probably takes him twice as long to read and grade papers than it would any other teacher."*

She added that the students are so comfortable with him that he's more of a father figure to them than a teacher. "They all go to him for advice, even the seniors."

Kim Caceres, 17, said that she will miss him when she goes to college next year, and while the two will still keep in touch, she said it won't be the same as having him around all the time. "If you have any sort of problem or a question, you go to him. He's wonderful."

"The kids and I have a rapport that's unique, like they want me to be their parent type of unique," said Panteloglou. "A lot of the kids come from homes where they don't have that stable family environment, so at school I try to help out a little bit."

While he has no idea how many other teachers with physical or vision impairments are currently working in the New York City public school system, Panteloglou has heard about teachers who are blind and bring seeing eye dogs into the classroom. The Dept. of Education has 50 teachers with visual impairments on record in the New York City public school system, though a spokesperson said there could be other people out there who haven't registered for visual assistance. Panteloglou said that some "cute" stuff happens from time to time, especially due to his color blindness. "I was talking to the kids one day, and I was looking at the fish hanging off the [classroom] ceiling, and I said, 'It would be cool if I painted my walls blue, so I can feel like I'm in the middle of an ocean.' A kid raised his hand and said, 'The room is blue.' I had no idea. It was blue for years and I didn't even know it."

My editor, who wasn't exactly predisposed to liking me, for whatever reason, loved the story.

And in that story, I found my calling.

CHAPTER TWELVE

Today I will stay with you.
I will be right here, right now.
I will fight my desire to retreat to our yesterday's
Where I can still find us.
I will resist the pull of practicality
That keeps me worried about our tomorrows.
Please keep looking for me. I never left.
Today I will stay with you.
I will be right here, right now.
—Mara Botonis, *When Caring Takes Courage*

The days of 2010 came and went, days where I could barely muster a deep breath. I was always saying the wrong thing and pissing people off. Potentially innocent black type on a page, emails and texts from friends, teachers, my boss, the director at my internship—they were all ripe for distortion and misinterpretation due to their inherent lack of actual tone, and I cast a net of paranoia and fear over all of these interactions.

In reality, I was crushing it at my internship and in my college classes, and I loved working with the kids at P.S. 150. I loved it so much that I started to go back and forth in my mind between writer and teacher, as a career choice. The kids brought me so much joy, and demanded my immediate attention, which was good for me; but after just three hours I was so exhausted, I didn't know how teachers could do it. To top it off, I had even managed to make and keep a few friends.

Through all of this, alcohol became the way I propelled myself forward, creating a life that looked good on paper and on Facebook. I figured I was drinking like everyone else. I didn't get drunk every day, or even every weekend, and I could go weeks at a time without picking up a bottle. I was young and carefree, scurrying from bar to lounge to club to party to dinner, sipping here and there and everywhere just like everyone else.

But then, I punched Anthony, and then, I lost my cell phone in a drunken stupor, and then, I was sick for twelve hours the next day, again, convulsing, sweating, hyperventilating.

Hoping to control myself, I switched from wine to vodka to beer. I cut out alcohol for weeks, even months. All the old tricks. *How could this keep happening?* I kept asking myself. I was a smart, responsible person. It felt like someone had a high-heeled voodoo doll and a vendetta against me.

On the night before Thanksgiving, I went on a date with a girl for the first time, something I had always known I would want to gather up the courage to do one day. I liked men, obviously—but I was also pretty sure I liked women.

Because she was a girl, I justified that it "didn't count" as cheating on Anthony.

She made me so nervous that all I wanted to do was drink enough to be able to get over my anxiety . . . and have sex with her. But I kept throwing back drinks far past that point, and ended up throwing up in the Gold Street Diner bathroom, my head spinning.

I called my lifeline, who, naturally didn't know I was on a date.

"I'm drunk. I need you to come get me," I said. Anthony was furious.

"I'm tired of this. Whenever I have plans of my own, you're always ruining them with this shit." He hung up.

My date entered the bathroom, walked me to my apartment, and we got into bed. I leaned over and gagged into the trash can.

"Attractive," she mused sarcastically.

Then, it all went black.

I woke up to fourteen missed calls from Anthony. Turned out, he had taken a cab downtown, spent an hour looking for me and trying to contact me, then went back uptown.

On Thanksgiving Day, after six hours of retching, shaking, and convulsing, I landed at New York Downtown Hospital for alcohol poisoning, my fourth time since I started college. It had almost become a routine.

"Ok, let's go," my dad said knowingly, grabbing his coat.

In the emergency room, while hooking me up to an IV, the nurse whispered to the doctor, "She's the ninth one today."

There were three college dormitories within a four-block radius of the hospital.

I am never drinking again, I resolved.

Despite what had happened, Anthony came right away.

"How can you say you love me and do this to me?" Anthony asked. "Don't tell me you love me anymore." But he stayed by my side the entire time.

I was released at 6:00 p.m.

My family waited for me to eat dinner, and as they ate turkey, antipasto, and stuffing, I drank ginger ale and sipped clear broth.

* * *

My internship at the *Downtown Express* had ended, but several months later, James, their new editor, called me up and asked if I'd be interested in reporting for them—not as an intern again, but as a paid reporter.

"Yes!" I exclaimed. "Just let me know when I start."

I went in to meet him dressed in a pencil skirt, blazer, and trendy work top I got from Express—one that only showed a slight amount of cleavage.

He immediately set me out to work, telling me he had a feeling I would be good at certain types of stories.

He sent me to the New York City Rescue Mission, a homeless shelter and recovery program down on Canal Street that was looking to raise money to build additional floors to make room for more people.

I loved covering that story more than anything, and I kept asking to go back: to cover Thanksgiving, to cover their graduation ceremony, to cover their SOUPerbowl party, where there was no alcohol.

I loved interviewing the men about their families, their experience in prison, their desire to start over.

For a story on their Mother's Day Banquet, James sent me up to a group home in Harlem to interview two of the mothers who would be in attendance at the luncheon.

"I went back to doing crack, because I just needed an escape," said one mother. "There was so much going on. I just wanted to escape."

I looked her in the eye and said, "Yes. I know exactly, exactly what you mean."

No matter how much I drank, the discontent, the restlessness, never went away. The desire for alcohol was like a child's fever for toys: more, more, more. I made promises I failed to keep. I worried my parents sick. That damaged, invisible little girl was laughing a disturbingly flirtatious laugh, trying to drown out the whisper of the woman I was on my way to becoming.

Convulsing on the bathroom floor for eight hours at a time, dizzy and dehydrated, was not my idea of a good time. I hung out with people I didn't like and went places I didn't want to go, drinking up any opportunity to be social and depending on the alcohol to create the good time for me. Each time I said, "never again," during a hangover from hell, I meant it. The will was there. But the problem was, it was nearly impossible for me to get sober alone, without support.

One day, I texted Dr. J that I felt like I had a split personality.

I can't implement what we work on sometimes, and its like I'm a different person, I said.

She wrote back:

You don't have a split personality, although at times I know it feels like you do. It's like learning anything new—it's not

always gong to work no matter how hard you try. It's just
continuing to try that matters. Go enjoy the beautiful day.
Be mindful of all the things you see, smell, and hear. Stay
focused on the positive changes, no matter how small, and
give yourself permission to fuck it all up. We are all fallible.
It's how you try next time that matters most.

Next time I saw her, she said, again, "You don't have these episodes when you're sober."

But I wasn't ready to hear that. I wasn't ready to stop. And I sure as fuck wasn't ready to think about a world without an escape route.

* * *

On September 11, 2010, the "Ground Zero Mosque" issue surfaced.

The neighborhood was once again at a level of maximum security, streets shut down, barricades put up, and police everywhere.

All of the city's elected officials had jumped on the bandwagon to preach religious freedom and make public their support of the project. People were calling my father, telling him that they were going to kill us because Community Board 1 was "in support" of a mosque, even though he, like other board members receiving these calls, weren't for or against anything.

How did they even find our number?

This was exactly what they were trying to avoid by doing what they called "tabling the issue."

Over dinner, baked chicken thighs and pilaf rice, one of the few dishes my mom cooked, my dad explained the situation.

"The issue was never whether or not they had the constitutional right to build the center. That's what these bigoted people are making it out to be, and now what politicians are making it out to be. Did you know that there are already two other mosques in Lower Manhattan, including one right here on Fulton and Cliff Street?" he said.

"You also can't throw a brick in Lower Manhattan without hitting a *For Rent* sign hanging in a nearby window. Given what the 'Cultural Center' has come to represent, the simplest thing would have been to move it. This Imam claimed he'd held out an olive branch to 'mend fences' between the Muslim community and Western nations, but given how emotionally charged this issue has become, reconsidering the location could have easily accomplished that goal."

I nodded, picking at my chicken.

"A major investor in the project said he would sell for a good enough offer. Donald Trump offered him a twenty-five percent profit, which he turned down, making his claim that this was about mending fences—a load of crap. The heart of the debate is about money, real estate, and politics."

These were the issues that ultimately cast a dark shadow over a "sacred day," meant for honoring the fallen.

On the scene, when James confronted a man ripping pages out of the Quran and literally wiping his ass with them, he had an engorged black eye to show for it.

All of it reminded me of the news stories I had seen so many years before, equating "Muslim" with "Taliban."

Equating any dark-skinned person with "terrorist."

People throwing garbage and rocks at the bodegas and delis owned by people who met those descriptions, looting their stores.

People shouting "You knew! You knew!" at the men who operated hot dog stands on the streets.

"Never forget" was supposed to be our motto. Originally— explained Mark, who I was now taking a second poetry class with, even though I was probably one of the worst poets to put pen to paper—the motto was used in reference to the Holocaust as a way to remember the people who died as individual souls, not statistics. It was supposed to be a way to remember that mankind will never stop perpetuating evil, killing innocent people along the way.

"We regenerated that motto on 9/11 because we were not supposed to forget what had happened to us, what we'd become, all of the lessons we learn from collective memory," Mark explained.

As Ecclesiastes said in the Bible, "What has been will be again, what has been done will be done again; there is nothing new under the sun."

And there we all were. Nothing new.

* * *

"Why do you care what you look like all the time?" I asked my mother on a late car ride home from a wedding in 1996.

"After a certain age, you can't go outside without lipstick," my mom said as she meticulously reapplied.

When I was four years old, I marched up to the salesgirls on the ground floor of Bloomingdales and declared, "Look, I can put lipstick on perfectly without a mirror!" I demonstrated, and the girls in fancy black suits with long lacquered nails laughed and said, "That's very good!"

I sauntered away, swishing my hips from left to right, hand poised, and wrist limp, making my way up to the children's section feeling very satisfied with myself. I was a little adult, and I was a pro. But I still clung to my mother's legs whenever she told me to go play with the other kids, or get up on stage when a magician needed a volunteer; the little girl who covered her ears when mom tried to mention sleep away camp.

My aunt and my mother always criticized each other's appearances. I saw it as normal, and thought the whole world would judge me the way they judged each other.

"I've got it together!" I wanted to broadcast to everyone, because I still only saw myself as others saw me. I still felt so damaged on the inside that I preserved with compulsion how I appeared on the outside, the part that was still attractive and seemingly scar-free. It was one of the only things I could control when chaos came at me from all sides, showing everyone, but mainly, myself, that I would not be destroyed.

Grandma, even in her elderly years, had always looked beautifully put together, makeup flawlessly done, wearing a stylish outfit, and sporting manicured nails.

The first thing my aunt would say upon entering my grandmother's hospital room—a place she now found herself frequently—was, *"Look at her hair."* With a small plastic comb, she'd lift her mother's head and try to manipulate the thin white strands to resemble the style my grandmother had always sculpted each day. My aunt also insisted on putting lipstick on her each time she was in the hospital. Lipstick was her attempt at preservation.

If I put the lipstick on her, then this isn't happening.

I fell into the habit of putting "lipstick" on things, too. I wanted to be strong for my aunt and my mother, so, I kept myself emotionally "covered up," not fully acknowledging just how scared I was of what was happening to Grandma. I suppressed those fears, and just like holding a life preserver under, it exploded with even more force when I least expected it. Most often, it exploded onto Anthony, who I expected to fix everything, to comfort me, which he couldn't. Nobody could. No amount of reassurance in the world would have been enough.

The hospital was an endless, exhausting rotation of despair and goodbyes and new hope.

Doctors never expected her to make it, through the pneumonia, through the heart complications, through this fall and that broken hip and the pneumonia again, but she was so fucking tough, she survived.

She proved them wrong, but we lost more of her each time, piece by piece, traumatized and disoriented by each hospital visit.

Whenever they took her blood, she felt like she was falling— she cried out for help and gripped the rails as though she were going to fall through, trying to steady herself.

"Helaina, I'm falling," she would start out soft, but grew panicked. Her hands would shake.

"I'm not going to let you fall," I said, thinking of her standing behind me on the windowsill as I sat and watched for my mother coming home.

When I was the one put up in the hospital bed—alcohol poisoning, of course, or food poisoning, or some reaction to a new medication—I felt trapped, short of breath, listening to the sounds of other people moaning, homeless men screaming, nurses whispering. I'd watch the slow drip of the fluid into the IV shoved into my hand, and my father, wearing a black sleeveless workout shirt and gray striped Adidas pants, would stand with his hands and on his hips, looking disapprovingly around for some help.

Surrounded by the same monitors and tubes, one feeling among many was the same for both of us: *How does this keep happening? What's going to happen to me?*

Everything I loved, everything that was good about the world, was shaking in that hospital bed, becoming teary eyed whenever the nurse came to change the bedpan and the bed sheets. Grandma was embarrassed, of course, but most of all, she was afraid of what it all meant.

* * *

For my twenty-first birthday, we took a trip to Paris, just my mother and I.

Technically, it was for both of our birthdays, and it was a few weeks before mine, but we were there on her actual birthday, June 11. We decided consciously, this time, to leave my father behind, since we loved to walk around forever and go into all of the shops and he—well, didn't. He had always tried to be a good sport, but we would feel rushed because we knew he was waiting.

We went to Buddha Bar, and I told the waiter that my mother was going to say she didn't want dessert, but to please bring some anyway so we could have the candle, *wink wink*. My dad had taught me well.

They brought out a giant cake that could have served about twenty people, this beautiful chocolate fondant creation decorated with orange slices and flowers and served with a sparkler.

The waiter left us with it after we finished singing, but never came back with forks or spoons.

"Oh my gosh, this is probably going to cost like $80," my mom giggled, sticking her finger in the frosting and tasting it.

"It's okay, it's on me," I said, able to make offers like that now that I had a debit card and two paying jobs. I looked around to see if anyone was going to bring us new forks and plates, but nobody seemed to care.

"Maybe I'll just take them off this table," I said, getting ready to get up.

"No!" she giggled. "You can't do that at a place like this. Just wait."

I started to take an orange slice off the cake, and my mom picked little pieces off with her fingers.

Suddenly the waiter came rushing over.

"No, no, no!"

He proceeded to try to communicate, in broken English, that the cake was just for show.

I suddenly realized I had seen the cake making its way to all of the tables where people proceeded to sing, but I thought that was just the kind of birthday cake they served. The waiter took it away back to the kitchen, grumbling.

"Oh my God, he must be cursing us back there, calling us stupid Americans!" my mom said.

She and I looked at each other like two teenagers who had just gotten caught by the principal, our hands over our mouths in shock, holding in giggles that came first from our nose, then our throat, finally exploding into laughter that carried itself up to the ceiling, framing a memory that, along with all of the fond memories of shops and cheeses and markets and museums, we would never forget.

* * *

As Dr. J tried to re-introduce me to a reality that wasn't as awful as the one I always made up, I was confronted with a very real one.

A week before my twenty-first birthday, Grandma fell again, and this time would be different.

We found her on the kitchen floor in the morning, just lying there, staring blankly at the wall.

"Where am I?" she asked. "What's happening?"

Her wrist was swollen, and the steel medical alert bracelet was cutting into her skin. Two EMTs arrived and began filling out paperwork, looking bored.

"I guess we'll take her to the hospital," one of the EMTs said with a sigh as he tried to get her bracelet off.

She began wincing despite herself—trying to be brave.

"Leave her," I said as calmly as I could. "She's in pain."

The invisible girl started arguing with me.

Do something!

There's nothing I can do.

You're letting them do this to her.

Dr. J would say there's nothing I can do.

Like a doll, Grandma couldn't stand up on her own, so the EMTs put on blue rubber gloves like they were getting ready to handle a wild animal and gruffly hoisted her up. She softly cried out in pain despite herself, and something was hoisted inside of me. I wanted to bash their heads through the mirror, angry at them, angry at everything, angry because I knew exactly what was going to happen now—it was going to be hell.

They strapped her down like a mental patient.

"She has to go in the ambulance," they said, even though we were literally across the street from the hospital.

"I didn't know there were so many things wrong with me," Grandma said.

In the ER, an Indian nurse hurried in and started to roughly examine my grandmother's breasts and arms. For what felt like the millionth time, she winced in pain. This nurse was handling her in a way that no human should be treated, let alone an old lady. I thought about what Dr. J had told me about communicating with people, feeling the boiling anger and panic start to flash before my eyes.

"Can you please try to be gentle?" I asked politely.

"Do you want me to take blood or not? If you don't want me to, I won't," she snapped as she roughly twisted my grandmother's arms, looking for a vein, throwing her around like a rag doll.

"Yes, but can you please be gentle?" I asked again, exercising so much control over my voice and my tone that I could feel the anger pummeling against the backs of my teeth, rattling them, begging to explode.

She shoved the needle in, and my grandma made a face I'd never seen before. She began to cry and look away.

"They won't do an x-ray without blood tests," barked the nurse.

My grandmother was wilting on the bed, in silent tears. "You're a tough cookie," I said to her as I held her hand and dug my foot hard into the floor. I began to feel dizzy, a familiar whir of helplessness and desperation and sadness and anger all whirling around inside me. I looked at my mother, desperate for backup, but got none. The nurse flipped her on her side to change her.

"They're torturing me, look," my grandmother quietly said as she showed me her arm, slightly panicked. My mom began crying. Enough was enough.

"You're being too rough with her," I said to the nurse, sternly but still not raising my voice.

"Fine, you change her," she said, throwing down the gown on top of my grandmother and abandoning us. I stood there with no clue what to do, helplessly looking at my mom for some kind of support.

"What should I do?" I asked.

My mother immediately turned on me.

"I don't know, it's your fault she left! Are you happy now?" She cried, wiping her nose. "You don't know how to talk to people."

I looked away. Dr. J's voice moved in: *Focus on what you're doing. Don't engage with her. She hurts you when she's hurt.*

"Ready for the princess dress?" I asked as I held up the washed-out blue hospital gown. She nodded, and I began to change her the way she used to change me, making little noises, "ch-ch-ch" when I needed to turn her gently her on her side or move her arms.

"You're my little angel," she whispered.

"You're mine," I said as I gingerly moved the IV along with her body.

"I should've stayed home with you, Helaina. It's safe there," she said, asking me to take off the swollen medical alert bracelet cutting into her skin.

"I can't Grandma, not yet. It's ok," I said. "You're safe. I'm here. It's going to be okay."

I had a sinking feeling that I was lying.

That night, I smoked a bowl, looking through the black metal bars of the terrace, out over the trees that obscured the twinkling lights of the Brooklyn Bridge. The courtyard below seemed to beckon me, the green grass appearing as a rusty brown abyss, empty and dried out.

Had I been sober instead of smoking weed—which I had now taken to doing on whichever nights I couldn't drink—I would have realized that I could not afford to go to these places. The weed kept me paralyzed, paranoid, following the spiral of these darker thoughts. But the invisible girl inside me craved it, because it gave her everything she needed to survive.

The next morning, I arrived to find Grandma's hospital room splattered with blood. She had been trying to escape, to go home, and had ripped the IV out over and over.

Now, they had found a way to literally attach her to the wall by a cord.

I want to go home.

I just have to get home.

What does home look like?

Feelings of desperation flashed through me.

"Please don't do this to me," Grandma said. "Why are you doing this to me?"

She thought I was responsible for what was happening to her. She thought I had hooked her up to the wall.

"Trust me, it's okay," I said, taking her hands in mine. It didn't matter how many times I told her she was going to be okay. She didn't believe me.

"You've always been a little girl who listened," she said, catching her breath. "Today, you're not."

What had once been our own happy piece of the universe, so safe, warm, and happy, was gone. That night, I tried to remember what it was like to cuddle up together as a child and read my favorite book while she smoothed my hair, but as soon as the warmness of the memory touched down, something stung me sharply, and it vanished. I was cold once again, surrounded by beeping machines and random cries coming from other rooms. The two of us lay under an unforgiving fluorescent light, shining a harsh reality on what had become of our world.

* * *

I felt permanently responsible for her life in a more direct way than I ever had before. I blamed myself for everything I couldn't fix. Showing up every day after class wasn't enough. I took her pain on and felt like everything was going to fall apart if I wasn't physically there to control it. I felt responsible for her in the way a guardian angle would, needing to literally watch over her every second to make sure she was safe.

The next day, she wasn't responsive when I arrived in her room. She was sort of swaying back and forth, sitting up in bed, holding a basin as if she were going to be sick.

"Is there a nurse that could come in here please? She's not responding," I said, trying not to panic, but trembling as I sat on the foot of the bed, watching her and not knowing what to do.

A doctor in blue scrubs came in, and tried to talk to her.

"Lucy?" he said. "Lucy, can you hear me?"

She didn't respond.

"It's probably the medication," she doctor said, not looking up from his clipboard. "Just give it an hour or two."

A few blocks away, the first Taste of the Seaport event was being held to raise money for local schools, and I was on assignment to cover it. Like I had ten years before, in fifth grade, I wiped my nose, kissed Grandma goodbye, and tried to push my fears about her dying out of my head as I left to report a story for the newspaper.

We were a few days away from my twenty-first birthday, and Anthony had rented me a room at a lounge on the Lower East Side. We had food, balloons, and champagne. I asked my mom if we should cancel it, and she said Grandma would have wanted me to have it. Anthony suggested I invite my mom, so I did. I wore a sparkly blue sequin dress, my mom enjoyed herself until Anthony put her in a cab around 11:00 p.m., and he watched my drinking, which I was great about. I barely touched anything but champagne, as far as he knew. But when he left to use the bathroom, and to put my mom in a cab, I chugged vodka like my life depended on it.

* * *

Grandma would have to go back to the nursing home in the west village for rehab, again.

This time, she was smaller, weaker, and more confused.

The Day Room had a pile of games in the corner, a couple of half dead plants, and some drawings taped to the beige wall. It reminded me of my elementary school: a smelly, scary, disgusting prison. Everyone was wearing the same red socks with little white lines on the bottom to keep them from slipping, even though they were all immobile, anyway.

I hated seeing Grandma there, not only because it was painful to watch, but because it was like we had all failed to keep her out of there. She was *not* some corpse waiting to go, she was the love of my fucking life, and, in that Day Room, she was just staring into space like all of the people who were there, but weren't there. She needed someone to constantly talk to her to keep her mind going, but there were no nurses in the room at all.

When I went to visit her, I tried to make extra time to talk to the others who were cognizant enough to hold a conversation. There was a woman named Regina, a little old lady I always went over to, who told me "I'd like to put you somewhere where there is glitter and glamour." I usually brought sunflowers or chocolate, for her, for Grandma, and for another woman named Eve. Sometimes Anthony would stop in with me, and we would all hold hands—I would hold Anthony's hand and my grandma's hand, he would hold my hand and her hand, like a motionless ring-around-the-rosie.

An internal argument between me and the invisible girl started up constantly while I was there.

You have to do something.

There's nothing I can do.

You have to do something. You have to save everyone.

I can't.

You should just kill yourself.

I felt responsible for all of them, and turning my back to get on the elevator on my way out, I felt I was abandoning them. If it was after 7:00 p.m., people were in their rooms, in the darkness, screaming and crying "hello" or "help." It reminded me of the fear I felt as a child, only it was much more horrifying for them, because their parents were nowhere to be found, and they didn't know where they were. Or worse, they knew exactly where they were. All freedom, all ability, all choices, all hope had collapsed.

Stepping into the cool night air, leaving the dark building, I fell apart. It never got easier. I stood frozen on the curb, ashamed to be outside. I didn't want my freedom when so many people didn't have it. I wished I could break it off into pieces and hand it out. *How could people die this way? Why is everyone abandoning them?*

No matter how painful it was, I showed up like clockwork. I punched that square button with a picture of a blue stick figure in a wheelchair that activated the double doors, and I whizzed right through them, signing in at the desk. I waited an extraordinary amount of time for one of the two broken-down elevators to arrive so I could get to her, to Regina, to Eve, and to Grandpa, who didn't recognize any of us anymore, but who I usually stopped to give a kiss to. My aunt stayed by his side far more diligently to feed him and talk to him, despite the fact, my mother later told me, that the two of them actually had a volatile relationship while she was growing up.

Dr. J tried to convince me that I was doing enough for all of them, bringing them joy when I could.

"What else can you do?" she asked, leaving me with the obvious answer.

The fact that there was nothing else made me even more depressed.

She reasoned that I should not drop out of college to sit with her 24/7, that missing a day or two out of the week didn't make me a bad granddaughter.

"Bringing joy to the other people when you have the time is more than enough. Only you can make yourself feel guilty," she said. "You've done so much more for her than most grandchildren would do. Most of the people in there have nobody."

That made me feel even worse.

* * *

"The Abilify would augment the affects of the SSRI, if increasing the anxiety medication doesn't help," said Dr. C during our summer session. "You've been doing well, haven't you? This is because of what's going on with your grandmother, right?"

"Yes," I said.

"Are you still smoking weed?" she asked. "Drinking?"

"Yes," I answered.

"But you're using it smartly, recreationally too, right? Not overusing?"

"I don't think so," I answered.

"As long as you're not only using it when you're upset."

I don't use it when I feel bad, I use it when I want to feel good.

I never did end up taking the Abilify, though. Dr. J explained that with everything going on, the stress of school and work and my personal life, the sadness, the anxiety I was feeling seemed appropriate: a totally normal response.

Dr. J was trying to gently lure me into the acceptance faze, but the invisible little girl saw "surrender" as defeat, instead of freedom.

"Half the battle is stopping the fight against things that you can't change or control. What you can do is enjoy the time you have with each person as you have it, being present in each moment and enjoying it as it is," Dr. J said.

I looked at her like she was crazy.

"Enjoy it? Have you been listening to anything I'm saying about how awful it all is?" I asked in disbelief.

"Yes. And, you do have the choice. Be stuck in the 'can't' or figure out how to live in the 'can.' One will definitely be more challenging, although it will decrease your suffering," she said. "Unfortunately, there are also a lot of things you can do nothing about, and you have to work on building acceptance toward that."

"I think I'm going to need a lobotomy to do any of that."

When I left her office, I didn't get a lobotomy, but I did the next best thing: I got wasted.

* * *

One day during the summer I arrived to see that they just left Grandma in the hallway, staring at the back of someone else's head. Her hair, always coiffed perfectly, was smashed down. She wore no lipstick. Her nails were not done. It made my heart break to see her, to see all of them, lined up in this way, like they were waiting for death.

What had all of them gone through in their lives to end up here?

What had they faced, overcome, to end up like this?

Why do any of us fight and fight through life if this is this how it ends?

All of that surviving—for what?

"Helaina!" she said when she saw me, her usual smile replaced by nervousness she tried to hide.

"I don't know where I am or where I need to go," she said, a flash of panic on her face, where all the happiness had left.

"It's ok, you're in rehab for your hip, but I'm here. We're going to go up to physical therapy now," I said.

"I'm so scared. When you leave, I'm all alone."

This stabbed me like a knife.

"You were always so good at being alone," I said, squeezing her hand and squatting down to meet her eyes. "Please don't be scared when I leave. I know that you're safe. I wouldn't leave you if you weren't safe."

As if reading my mind, she said, "I'm not as tough as I think I am." Then, like a scared child, quietly, "I want to go home."

I took her up to therapy and promised I would be back before she knew it. I treated every time I saw her like it would be the last time, worried that she might die before I got to say "goodbye."

I didn't realize, then, that just getting to say "goodbye" doesn't come close to being there for someone's entire life.

* * *

My grandfather died fifteen minutes after I left the nursing home that day. I was already sitting down at some Mexican restaurant on West Twelfth Street with Anthony, deciding which one of the twelve varieties of margaritas I was going to order first.

"What?" I shouted into the phone when my dad called to give me the news. I flew out of the restaurant, everything around me melting away.

I hadn't even seen Grandpa that day, having spent all of my time with Grandma.

I didn't get to say goodbye.

One of the nurses said she saw, at the time of his death, my grandmother reaching her arms out saying, "Goodbye, see you soon," from her own room.

The floor manager insisted that nobody told Grandma that he had died.

* * *

The ride over to the funeral parlor from the nursing home with my grandmother was so painful, I thought my heart would actually just give in right there, finally reaching its natural limit, if someone really could, in fact, die of a broken heart.

"I wish I didn't love Lucy so I could get the hell out of here," said Uncle John once we arrived at the funeral home in the Bronx. He was fidgeting in that gruff, Irish tough guy way he fidgets, smelling of cigarettes, pacing, rushing three steps forward and stopping, then doing the same in a different direction, adjusting his baseball cap.

"I didn't think she should have come at all," I said, fidgeting with my phone.

Everyone huddled over Grandma's wheelchair. She looked so small, bewildered, and confused under her lipstick and silk shirt that had become too big.

This can't actually be happening.

"Do you want to see him in the casket or should we close it?" my mother asked her.

"Why, he's dead?" Grandma asked.

The dementia caused her to forget the most painful details, which we had to remind her of over and over and over: the nursing home, the hospital, the funeral home, his death, feeling the impact over, and over, and over.

"Yes, he's dead, that's why we're here," my mom and aunt said in a jumble together.

Grandma turned to me and asked, "What do you think?"

"I think we should close it," I said, and everyone got mad at me.

A month later, Grandma got to come home again. Now, she qualified for twenty-four-hour care, but was horribly depressed.

The rotation of home health aides the agency sent made her cry, because their voices were sharp, or their touch was rough, or they didn't let her get up to do things herself (which she physically couldn't anymore). One of them cut her leg by accident and didn't report it, the other one saw her cut leg and didn't report it, either.

"I just wish I could die already," Grandma would say.

Me too, I thought.

Instead, I said, "But I can't live without you," and gave her kiss after kiss until she smiled.

I started to arm myself with a bag of weed at all times, so that when I couldn't get to a bar to drink away a pinched nerve, I could light up immediately on the terrace. I tried to hide it from my parents at first, then became reckless, leaving rolled joints on the floor of my room—which Gucci would sniff, and fortunately, decide he wasn't interested in—and going outside to smoke while they were still awake watching TV.

* * *

At 6:20 a.m. on a Tuesday morning in March 2011, the air was strangely moist, the temperature, stubbornly cool. After saying goodbye to a stranger and making my exit down a hallway I did not recognize, I scrambled through my bag for my phone, thrashing through lipstick and eyeliner.

Gold Street?

I was three blocks from home. I tried to use my phone and stared at a black screen, then remembered it had died the night before. It started coming back to me like sucker-punches to the gut.

I told my parents I would be coming home, and I hadn't.

Never again, never again . . .

I knew they would be worried sick.

I had spent the last several months reassuring them that I was fine, that they could stop worrying about me and the drinking. But my mom was still waking up to the sound of retching and various objects (or myself) clattering to the floor. She got into the habit of staying up almost every weekend night that I went out, but always claimed that she had "just woken up." She'd appear in the small space between her room, my room, and the bathroom to ask how my night was, trying to see what kind of condition I was in. When I started going out on weeknights, the same pattern held true. How my mother was able to function on so little sleep, I will never know. I always told her not to worry, and then I always did it again.

My mother hadn't been able to sleep all the while that I was drunk and passed out at the stranger's house.

She emerged from her room in tears, telling me she texted Anthony to see if I was with him. *Great.* Of course, I wasn't. Now everybody was sleepless and worried.

Several minutes after putting my BlackBerry on the charger, I received a text message from my friend, who I was with the night before. The guy she'd left with and the guy whose place I'd ended up at were not friends, as we had thought, even though we met them all at the bar together. In fact, they didn't even know each other. The stranger was a random person who had approached the group and offered to buy everyone at the Stone Street bar some drinks.

After the usual ritual of throwing up a few times, taking a sleeping pill, throwing it up, and not being able to go back to sleep, I spent seven hours in pain, nauseous, heaving, dizzy, and crying. I was still in awful shape by 4:00 p.m., but I hadn't seen my grandmother the day before, and missing a day was like missing a year.

I was doubled over on the couch as Lynette, the Tuesday aid, wheeled her in. I could barely sit up. I felt like death. My stomach was killing me from ten hours of retching, trying to expel at least ten drinks, plus the Ambien, Nortyrptalin, and Celexa. I had only gotten two hours of sleep.

I held the couch for balance and positioned Grandma's wheelchair so I could sit close enough to hold her hand. She looked straight ahead, so I took both of her hands in mine and gently turned her face toward me. For all that she could not see, understand, or remember, she could still tell that something was not right.

"What's wrong, Helaina?" Grandma asked, her eyes full of worry.

"I'm sick," I said. Her face crumpled and she looked as though it were she who was in pain. I realized then that as much as I suffered her pain with her as though it were happening to me, she had always suffered mine too.

"Oh no," she said. "My baby . . ."

"It's ok," I lied. "I'll be better soon."

I paused for a moment to gently guide her face back toward me, as she had begun staring at the wall again.

"Remember when you used to take care of me when I was little?" I asked.

She nodded and smiled.

"You used to come downstairs with a piece of bread soaked in wine and lay it down on my stomach when I was sick. You said it was an old Italian tradition."

She smiled and said yes, though I could see she didn't remember.

My father didn't like that ritual very much, so we only did it when he wasn't home. It was rare and exciting, and at a young age I became intoxicated and spellbound by the smell of wine.

"When you're sick, I'm sick," Grandma said.

My eyes began to tear up, and I tried my very best not to cry. I knew she'd be able to tell.

I started to sing, "You Are My Sunshine."

Whenever I sang it to her, she usually came in right before the end, finally recognizing and remembering the words, with a very emphatic, "How much I love you."

That day, she took my hand in hers, looked me in the eye, smiled, and in the gentle, warm voice I recognized from so many years ago, recited the entire song like a poem.

I knew that there was a second verse, a sad one that I didn't like and never sang, about "dreaming I held you in my arms and waking up to see you weren't there, and crying," so we never sang that one.

After my grandmother left, my dad appeared in the doorway.

"You know," he said. "I didn't quit drinking for you or Mommy. That was part of it. You have to quit for yourself."

The next day, good as new, I went back up to Grandma's house.

Our new thing was "dancing."

Or rather, simulating dancing.

I downloaded a few cheerful-sounding songs off of Sia's 2010 album, "We Are Born." This was *right* before she exploded onto the pop music scene. Those songs had lots of bells and tambourines and cheerful lyrics, plus, clapping sounds, which made my grandma's body feel motivated to dance. She would raise her arms and twinkle her fingertips to simulate rain and glitter, reaching them out in front of her and shaking her wrists, like she was a wizard sending a love spell over to someone. She let me take her hands in mine, moving them around, even if we were only dancing with our top halves. When she became tired or out of breath, she playfully tossed them away.

Several years later, Sia's "Chandelier" would become a huge international hit. Some girls would see it as a party-girl anthem, a cheer with tiny holes of regret poking through the melody. The rest of us who knew better would see it as a raw ballad of surrender, sadness, maybe even regret, and a Google search will confirm that Sia had been sober for five years.

* * *

In spring of 2011, right before I graduated college, I found myself in the Time Warner Building on Columbus Circle sharing iced tea and cookies with Dr. Patricia Bratt, a psychoanalyst and a director of the Academy of Clinical and Applied Psychoanalysis and the Boston Graduate School of Psychoanalysis.

For my senior work thesis, I was writing a collection of essays based on my experience on 9/11 and living in New York City in the years after.

Dr. Bratt accepted my request for an interview about her work with adolescents and children who have been through trauma, and how that trauma manifests in different people— namely, people like me, who had experienced all of this out of control behavior that didn't exactly fall under the DSM Manual categorization of post-traumatic stress disorder.

Her response to my initial email woke up something in my brain that, until then, had been dormant, unaware of the need for answers it was not actively seeking:

*It is very hard for a young person such as yourself to recover
from a catastrophe like 9/11 without continuous adult
intervention to reconfirm the validity of your feelings. If your
environment didn't provide a supportive and secure foundation, it's very possible to see, in you and many children,
regression, depression, or withdrawal. You could be faced
with manic, risk-taking, aggressive behavior, or even suicide.
Sex, drugs, all sorts of addictions could manifest. Everything
that ordinarily characterizes the fragility of adolescence could
explode exponentially.*

I had prepared questions ahead of time, and I was ready to
find some answers.

We sat across from each other in a floating island of chairs
overlooking Central Park, and I took out my notebook and the
white a tape recorder I had just bought at J&R.

Looking across Central Park, it felt difficult for both of us
to connect with those days of uncertainty, chaos, and persistent
reminders of potential disaster; but we both knew the shakiness
just talking about the events triggered.

"Thank you so much for meeting me," I said.

I was still coming down from the anxious rush of train trans-
fers I didn't usually make, then finding her office building and
calling to her to let her know I was there.

"Sure! Do you want anything? Are you hungry?" she asked.

I had eaten lunch already, so I ordered a chocolate chip cookie
while she ordered a tuna nicoise salad.

I took a deep breath and hit the red button on the tape
recorder.

"So, do you think kids are really naturally resilient?"

"Some people believe that. There's definitely discussion about whether resilience is a 'fixed' or learned trait," she said. "I think it needs to be taught to young children just like any other skill, even before something bad happens. Things like flexibility, confidence, personal problem-solving skills."

"I feel like I never learned any of that," I said. "I don't think I had any resilience."

"I wouldn't be so sure. You managed to stay focused enough to get yourself to college, you've reached out and connected to me. You kept fighting through a mental health system that was relentlessly unhelpful. It's human nature to look at negatives first."

"Maybe," I said, looking down.

"I think you *were* resilient, even when the world was overwhelming," she said, and our food arrived. I left the warm cookie where it was for the time being. "I've seen a lot of kids act out their childhood in extremes."

I pondered this for a second before describing what happened after I broke up with Vin.

"So you were acting out sexually. Maybe you were telling people that you felt out of control, so your body acted out your story for you," she said.

"Things typically go 'out of control' at the developmental level where you were traumatized. So, if you were six, you might regress to being infantile, throwing tantrums. In the case of sexual abuse, you might start injuring your body or develop an eating disorder."

I thought about all of the episodes of crying hysterically, throwing things, screaming, and crumbling on the floor, something I must have thought out loud, muttering, "I thought I was just a fucking psycho."

She smiled.

"No, you weren't. Children need to know that the adult world is there to protect them as best it can. Otherwise, you'd always be asking yourself, 'What's wrong with me, with everyone else, with the world?'"

She paused briefly to motion for the waiter to refill our water glasses.

"You would begin to doubt all your perceptions, feel life is too fragile, and start challenging all rules and boundaries. After all, if nothing is as it seems, why should rules be followed? Why do things to safeguard yourself in an unpredictable, chaotic world?"

"But I'd always been a rule follower. I was never one of those kids who flipped off a teacher or talked back. I never really committed any crimes, unless you count sex in a hotel staircase or underage drinking."

"You knew better than to meet these guys you didn't know and go off with them, I'll bet. But we all have this need to fill a void, to be connected, and when you can't trust your own perception, you look for external validation."

"Through sex?" I asked, grateful that I didn't have a tendency to blush, but most likely giving a tell by the way I kept grabbing for my water glass over and over.

"What kind of emotional validation does an adolescent get?" she asked. "Sexual relationships, affiliation with groups who want to 'go to war' with other people, adults, 'the system'? It's a time of natural, boundary testing. Couple that, especially in early adolescence, with trauma or catastrophe, and you've lit an explosion of identity crises, hormonal overload, impulsive and compulsive behavior. Potential chaos."

"Everything felt like chaos," I said. "My therapist says I created a lot of my own chaos without even knowing it."

"Sometimes we unconsciously make choices to dredge up certain feelings to see that we are able to get ourselves through new disasters. It's the same reason kids go to horror movies."

Not this kid, I thought.

"There is a psychological addiction, almost a compulsive draw to the chemical reaction. Everyone likes a thrill, but in a post-traumatic emotional state you can be training your brain to need-and-survive the threat. The adrenaline rush can become addictive."

She set down her fork, finishing her salad, chewing her last bite. I waited, almost in a trance.

"The feeling that danger is imminent and that we can find a way to survive is exciting. Some people deal with trauma exposure by becoming risk averse, others jump in and keep re-creating threats. People in law enforcement, the military, or emergency medicine confront this adrenaline-loop-challenge every day. They have to be charged up in a prolonged adrenalized state, then come back to mundane reality. It's not an easy transition."

CHAPTER THIRTEEN

These past ten years have shown that America does not give in to fear. The rescue workers who rushed to the scene; the firefighters who charged up the stairs; the passengers who stormed the cockpit—these patriots defined the very nature of courage. Over the years we have also seen a more quiet form of heroism—in the ladder company that lost so many men and still suits up to save lives every day; the businesses that have rebuilt; the burn victim who has bounced back; the families that press on.

—President Barack Obama's remarks on the tenth anniversary of the 9/11 attacks, as released by the White House

J ust get over it! Move on!"

James and I were the only ones left in a restaurant on Front Street by the Seaport, and the bartender, who I knew, raised an eyebrow at me.

Well into his fourth Jack and Coke, James was rambling on about how he was "so tired" of hearing about 9/11. Writing for the local newspaper of Lower Manhattan, it's safe to say he'd been inundated with it all year.

"You don't see anyone making this big a deal over Katrina," he said, loudly. He whipped out his phone and showed me pictures of his home in New Orleans, which had been destroyed by the 2005 hurricane.

"I was getting promotional emails around the five-year anniversary, saying that girls named Katrina would get into clubs or bars and drink for free," he said. "I would love to see the same for guys named Osama."

The bartender shot me a meaningful look. I nodded and made the universal air sign for the check.

"I understand," I said. "I get it. People have moved on down here, you know. But moving on looks different for everyone. Sounds like you're pissed that people don't really know or respect what you went through personally. I would be too."

"Nobody . . . knows," he said, trying, and failing, to button the last button on his corduroy blazer, then reaching for his puffy green down jacket. "I mean, I don't care, man! I don't care. But I had to just move on. So everyone else should too."

I handed the final check to the bartender.

"Sorry about him," I said.

"Don't bring him back here," he said in return. I nodded.

* * *

With the anniversary approaching, I reached out earlier that spring to a few publications, thinking maybe they would want to hear my story. I had made a decision to write about my experience on the day of September 11, 2001 with Mark Statman as an independent study, which turned into a year-long project, rounded out by a collection of essays for my senior thesis project.

Mark made one last observation before we concluded for the year.

"I tell this to my wife all the time, when we talk about our son: you need to feel safe before you can feel happy, or feel love, or anything else. You have to feel safe."

When I let other people hold the pen, it didn't quite go as I had hoped. *The New York Daily News* ran a story in June that made me look a little worse for wear than I'd hoped I would, but I was glad to have it out there.

Until I read the comments.

"A slap on the ass and a black boyfriend ought to set her straight."

"Just another ballad of Jewish suffering."

"If it was so bad, why didn't you move?"

It wasn't as painful to read as the story that ran in the *Chicago Tribune*, though.

I had sent some notes to the editor, and on the morning after Osama bin Laden was tracked down and assassinated, she told me she really thought we should run something for the next day.

The only problem was, I had woken up with this mysterious inability to open my right eye. Tears streamed down like a babbling brook, and every time I tried to open it, I couldn't. I hopped in the car with my parents on the way to the eye doctor, firing off emails to my professors and the supervisor at my internship, when I got the call.

"I really think we should run this," the editor said. *Run what?* I hadn't even thought about what my Op-Ed would be about. I explained the situation.

"I think we should wait. I don't even remember what I sent you . . . I won't have a chance . . . let's just wait until September?"

"Ok," she said. But then, twenty minutes later, she called me back. She was determined, and I wasn't going to blow the opportunity altogether.

"I'll put together what I can then call you for a fact check to go over it with you," she said.

It turned out I had managed to develop two ulcers in my right eye, by the way, which I was almost sorry I could open again the next morning.

I thought there was so much left without an explanation in that Op-Ed, that it almost appeared like a laundry list of every shameful thing I'd ever done, blamed on bin Laden.

Surprisingly, though, based on the comments, it seemed like people were inspired, and even humbled.

Someone else, though, was angry.

"Take your pity party somewhere else and take responsibility for your actions," he wrote. *"People lost their parents. Those are the people who deserve sympathy. Sounds like you were just another American teenager."*

Trevor jumped in to my defense in the comments section, as did other people.

But that was the end of my ever reading the comments section.

For the anniversary, I decided I was going to write something myself, something better—because I was going to get in touch with my former classmates to see if any of them had gone through the same thing.

Through Facebook, I began getting in touch with them, and managed to find sixteen people who were willing to sit down to talk or hop on a call. Over the course of many interviews, I heard about struggles and pain that could have been lifted from my own story.

"I thought I'd never be normal like my friends were."

"I couldn't just relax and have fun. I panicked if plans changed."

"I cut myself. I banged my head against a wall."

"What seemed like a small problem to others felt like a tragedy to me."

"I felt branded, wounded, damaged, and crazy."

"Getting upset was never just getting upset—it lasted for hours, days, and months."

"I cut off friends at the first sign of betrayal, but mostly they were paranoid delusions."

Only a few of my former classmates had tried therapy, and those who did became lost in the same labyrinth of misdiagnosis and prescription pills. Some had become shut-ins, some became addicts, but whatever their story, normal teen angst seemed to be amplified, and their parents—caring, supportive—watched helplessly as the happy children they loved receded into a dark place nobody could reach.

The most common thing I heard was, "I've been waiting ten years for someone to ask me my story."

Like James, they felt that their pain had just been passed over.

They didn't volunteer themselves, to other people, to the media, because they didn't want to sound like they were "bragging." They did not believe anyone would understand—or that it mattered. Or, they were horrified listening to ill-informed, insensitive accounts of the day from people who hadn't been there, people who "didn't know what it was like to know that your parents could no longer protect you," that no one could. They were annoyed with the politicians who used 9/11 to grandstand on some sort of issue, or attack their opponent for saying anything questionable about New York or New York Values.

The main reason they stayed silent, though, was because nobody ever asked.

* * *

James, full of Jack and Coke, walked with me over to the water, where we sat on a bench, the reflection from the Watchtower sign creating a red path of light across the water that led right up to the pebbles and garbage on shore at our feet. I lit up a cigarette, then lit up another one using the one in my mouth, and handed it to him. It was chilly, but not freezing, the breeze from the water prompting me to pull my leather jacket closed more tightly.

"You could always write your story," I offered. "I'm going to write mine. I don't know if anyone will care, but, we'll see."

"It only takes one person to care," he said. "Look at Mitch Albom. He was a sports writer. A sports writer!" he shouted into the river to nobody in particular, but consequentially, to me. "*Tuesdays with Morrie* got only one 'Yes', and it turned out to be the best-selling memoir of all time."

"Well, if you ever decide you want to write a book about what happened to you, I promise, I'll read it," I said, dropping my cigarette and stomping it out. "I'll talk to you soon. Get home safe."

I headed over to a bar across from the former Fulton Fish Market, where I was meeting a man named JC who had promised me a ride on his motorcycle as a thank you for writing his brother's story for *amNewYork*.

I arrived to see him leaning on the bike outside, wearing black boots and a long braid draped over his shoulder, underneath a red bandana. He was wearing a leather jacket that was covered with patches and words, on the back was an American Flag, an Eagle, the Towers, and a message: *Never Forgive, Never Forget*.

JC, his sister, and his brother all worked in the World Trade Center. He and his sister got out in time. His brother, an electrician, did not. His brother's motorcycle was now parked in the window of the 9/11 Memorial Preview Site on Vesey Street, decorated with tiny illustrations of Curious George, his favorite character.

"My brother was the kind of guy you wanted your daughter to date. He always said it was distracting working in that Tower, all of the pretty girls who worked there. But he was shy," JC said, stopping to turn his beer bottle upside down into his mouth. "He tried to make eye contact with them, though."

I took a long sip of my White Russian, which I didn't even want.

"They never found him, but every year the Medical Examiner's Office holds a service for the victims' families, people who maybe only had found an elbow, or a kneecap, who didn't have anything to bury," he said.

The family hosted a service for his brother before any remains were found, a memorial that eight hundred people showed up to, people he didn't even know.

"You don't realize how many lives someone touches until something like this happens," he said. "The mayor wants this to be the last year we hold the ceremony with the names read, but I don't need his permission to remember my brother. I think about him every day."

He got up to get another round, and I checked my cell phone. Nothing from Anthony, so I was still in the clear.

"You know," he said when he returned, with another White Russian for me, "I tried to enlist in the Army, but they denied me. They could tell I was out for revenge. They told me, 'Come back in three years, and if you still want to go, you can go.'"

"You didn't go back, I'm guessing."

"No. That's probably for the best. Those guys want to put you in a burka, you know."

"You're still a devout Catholic?"

"Yes."

"Lots of people lost their religion after what happened."

"Lots of people did. But God doesn't do these things," he said, clunking his beer down on the table, shrugging his jacket on, and holding out his hand. "People do."

With that, we stepped outside, he handed me a helmet, and we were off on his motorcycle, heading toward the Brooklyn Bridge.

* * *

Six weeks later, on October 27, 2011, I woke up after my Halloween party and ran to the bathroom. When I was finally able to pull myself up off of the cool tiles of the floor, I looked around the apartment and thought, *what the fuck happened here?*

My Blackberry was resting in a puddle of spilled Rum. There were chicken nuggets on the terrace. The floor was covered in sticky black footprints. Somehow, blue paint had gotten all over my nurse's costume.

I picked up my digital camera, scrolling through for clues.

I'd had the balls to invite the guy I'd cheated on Anthony with a few nights before, a guy I had no interest in, who I thought was gay, frankly. But after enough drinks, I had pulled open the snaps of my dress that closed all the way down the front, and my body had gone into autopilot. Sick as a dog the next day, I had asked Anthony to leave work early to meet me at his apartment because I wasn't feeling well, and I needed him.

I put the camera down and took a deep breath. I crawled back into bed and turned to look at Anthony, who was still asleep, and it all came back to me.

I had said I wasn't going to drink until midnight, and I hadn't. Then, at midnight, I made a drink that was 90 percent vodka, 10 percent juice, and mixed it with weed, something I knew I couldn't do.

Then, nothing.

I ran back to the bathroom, stayed there for a while, and climbed, once again, back into bed, blotting my forehead with a wet, cold paper towel.

Anthony turned to me and said, "How much longer are you going to keep doing this to yourself?"

I picked up my Blackberry, which, miraculously, would work for a few more minutes, and sent an email with one line to Dr. J.

"Do you know of any twelve-step meetings people under the age of fifty go to?"

I was surprised that I'd even though of it, but the thought must have been waiting in the back of my mind after I read about those meetings in Caroline Knapp's *Drinking, A Love Story* a few months before.

The seed had been planted, all the way down there at rock bottom, just waiting to see some light.

PART FOUR

CHAPTER FOURTEEN

There's something about sober living and sober thinking, about facing long afternoons without the numbing distraction of anesthesia, that disabuses you of the belief in the externals, shows you that strength and hope come not from circumstances or the acquisition of things, but from the simple accumulation of active experience, from gritting the teeth and checking the items off the list, one by one, even if it's painful and you're afraid. When you drink, you can't do that. You can't make the distinction between getting through painful feelings and getting away from them.

—Caroline Knapp, *Drinking: A Love Story*

D r. J sent me a list of meeting suggestions, so, that Friday night, I went into the basement of a church on the Upper East Side. The name of the meeting was Fearless, because apparently, there were so many of these meetings in New York City that they each had names.

"Be careful," my dad said before I left to get on the 6 train to Seventy-Seventh Street. "You don't know what kind of people will be there."

I was less afraid of the people who would be there than I was of drinking again.

As soon as I entered, I wondered, *am I in the right place?*

It was a plush room by a fireplace, with well-dressed people talking and laughing.

A sign hung over the mantle:

False

Evidence

Appearing

Real.

Everyone looked so happy, so comfortable.

The woman next to me held out her hand.

"Hi! I'm Mary," she said.

"Oh hi! I'm Helaina . . . er, this is my first meeting."

"That's terrific!" she said back. The woman was in her forties, had blond hair done up in a clip, and wore a purple cashmere sweater with a satin scarf. She smelled like Chanel No. 5, which wafted off of her wrist as she scribbled down her number for me on the back of a piece of paper.

Wow, I thought. *She's friendly.*

"Try to make ninety meetings in ninety days," she said. "Call me or text me anytime just to say hi, or if you have any questions."

I smiled gratefully, and with a few minutes left before 7:00 p.m., decided to walk over to the front of the room where two women were sitting at a table covered in brochures and books.

"Hi," I said to the woman with the black hair first, smiling at the woman next to her, an older woman with straw-colored hair and blue eyes.

"This is actually my first meeting, I'm not sure if I need to do anything . . . ."

"Welcome! That's fantastic. No, nothing you need to do, except you can take one of these," she reached underneath the table and handed me a manila envelope.

"Here's your newcomer packet. It has a copy of *Living Sober*, a meeting book, and some pamphlets."

"Thanks!" I smiled and went back to my seat.

Why would Dad have told me to be careful? This is awesome!

Someone rang a bell, and the woman with the dark hair began talking about how the group was not affiliated with any religion, and was not governed by anyone in particular. She said that everything that was said in the room should stay in the room.

I guess everyone really trusts each other.

"Is this anyone's first meeting?" she asked.

I didn't raise my hand, but she didn't call me out on it.

"Is anyone counting days from one to ninety?"

Some people announced how many days they had, and I thought they sounded like a lot: thirty-eight, sixty-six, eighty-six. Those paled in comparisons to the anniversaries, though: one year, seven years, twenty-five years. Everyone clapped whenever someone announced their number, so I clapped too.

After all of that business was done, the woman with the straw-colored hair began talking, telling her whole story, explaining how drinking was a relief, something to look forward to, how she felt coddled and taken care of, which I understood. I nodded.

"Now, I have to get out of my own head and in the moment. My sponsor asked me today, 'Are you ok?' If you don't feel okay, you're thinking about the past or the future. In this moment, you're okay." Fifteen minutes later, she ended with, "The war is over. You never have to drink again."

Someone passed around a basket.

"You don't have to put anything in there today," Mary whispered.

After that, people began raising their hands and saying what was on their mind. One girl who looked about my age said, "My family keeps asking me if I'm sure, but I know that I'm sure, because people who drink normally don't have the thought, 'Am I an alcoholic.' So it doesn't matter if they don't understand. Only I need to understand." A man held up a finger signaling that her time was up.

I listened to other people talk and took notes on the back of a pamphlet, because I liked the way they put their feelings into words. With ten minutes left before 8:00 p.m., I raised my hand.

"I'm Helaina, and I think I'm an alcoholic, this is my first meeting ever . . . ."

Suddenly the room erupted into this roar of applause, like I had just scored the game-winning home run.

"I chose this meeting because of the name. I've been living in fear for ten years." I told my entire story, what happened on 9/11 and after. I'm sure I went over the three-minute sharing period, but nobody stopped me or told me to wrap it up.

"I'm afraid I wont be able to handle it when the impulse comes," I concluded.

At the end, they all stood in a circle and held hands and said something. I held Mary's hand, and some stranger's hand, and just watched the group. One last round of applause, and it was over.

But before I could put my pen back in my purse, a small group had formed around me.

"Could I give you my number?" asked a Japanese girl in a bomber jacket with a huge scarf wrapped around her neck. "I related to what you said so much. We should have coffee."

Startled, I said, "Of course, yes . . ." and took down her number.

More women moved in, some handing me their business cards, circling their cell in red pen, another invited me out to dinner with the group.

Holy shit, where were you guys when I was in school?

One last woman made her way through the crowd.

"Here's your newcomer packet!" she chirped. "I'm Emma."

"Oh, I already have one, but thank you." I said.

I took her number, too, and walked twenty blocks up to Anthony's new apartment on Ninety-Fifth Street.

After he sold his business for much less than it was worth and began working in the flower market doing wholesale, he had qualified for some sort of rent discount program in a fancy doorman building.

After he went to sleep—he woke up at 4:00 a.m. now for work at the market on Twenty-Eighth Street and Sixth Avenue—I sat on the toilet of his studio apartment reading through the contents of the newcomer packet and smoking a joint.

The following Wednesday, after another, much larger meeting at another church, I sat with Emma at the diner on Eighty-Ninth and Third on the Upper East Side. Emma, it turned out, had a condition that deemed her legally blind. She could see patches of color, almost like tunnels, and could also recognize people when she was very close their faces. She reminded me a bit of a Barbie, save for the fact that one of her front teeth crossed slightly over the other, and, well, there was the eye thing . . . but she was exactly what you'd expect from an Upper East Side real estate agent: blonde highlights, a furry coat, sequin Ugg boots, shimmering lip gloss, and the latest Gucci bag, all covered in a cloud of sweet smelling French perfume.

"How many days do you have again?" she asked. "Twelve," I said. "I haven't had a drink in twelve days."

"Are you doing any other drugs?"

"Well, I smoked weed," I said. "Sometimes."

"You *smoked*, or you *smoke*?"

"Once in a while, I still smoke," I said, stumbling over my words because I knew what was most likely coming next. She was going to try and stop me.

"Well, maybe you should stop counting days then."

"What! Why? I thought this was about alcohol," I said.

"Think about it this way," she said as she held up the menu right to her face so she could read the offerings. "Are you reaching for something outside of yourself to feel something?"

Fuck.

On the way to Anthony's, only a few blocks away, I called one of my professors from college who I still kept in touch with. He told me to call him after my meeting, a meeting he knew I was going to because it was my explanation for not going to see his son's band.

"What's your program?" he asked.

"What?"

"*What's your program?*"

I had no idea how to answer that.

"Helaina," he said with an exasperated laugh. "I'm trying to tell you I'm in the program too."

As I rolled a joint, I listened to him explain how he had a hard time with the notion of giving everything up.

"As a writer, I worried plenty about how much I would suck. But I've done some of my best writing in sobriety," he said.

I continued to read *Living Sober*, thinking, *geez, this book could be about me, and it was written forty freaking years ago.*

I wanted to finish what weed I had left, so, three days later, I smoked my last joint, making my official sobriety date Saturday, November 12, 2011.

"Okay," I told Emma at that night's meeting. "I'm ready. But I'm kind of afraid."

"Of course you're afraid!" Emma said. "We're all afraid. We all live with this fear in every aspect of our daily lives that other people don't. Why do you think we all drank?"

I was just one day sober when I accepted an invite to a sober party uptown after the meeting. The people at this party could have easily been gathered together inside the hottest club West Chelsea had to offer. Not only did they look cool as hell, but they were the happiest crowd of people I'd seen in a long, long time, and the most cheerful I'd ever seen sans alcohol. All of them were in the program—some had five years, some five months, others had decades.

I awkwardly stood in the doorway clutching a red plastic cup full of seltzer and watching dozens of people laughing, chatting, dancing, and singing, doing everything they normally would have if there had been vodka in the punch. I could barely move from that doorway, staring at my phone which was not getting any messages or emails, looking out at a bunch of people I didn't know. They looked like they were comfortable with themselves. The laughter was real. The friendship was genuine; you could almost feel the warmth radiating out of them. They all had this ease about them that, even at my drunkest, I couldn't quite cultivate.

Best of all, none of them looked like they were dying to escape—but I was. I thought about booking it, right there. Whatever social anxiety I had managed to stifle was springing up like a Jack-In-The-Box, telling me that I needed to get out of there, fast. I could easily get more weed. I could easily get a bottle. I could try again next year.

But someone saw me standing there, in the bathroom door-frame, and they pulled me into the room, and they sat me on the couch.

Two hours passed in a happy rush, and I left feeling like I had just won some sort of award.

After that, Emma and I started meeting at a diner to read out loud from our own respective copies of another book, one that talked about what work we had to do to make me better, to make me stop drinking, but also, to try and figure out how to have a life without it.

How to have a life at all, I thought.

I had spent so much time just "getting through life" that besides being a good student, a good writer, and a loving grand-daughter, I had no idea who I was.

"We're going to get you back to the girl you were meant to be before 9/11," Emma said. "Before you picked up your first drink."

I hit that program hard—since I was only a few months out of college, I took to stepwork like it was a make-or-break senior work project, a final exam. I finished work in two nights that took some people months, dragging their feet along. I wanted this, badly. Emma called me her "perfect little student," which felt a little condescending, but no matter. I'd take the compliment.

* * *

I learned the "one day at a time" mentality, which made life easier, and provided a lot of relief.

"Just worry about the next hour. The next few hours. Stay here, because you don't have to worry about being sober tomorrow, or what's happening tomorrow. Stay here."

I went to a meeting every day. I called three girls every day just to talk. I stayed out of bars. I went to movies with Anthony and cuddled with his dogs more. When the Christmas season rolled around, I felt happy, going upstairs and trying to simulate decorating the tree with Grandma and one of the new, more caring home health aids my mom had lobbied for.

But I braced myself for the big night, because, during Christmas dinners past, you could always find me ducking into my room to hide between courses. I felt incredibly uncomfortable at the table. I usually held tight and counted the minutes before I could escape and meet up with my friends for a drink (or four). None of my new friends, either, punched the air and declared, "Yeah, I'm going home for the holidays!" It was more like a dejected sigh of resignation. Understandably, many of us either drank to get through it, or got through it to drink.

The weekend before the holiday, I walked outside to find myself in the middle of SantaCon, a weird parade of young people dressed up as Santa or scantily clad Mrs. Claus who were taking to the city's bars and restaurants, later spilling out onto the streets where they continued drinking.

The original idea for SantaCon, I later found, started off as a very merry concept. People would dress up and parade through the streets spreading goodwill and good cheer, singing Christmas carols, giving out gifts to strangers, and collecting cans for charity. Unfortunately, whatever that once was had been completely overhauled into an event where adults acted like out-of-control kids.

That day, the "SantaConers" started early, and the neighborhood smelled like one big brewery. Last time I checked, walking down the street and drinking from clear, plastic cups full of beer was illegal, but it seems to be tolerated on SantaCon day. By 1:00 p.m., people were urinating in public, passing out in the street, keeling over on the sidewalk, screaming profanities, and throwing up in the park.

My elderly neighbors were pushed and knocked over, and children were shoved aside. As they dodged profanity-screaming elves and belligerent reindeer running amuck, I heard one little boy ask his father, "Daddy, why are Santa and the reindeer acting like that?" Another little girl hid underneath her mother's coat, and others literally ran away crying, repeatedly looking back over their shoulders in terror as the crowds gained momentum. A bunch of drunks were shouting the words to Jingle Bells as though preparing to charge into battle—think Gerard Butler shouting "This Is Sparta!" in the movie *300*.

All I could think was, *Holy shit, I'm glad that's not me.* Not that it would have been me—I wouldn't have been caught dead at a pub crawl. Still, as someone who understood the need to take a vacation from reality, I saw something familiar as I looked into the glazed eyes of one slutty Mrs. Claus: the need to get obliterated, and what a mess it looks like when you do.

"Hey, do you want me to cover this Santa thing that's happening?" I called James on his cell.

"Yeah, go for it," he said.

I went into a deli where a group had congregated, hoping to get some quotes from people who were actually standing still.

One young man dressed as Jack the Pumpkin King could not have depicted a Nightmare Before Christmas any better.

The command, "Don't take my name," indicated that there was enough self-awareness to cause some semblance of embarrassment.

"Okay, so, what brings you guys out here today?" I opened, not putting too much thought into the question. I had a feeling they would say whatever they wanted.

"Wait a second," a slutty elf chimed in as I took notes on my iPhone. "You're clearly not a recorder."

I looked at her, confused.

"She said she's a recorder, but she's not," she slurred suspiciously, raising her voice, looking at Jack the Pumpkin King. "Does she look like a flute to you?"

"Reporter," I clarified. "I'm a reporter."

After letting the realization marinate, she huffed her reply.

"That's not a Christmas character!"

I had to admit that the tamer members of the bunch looked like they were having a great time, and that triggered something that I had struggled with my whole life: fear of missing out. Such a feeling was an evil Grinch that presented itself whenever something was going on without my involvement. The Grinch pointed a big hairy finger directly at my fear of what other people thought of me, whether I looked popular, cool, or pretty enough. Watching them parade by, erupting in laughter, I heard my aunt's enabling voice in the back of my head.

"You're young, you're supposed to go out and have fun," she would say. "When I was your age, I had one thousand friends and we went out every weekend. This is your time."

Actually, it was not in the back of my head. It was right in front of me, on Christmas Eve. Talking to her and my mom together was often like going into the *Shark Tank*, but instead of hundreds of thousands of dollars in investment capital, you got "all in fun" criticism and unsolicited opinions. I braced myself. Throughout the day, my mind had replayed old tapes, churning up anxiety and forming negative expectations that created a nice big bubble of dread in the pit of my stomach. I wasn't sure if I was ready for the well-intentioned, unsolicited advice that would salt the wounds of my own insecurities.

"Are you going to any parties?" my aunt asked as she spooned her baked ziti onto my plate, knowing that I don't eat pasta.

"Yes," I said, with hesitation. "There's a party at this girl's house. . . ."

"What kind of party? Is it on the Lower East Side? Where are the cool people going these days?"

In hindsight, I know that telling her it was a sober party was a mistake.

"What are you going to do, have no life anymore?" she cried in response.

"Those people are lame. Go do something fun. Live it up!" my mom said.

Fortunately, I had been given one of my gifts early: nearly twenty new numbers in my phone, all belonging to friends and other women in my support network who would listen, laugh, and help me feel true relief. Calling in their support was more comforting than any amount of Baileys.

I furiously texted Emma, who reassured me, "Soon, you are going to be able to go anywhere and do anything you want. This is a very short period of time that you are using to get ready for the best years of your life."

Throughout the night, I surreptitiously and periodically backed away into my room, reaching out to girls who knew how to turn off the valve that began steaming inside me when my uncle raised his voice. We ran through a list of what I was grateful for, because it's easy to see what's wrong and get annoyed, but it takes practice to start learning how to see the good in people and in each situation.

Perhaps even more useful was the advice to "Hum a little tune, and pretend that you're watching and listening to someone else's family."

Learning to be patient and to accept my family as they are, instead of how I wished they would be, took time. They were fallible and flawed, just like me, just like all of us. When I stopped expecting them to be anything else, though, I started seeing the best in them, which wasn't hard once I had the right lenses on.

Eventually, I was able to stay present, no longer jumping out of my skin or chomping at the bit to escape any given situation. Despite temptation, I continued making my own transition to adulthood, gripping reality tightly even when I wanted to let go through hot toddies and spiked cider. There were days that I wished I could drink up a bit of that warm, fuzzy feeling of relaxation to take the edge off, but I was to remind myself that I usually couldn't stop at "a bit" and that the trade-off was better.

Eventually, I found what Emma said to hold true: I could go anywhere and have a good time, and I never felt like I was being short-changed just because I wasn't drinking.

My nights started to balloon up with authentic laughter and fun, sometimes at a "normal" party, sometimes at a sober one, sometimes at a dinner party full of drinkers. Regardless, I knew for sure that I was definitely not missing out on anything, despite what my aunt liked to insist.

The realization that I finally knew what real peace and happiness felt like was a very merry feeling.

* * *

Emma and I hit a wall when I got to step five. She took issue with the fact that I took sleeping pills, something she had previously abused back while she was still drinking. I had long since stopped taking them to go back to sleep in the mornings, ever since Aaron was out of the picture; but she told me to tell her every time I needed to take one.

Before long, she decided to drop a bomb on me, at the advice of her own sponsor, someone who belonged to a sub-group of the program who encouraged people to throw away their medications and live their lives like foot soldiers who would forever be sick.

"You should go to a meeting for people who use drugs before we go any further," she said.

"I don't abuse them," I told her. "I take them when I can't sleep, which is most nights."

"Then maybe you need to find someone who's okay with that," she said.

She still hosted my ninety-day celebration in the party room of her Upper East Side apartment building, just a block from Anthony's building.

If you were there, it would have been easy to see how I put on six pounds in those first few months. There were tons of cupcakes with cartoon character's faces on them, candy, cookies, pies, and more two-liter bottles of carbonated drinks than you could count lined up on a marble tabletop next to a bucket of ice and highball glasses.

Anthony sat off to the side and spoke to a middle-aged woman I had become friendly with.

"Do you see a difference?" she asked.

"It's like night and day," he said. "It's unbelievable."

"Just wait," she said. "It keeps getting better."

After the natural high from my party faded, the reality of trying to find a new sponsor set in. I was already sitting on this notebook full of what's known as "moral inventory," a giant list, with a bunch of columns, detailing everything from the past twenty-two years of my life that I felt bad about. The people who hurt me, the people I felt betrayed me, what they did, what I feared, family, friends, ex-boyfriends, everyone was on that list. I was supposed to figure out what my own "part in it" had been, which was a tall order.

Another woman in the program who also had PTSD said she would read it with me, if I wanted. Her name was Tina, and she always seemed a bit harried, thinking about something else, just a little bit ahead of where we were.

But there was also an understanding between us, the idea that, after what we had been through, we were a bit more fragile than the rest, and I trusted her to be honest with me, but to be kind, too.

"Your part in that one is selfish," she said as she began ticking off my "part" in relation to one particular name on my list.

"Being self-centered. Dishonest, too. Write it down," she said, pacing the room as I sat, open-jawed, across from her with my notebook.

"How?" I asked.

"You were so worried about your own needs and your own feelings that you didn't care what it did to Vin. You stayed with him when you knew it was the wrong thing. You cheated on him. You tried to keep him away from other people. You told him what to do to try to make yourself feel safe."

Oh boy.

"Yeah, but, he ruined my life."

"Has he really ruined your life?"

I thought about it, but I had nothing.

"He hasn't ruined anything," Tina said. "If he has, I can't see it."

Five hours later, we had done "the fifth step." She understood all of the baggage I carried around with me, the hurt, the shame, the embarrassment, the resentment, the traumas that had spawned from that initial big one, creating evil offspring that I had to learn to let go.

As we walked to the train, she left me with a couple of parting suggestions, which were "only suggestions."

"You should try to change the voice in your head to something kind and forgiving. How would you talk to a friend if she told you these things? You have to be soothing to yourself."

I nodded.

"And stop letting these things and these people have so much say. Consider the source. Consider the quality of the people who are bothering you so much. How much weight do you want to give those opinions?"

She had a point.

Before I descended into the subway station, she added one more thought.

"Something has definitely been looking out for you. After hearing all of that, I think you're lucky to be alive. Have faith in something."

* * *

The cravings subsided after ninety days, and that was no longer the harder part, especially not with a community and support network around me. It was being totally present in the mess of my mind, and being willing to clean it up, slowly and painfully, and the fact that I needed prescription medication to sleep was making finding another sponsor incredibly challenging. I didn't really understand why, since the "rules" said that it's perfectly acceptable—encouraged, even to seek outside help from doctors, which other people in the program are not (unless, you know, they actually are).

Right at the cusp of my wit's end came Ava, who turned out to be just as life-changing for me as Dr. A, and who I butted heads with just as hard.

When I first saw Ava after we spoke on the phone, I thought, *no fucking way*.

She was stick-figure thin, wearing black leather leggings and four-inch red wedge heels. She was also wearing a big, shaggy white vest that looked like it was made from a sick, old lamb, and had long, straight, jet black hair streaked with bright blue. Several tattoos stuck out from under her sleeve.

"I can't lose another sponsor," I told her in the beginning.

"I will take you through all twelve of these steps," she said. "I promise."

It was not an easy road. My first year was chaotic—being fully present and awake, with pores all open, was painful. That scared, invisible girl emerged with full force, with stronger panic attacks, throwing bigger tantrums, creating bigger fears, and there was no pacifier. I was saturated in reality.

"Taking your own fears and anxieties out on other people because of what you went through is not fair," Dr. J said. "It's one of the reasons that people left, quickly. You have to do your best to keep that anxiety from spreading to the people around you."

I leaned on those first sponsors heavily, eager to do the work but also hoping that someone could talk me down from what was causing my urge to use, too. I was transferring this dependence off of alcohol, and off of Anthony, onto other people once again. Women, this time, so healthier, but still not ideal.

The program put a lot of emphasis on doing things for others to "get out of yourself." That meant anything from volunteering to making coffee at a meeting or just listening to a friend.

"I love animals, but I can't go into a shelter," I said. "It's too hard for me."

"Well," Ava offered. "Could you offer to help by using skills you have, like writing? Or maybe social media?"

So I began uploading photos and descriptions of animals coming into a Brooklyn animal rescue, posting them to two pet adoption sites every weekend. While some of the pictures upset me, my perspective slowly began to change, focusing on the people out there who cared enough to dedicate their lives to helping them. Because of them, these little guys would get a second chance at a good life.

Ava and I did another fifth step, working through the memories and the resentments that hadn't quite gotten shaken out of my head during that first round six months earlier

"You have to act like a woman of grace and dignity to be one, behave as though everyone were watching your every move, even if you think nobody is watching," Ava said as she smoked cigarettes outside the bedroom window of her apartment, in a neighboring building from Aaron that was part of the same complex.

I was about to turn twenty-three, so I guess I could be considered a "woman."

"Okay, got it. Only do what feels like the right thing. I'm with you," I said.

"Let's get out of here," she said, stubbing her cigarette out on the ledge. "I want pancakes. Bring the book with you."

We walked to the diner on the corner of Twenty-Eighth and Ninth Avenue, and I re-opened my notebook.

"You stayed in a situation that was abusive and unhealthy for a long time because of the fear of leaving," she offered as she poured syrup over her eggs and bacon at the Moonlight Diner on the corner of Ninth Avenue. "Going forward, you'll want to make a commitment to yourself not to stay in any relationships that aren't good for you, even if leaving is painful."

At the end of the third day—because this time, it took three damn days to get through it all—she said, "Victims don't want to take responsibility for their actions. They point to something someone else did to 'make' them feel a certain way, which keeps them from having to change anything. I can tell that's not you. You've always had a desire to get better, but you probably couldn't clearly see how you were keeping yourself from really being able to do that."

She told me to go home and do nothing but meditate for an hour. After that, I was free to do whatever I wanted.

* * *

Soon, it became time to address the social anxiety, which Ava framed like this.

"Instead of thinking about what you'll get from a party, or a dinner, and what people will be thinking about you, why don't you think about what you can bring to the situation?"

Once I started thinking about it that way, after clearing out all the self-doubt and paranoia and threat assessments, I was suddenly the first person to crack a dirty joke or break the ice and keep the conversation alive. I hadn't even known that person was inside of me, but when I focused on other people, I had less time to dwell on whatever I felt was still dark inside of me and what my own expectations were.

Ava had me make a list of all of the qualities and characteristics I wanted to emulate. I wrote them in a notebook with a really nice, sparkly pen, the kind that makes you want to write in your best handwriting, and I read them to myself every day.

Modest, confident, compassionate, grateful, tranquil, adult, I trust myself, I stay present with the person I'm with, I trust in a greater plan, I feel supported and protected, loyal, brave, content, self-reliant, self-sufficient, tolerance, stable, self-accepting, equal to other women, accepting of differences, accepting of powerlessness over others behavior, trusting, unassuming.

"Have faith, that one day, you will become all of those things."

As I neared the big one-year mark, on October 17, a few blocks away from our apartment, a man left a truck outside of the Federal Reserve building. It was the corner of the block where I got my nails done. The student, Quazi Mohammad Rezwanul Ahsan Nafis, believed he was going to detonate a one-thousand-pound truck bomb outside of the building—but the whole thing was a sting operation, so nothing was set off.

I remember texting Ava, and her response being, "We don't dwell in fear and self-pity," which I found very insensitive.

"I'm not dwelling," I immediately texted back in defense. "I'm just sharing this with you."

"All I can do is pass along to you what was passed along to me," she replied.

I grumbled to myself, texting Dr. J, who said, "She, like you, is just human. She doesn't have all the answers."

I was leaning on Ava the way I had always leaned on Vin, Aaron, John, Anthony, and Dr. J, clinging to them to keep from drowning. Now, almost comically, it was like I realized the water had only been two feet deep all along.

A small part of me, even though I was irritated, and slightly afraid, began to understand that if I kept looking for people to have the reaction I wanted, a specific message of comfort or reassurance, I was going to bring even more grief on myself when that expectation fell through.

Nobody else is going to make you feel safe.

So, I stopped thrashing around and grasping at them, and simply stood up.

Dr. J was answering my texts less and less, and the more silent she was, the more apparent it became that I could get myself through what felt like an "anxiety emergency" on my own.

* * *

The time came, exactly one year and one month after I got sober, that I had to break up with Anthony, who I had been faithful to for the past year, and on and off with for two more. I had tried everything to make it work, in sobriety: breaks, compromises, and acceptance. What I wanted—intimacy, emotional vulnerability, a strong connection, the ability to build a life together—was not unhealthy, but we wanted different things.

At his cousin's wedding, he looked over at me from the altar where he stood as a groomsman, and must have thought I was losing it. The officiant marrying his cousin and new wife could barely read, had a thick Staten Island accent, and looked like she had just been picked up from the hotel bar. But there I was, sobbing, taking a tissue from Anthony's sister, because I knew it would never be us up there. I felt tears rolling behind my ears, down my neck, as I tried to wrap my head around the concept of loving someone and still having to walk away from them.

At the reception, Anthony's relatives talked about how they hoped it would "be us next," and I sat at the table with the rest of his family, acting weird and sullen "for no reason."

At some point, my phone buzzed in my lap.

Did you hear what happened at that kindergarten? With the shooter?

I Googled it and saw "Sandy Hook" and "Kids dead."

What's going to happen to all of those kids?

CHAPTER FIFTEEN

This one moment—Now—is the only thing you can never escape from, the one constant factor in your life. No matter what happens, no matter how much your life changes, one thing is certain: it's always Now. I am not the content of my life. I am the Now.

—Eckhart Tolle, *Stillness Speaks*

I can't leave him," I told Dr. J that Monday. "It's right before Christmas. This is so cruel."

"So you're going to go through the pain of pretending everything is okay on Christmas and *then* do it?"

I sniffled, searching for another reason not to do what felt too painful.

"He keeps me safe," I said.

"How?" she asked.

Just one simple word took this veil off my eyes. I had no answer. I started a sentence, and stopped, and started again.

"You kept yourself safe," she said.

"You want a healthy, functioning relationship, and you're being hard on yourself for asking for what you want. But it's what you should want. You're not being selfish. You *should* be talking about moving in together after three years. That's the reality."

I wailed like a baby and threw myself, face down, on the couch.

"You can't hide behind a text, either," she said. "You have to call him."

* * *

I continued to take the freelance assignments I was offered, or that I went out and hunted down. I covered news about how a community rallied to support a toddler with cancer and a theater program that gave at-risk high school kids something meaningful to do. I even began to do restaurant reviews. At charity events, I covered red carpets where headset-clad PR people ushered celebrities along the media line, and I balked at the stupid young "reporters" who would ask celebrities dumb questions about their marriage or fashion or some food trend, when I wanted to know why the cause mattered to them and what their actual involvement was beyond lending a name to the organization.

I would get home and tell Grandma about what I was writing, hoping she would understand. The dementia was progressing like we knew it would, her body following suit, slowly caving into itself, hunching over, leaking from different places. Her breathing became more shallow, but she still clung to life, clung to me. There was always a home health aid sitting at the table where we used to sit together, but I quickly learned to be comfortable hugging and kissing Grandma in front of her. Grandma would be wrapped in a blanket, staring not at the TV but ahead of her, somewhere far off, and I would slowly get to eye level with her, and put my arm around her, and touch my forehead to hers, and say, "Hello, love of my life!" and she would smile.

My mother still bought cards from "Grandma" for my birthday, Christmas, and Easter. She'd hold the pen for my grandma to sign her name with, creating a wobbly scribble next to some X's and O's. My mother always wrote, "To Helaina, the love of my life," which is what Grandma had always called me. Grandma turned ninety-five, then ninety-six, then ninety-seven, and we got her gifts on holidays and birthdays and "just because." My mom bought her tops, scarves, and perfume to cover up the smell of ointment. I got her costume jewelry with big stones in hopes that she'd be able to see them sparkle, her eyesight lost to something known as macular degeneration. We didn't know how long she'd be around to use these gifts, or if she was aware that she was wearing them, but that wasn't the point.

"I'm so mixed up I don't know who I am," she'd say.

"I feel that way sometimes, too," I'd say as I nestled my head in her neck. "But you're the love of my life. That's always who you were and who you'll always be."

"How did you find me?" she'd ask, no longer recognizing that she was in her own home.

"I always know where to find you," I'd assure her. Some days I ran myself ragged trying to fit time in, and my dad would always try to get me to give myself a break.

"She won't even remember you were there, honey," he'd say.

"Maybe not," I'd respond over my shoulder, juggling a can of soda, a sandwich, and my purse, kicking the door to the staircase open and dragging my tote behind me on the stairs. "But I will."

Sometimes, I'd find her sitting in this big reclining chair in the living room, one that raised her feet up with the touch of a button. I'd sit on its big arm, wrapping myself around her— even when she had a cold, which my mom would get angry about, and I'd look at our reflection in those floor-to-ceiling mirrors, the ones I used to watch myself dance in as a child. Now, they reflected someone small, someone whose body was almost molded to the chair and withering away, fragile as wet paper. But when I looked down, directly into her eyes, I saw the same sweetness and strength that was always there. I would sing, "You are my sunshine," and she knew, deep down, that it was me. We'd tap on the table with our hands; I'd give her a thousand kisses.

When she said, "I don't know where I am," I would tell her, "You're home, and you're with me, and you're okay. I promise."

I'd touch her face, stroke her skin, bring her head onto my shoulder. This was all we had now, not many words, but a familiar feeling of comfort, and my best effort to make her feel that she was safe.

* * *

"So, explain to me how exactly you do what you do. Why would someone go to you?"

Mark Murynec was a "philosophical counselor," someone who helped people figure out who they were and what made them happy. I met him in the office he rented off of Washington

Square Park in the spring of 2013 to interview him for a story for the local newspaper.

"Well, if you have a headache, you take medication to kill the pain, and if you're sad, you take medication to feel better. On their own, meds treat the symptoms, while philosophical counseling helps treat the cause. There's nothing I can do to help a headache, but I can help you be happy despite the headache. Hopefully."

He continued to explain that some people see a psychoanalyst for fifteen years and still have the same problem.

"It just doesn't work. Psychology isn't bad, but philosophy can also help."

I pondered this and thought back to that Ethics class at the New School that seemed to open new windows of understanding for me. Mark had, in fact, gotten his Master's in Philosophy from the New School in '07, the same year I entered undergrad. His career had gotten my attention because I found myself, with over a year of sobriety and several more years of skill-building therapy under my belt, trying to find answers. I had cleared away all of this wreckage, learned how to just show up for life, and I was realizing that I had never gotten the chance to figure out who I *was*.

"What's the biggest difference between you and a conventional psychologist, in terms of your approach?" I asked, turning my attention outward to the list of questions I'd prepared.

"Psychologists believe that mind equals brain, so they treat mind and brain. But, as philosophers, we believe that humans are composed of mind, body, and soul. To a psychiatrist, your past is what makes you who you are. I'm not going to dig up stuff from your past," he said.

"How can you expect people to deal with the present if they don't also deal with the past?"

"Your past is an integral part of who you are, so it's easy to become mired in your history. I start with the basics, let people tell me what they want to tell me. The point is, who you are can change, if you're open to questioning yourself and everything you know."

I looked down at the page where I was furiously writing and could already tell I was going to have a hard time reading my notes back.

"How do you deal with people who come to you with anxiety?" I asked.

"We combat anxiety by living in 'the now,' right? But what if 'the now' sucks? That's when we have to make a decision to say, 'I don't mind being hurt, because at least I'm alive.'"

"Wow. That's one way to look at it. . . ." I mused. "You must have studied psychology. Seems like you know it well."

He smiled back.

"I took some in undergrad."

"What are the most common questions people come to you with, in the beginning?"

"Am I doing the right thing; who am I; what do I want; how can I change; can I change; someone else; am I wrong in feeling that way?"

"I'm sure you get lots of people looking for help in the relationship department," I said.

"Sure. Why don't you tell me about your relationship?"

I had walked right into the subtle shift between an interview and a session.

I cleared my throat and began picking at my cuticles.

"Well, I fell in love with a girl, which is a first."

"What's her name?"

"Grace. She's a year younger than me, and she's so sweet, and the sex is amazing. I mean, we can spend ten hours in bed and just go, and go, and it's so beautiful. I always knew I could be attracted to a girl, and there was this one time a couple years ago . . . anyway, she's different than all the guys I dated, or that I think I should date. They usually have a good job, a life plan, or a loving, supportive family. She doesn't have any of those. I met her in the program, and we had been best friends for almost a year, but something changed since we changed our relationship. Now, I care more about her lack of motivation in her career, her lack of financial security, her tendency to be flirtatious."

Being with a woman was a completely different experience. I had gone from someone who was pretty much closed off from intimacy and unavailable emotionally to someone who gave me a real run for my money in that department. We really, really loved each other.

We cooked together, we spent a lot of time in bed, just being affectionate and listening to music, and sometimes, I read to her from Buddhist philosophy books, which we'd then discuss thoughtfully.

"I mean, there are a lot of reasons this won't work long term, and I can tell I'm sabotaging it. My parents are pretty pissed about it, for one. Second of all, I'm being controlling, I'm acting jealous, and I'm not really enjoying it anymore because I'm worried about what all of the long-term implications of how she's living her life now will be on me, since I'm so emotionally invested."

"Okay, well, what does a good boyfriend or girlfriend do?" he asked.

I paused. I had no answer. After stopping and starting several times, I realized my only expectation was for them to have a stable job, an apartment, all externals, none of which came from me—these were things my mother would have wanted for me.

"It sounds like you're disappointed. But how can someone disappoint you and not meet your expectations if you don't really know what you want?" he asked. "You'd be surprised how many of us end up wanting what our parents want without realizing it, and without stopping to figure out what our own ideals are. So, what's important to you? What qualities?"

"Honesty, definitely. Loyalty, a sense of humor, family values, ambition," I said.

"And what makes you happy?" he asked.

Again, I had nothing.

"I don't know. . . ."

"Of course you do."

"Well, writing doesn't count, I suppose. I've always enjoyed that, but it's a job."

"What's your favorite kind of food?" he asked.

"Either Mexican or Thai."

"Do you like comedy? Who are your favorite comedians?"

I started to rattle off answers and understood how simple these questions were.

"Where do you like to go? What do you like to do just for the sake of doing it? Not as a means to an end, but in and of itself? That's how Aristotle defined happiness."

"I'll have to get back to you," I said.

"Sometimes," he said as he capped his pen, indicating that the session was ending. "The solution isn't to end a relationship but to love yourself more."

"How?" I asked.

"We don't take the time to identify who we want to be, what we want to be like, or how we want people to think of us. For example, you can say, 'I'm a great person.' But you'd be surprised at how many people can't start listing off the reasons why. So, some of my clients realize they want to volunteer, become philanthropic, help the poor, or just help their buddies or their own families more. The point is, they have to start somewhere."

"Anything you want to add that I haven't asked you?" I offered as my signature last question.

"With philosophy, you can get dark easily, or you can go the positive route," he said. "It just depends on what you want to believe in any given moment."

Shortly after that meeting, I would start to write stories about social good and nonprofits for Forbes and Huffington Post. Unpaid, hundreds of hours unpaid. I found a part-time paying job to pay the bills while I did that, knowing I wanted to commit to it. It was what made me happy—the world needed more headlines that didn't scare the shit out of everyone, that focused on the fact that the world was not all bad and horrifying. If I wasn't getting paid for it, it wasn't a means to an end, so it counted as something that just made me happy.

* * *

When things ended with Grace, which they did a few months later, the most important decision I made was one that was long overdue.

It was one that, I believe, was the final piece of the puzzle: I had to be alone.

No dating.

No flirting.

No sex.

Because there was still one person I needed to learn to trust, someone I had left out all along: myself.

I started making gratitude lists, shifting the focus to everything I was grateful for, even if on some days that thing was "water," because even that was something that many people didn't even have. I started holding doors open for people and smiling at them instead of rushing past them and keeping my head down, or sighing with frustration if they were "slowing me down" on the sidewalk. I started visiting the old lady down the hall to keep her company, because she had all of her marbles but couldn't see or walk, and had nobody else to talk to.

If I missed the train, I thought, "Guess I wasn't supposed to be on that train," and made peace with it being part of a bigger plan, even something as microscopic as that. In that time, aside from spending time with friends—friends that I could keep around for a while, now, instead of cutting them off (or turning them off)—I had to figure out who I was going to be as an adult.

I had to find a way to give myself everything I had always tried to grab from another person and glob on, like clay that my skin couldn't absorb. The old ideas I had about the world and the people in it started to meet these new ideas about who I wanted to be and *how* I wanted to be in it, and I needed to give all of that time. Because sometimes that is the only thing that will make things easier—time, and the ability to stay put when you want to impulsively run to something else, or someone else, to fill that time, with its long stretches and wistful sighs. Fortunately, during that time, Ava and Dr. J were like a tag team, drilling home the same points, with Dr. J sometimes cushioning Ava's more direct blows.

Ironically, I learned that the best way to move through what was uncomfortable and scary was simply by staying still; not running, not reacting, not shouting. Sooner than later, I'd find myself on the other side. I had to give the world the benefit of the doubt.

"Picking your battles is part of fight or flight," Dr. J said. "It's choosing a middle ground where you don't have to do either. You just chill."

Slowly, finger by finger, we were able to pry the invisible little girl's fingers off of me, until finally, she felt secure enough to let me go, joining the other kids and letting me head off to work.

CHAPTER SIXTEEN

By seeing the best in me,
She empowered me
By believing in me,
She transformed me
She grew old
And floated away
But her love remains standing
Eternally by my side.
—Giorge Leedy, *Uninhibited from Lust to Love*

I met Lee in the fall of 2013 after he pitched me one of his clients for a story. Lee is a good guy, with good values, one who put on a "front" during our first encounter at an Italian restaurant on Fifty-Fourth Street and Madison Avenue.

When I arrived, I saw him sitting in the corner, wearing a purple-checkered shirt under a blue blazer, brown hair tucked behind his ears, long on the sides but not all around. He was tall, about six feet, and had a slim build—not lanky, just tall and thin. He reminded me of a hybrid between Ryan Gosling and Bradley Cooper.

We started talking—I ordered the lobster, him, the Osso Bucco—and I quickly called him out on his bullshit generalizations about the power struggles between men and women and whatever other nonsense he went on about.

"I'm also writing a book about how we're always looking for happiness outside of ourselves," he said.

"I think Eckhart Tolle already wrote that book," I quipped, motioning for the waiter to refill Lee's water glass, which had been empty for a few minutes.

We parted ways with a weird hug, and as I walked back toward the office, leftover lobster in tow, I thought, *well, never gonna see him again.*

But he texted me the next day.

You really got under my skin. I can't stop thinking about you.

I would later learn that no, this was not a line, and that, like many nice Jewish boys, he didn't have much "game."

So I texted back, *"I'm free on Tuesday and Sunday night. Pick one, and be yourself this time. I don't know what that bullshit was. Just be yourself."*

I went upstairs to see Grandma, who was sleeping with her chin to her chest. She had lost many of her words, by then, but when we locked eyes, hers flickered with some sort of recognition. She didn't say much, closing her eyes, opening them, reaching out for the magazine in front of her, but too weak to turn the pages.

I nuzzled my head in her neck, which smelled the same as it always had, only the sour smell of medical ointment was stronger now. I held both of her hands, and sang, *You Are my Sunshine*, and she tried to mouth a few of the words.

I got up to go to the bathroom, and she asked, calling out to the air in front of her, "Where are you?"

I leaned over, coming up from behind, and whispered, "It's okay. I love you. I'll be right back."

"I love you, too," she said.

When I got back, she looked at me and said, "I'm dying," and again, "I'm dying."

I did not say, "No you're not."

I said, "It's okay."

* * *

As it turned out, Lee's actual "self" was kind, funny, patient, supportive, communicative as hell, and honest. He had dreams, aspirations, was a hard worker, and was happy to hit binge-watching Netflix together all weekend just as hard. I was able to make a decision to trust him, because I felt safe enough to let myself be vulnerable, knowing that I was someone who could walk away if it didn't work.

With Lee, there was no drama, no battle for control. He did what he had to do, and what he wanted to do, and he gave me that same respect. It was nothing to feel threatened by. Not having control over a lot of things, I found, can actually be very freeing.

I no longer defined love as this crazy, painful passionate plight of chaos. It wasn't about finding someone who would "protect me" or "take care of me." It's peaceful and sustainable, and it requires, for me at least, two people who are already whole to come together in order to form something new and wonderful.

I had been spending a lot of time in what some people refer to as the "graduate" program for friends and family members of alcoholics, figuring out what did and didn't work in my life, what traits and behaviors were no longer useful or necessary. I learned that being aware of what I did yesterday could help me understand and accept who I was today, so I could be the person I wanted to be the next day, a slightly better version of me, for my own sake, and for his.

Years of stepwork in both programs, and in therapy, resulted in some permanent rewiring of my brain. I could easily distinguish between the way things looked to me, or appeared to me, and the way they really were. I examined what would happen if all of my worst fears came true, following those thoughts until they dissolved, oftentimes never coming back. I figured out how all of my fears affected the way I made decisions, and the ways I was willing to be more flexible about those decisions on any given day. I learned how to show respect and tolerance to all of the people in my life. I was honest with my sponsors about what I did and how I felt and where I could do better. I started to do yoga regularly, even when I couldn't "get it right." I started to meditate, even if I didn't do that perfectly.

These tiny doses of calm became a permanent baseline; where there was once anxiety, there was now a deep breath and a shrug.

In September of 2014, I was constantly worried about my father's safety because of all the threats he was getting.

After the new Southbridge board of directors put wheels in place to convert the affordable housing cooperative into privately owned co-ops, my dad formed a group that challenged the way they presented their information—not very transparently—and tried to keep the vote from passing. The very vote itself had torn the community apart. Women were fighting and putting each other in the emergency room. People were looking down instead of saying hello in the elevator. The people who were "for it" wanted to suddenly own apartments they never paid for in the first place, and the people against it didn't like the idea of robbing other people of affordable housing, or of elderly people on fixed income potentially being forced out by rising rents and flip taxes.

When people decided to take sides, my dad went from being the guy who helped create after-school programs, the guy who stayed with your mother when she fell in the street until you could get there, the guy who ran the Halloween parties, to one solitary guy "standing in the way" of their making a profit. Nobody really cared that he was the guy who, on September 12, helped get everyone their medication and cell phones and food. People gave him the finger as they walked by, or they shouted, "I'm going to fucking kill you" or "I hope you drop dead." Someone threatened to have their dog attack Gucci, who was thirteen years old by then.

* * *

On the day that it finally happened, I woke up, kissed Lee on the head, and let him sleep a few minutes longer. The night before had been rough, because, on his way home, he had been attacked on the subway by a crazy guy. I'd told myself not to worry that he was unexpectedly missing for twenty minutes after texting "almost at our stop." He was okay, in the end, but it wasn't lost on me that after all those years of worrying about that exact thing happening, it did; and there was literally nothing for either us to do but get back on the train the next morning and hope for the best.

On the day that it finally happened, I rubbed the sleep out of my eyes and looked around our new home. Lee and I decorated it with photos of our trips together, pictures of the ocean and lakes and waterfalls mounted on wood. A mantra, *It's a good day to have a good day,* hung over my desk on canvas. I made coffee in the Kuerig he'd gotten me for Christmas, and stuffed some messy handfuls of gluten-free cereal into a sandwich bag, flakes dropping to the kitchen floor. I sat down at my computer and began looking through stories my writers had submitted at our news site that focused on people doing good things for other people (and animals). I was working thirty hours a week at a day job, and on the side, serving as Managing Editor at a site dedicated to good news only.

On the train, the taste of coffee still in my mouth, I thought about what Lee and I would do for dinner. I wouldn't obsessively worry about our relationship, its state, its future. Our life together was there, just like sleeping and eating and all those other things that are sometimes a little bit of work, but easy, natural. Nothing was going to yank it away.

On the day it finally happened, the walk to the office was pretty chilly, with hopeful spring daffodils defying the weather. People waited for their breakfast to be flipped from a spatula onto a piece of parchment from a food truck, and I texted my mom and e-mailed my dad as I hustled toward the corner of Park Avenue and Fifty-Second. As always, my mom had sent me five emails about sales on stuff I didn't need. I waited for the elevators at the bank that specifically went to floors two through twenty, and I said something silly to Dana, the secretary, as I walked in.

I'd worked there for a while by then, continuing to pursue my writing, just like most of us creative twenty-something's had to do, a bunch of cobblers mushing all these jobs together because we had to pay the bills. I passed the cubicles and offered a cheery, sing-song "Good morning!" loud enough for everyone to hear and tossed my coat onto one of the other two desks in my office that belonged to nobody, under a TV nobody ever activated. I flicked the lights off—one of many defenses against the still pervasive chronic migraine attacks— and lit a candle. I double clicked Pandora and brought up a list of calming music mixed with pop, rap, yoga music, and, of course, reggaeton.

On the day it finally happened, Dana came in and closed the door behind her. She complained about how the bosses treated her, how overwhelmed she was, what they'd said to her already that morning, how she couldn't take it. "Maybe you can set limits on your time today, and tell them what you can do, rather than what you can't," I offered. But mostly, I listened. Sometimes, people needed you to just listen, and it was usually easy to read who needed what and when. As Dana turned to leave, she said, "I don't know how you're always so happy all the time!"

How uncanny it was, indeed, that I had somehow become the "happy one." Not in this crazy, wide-eyed, come-drink-the-Kool-Aid way. Just, naturally happy, cracking jokes, smiling, asking people about their day, and listening. At first, I felt I was foolish to let myself be happy. I had always waited for the other shoe to drop, for something bad to happen to take it away;

people were malicious; people got sick, people turned "bad." People died. People tried to hurt you, to sabotage you. I had to train myself, when the feelings of happiness and love and calm came up, to trust it. To quiet whatever was swooping in to try to take it away. That took guided practice too. I had become my father's daughter, chatting with the guys who made the sandwiches at lunch, the FedEx guy, the waitress, giving off the air, most likely, of someone who had been through no pain at all, nothing hard in life, someone who was naïve and in for a rude awakening when the reality of the world hit her hard. At least, that's what I would have thought about myself, if I was in the other person's shoes.

But this feeling of joy that comes from cooking and singing along with Spotify, or taking an early morning walk and appreciating how clean and crisp the air is, before all of the cars and the people thicken it up, are simple pleasures I've never had room for before. There's a lightness behind it all, even when things rattle me—the sickness of a loved one, too much stress at work, something as simple as hunger or lack of sleep. I may not be a total Buddha who has found a way to watch it all unfold from up above on a fluffy cloud, but there's clarity, space between it all, that has replaced the deep grip that these external things used to have, the one that used to jerk me around in all directions.

On the day it finally happened, I walked over to the Citi Group building during lunch and sat in a women's meeting and was bored. *Bored!* It was such a luxury, my mind not racing ahead to the future, or dwelling backward in the past. Being where I am, that delicious slice of a present moment, even if it's boring, is a gift. "She is so put together, how much time does she have?" someone asked my sponsor. I had begun to rely on the meetings less and on myself more, but I would never completely abandon them. I resolved not to leave the community that gave me so much without trying to give something back. I had reduced my therapy sessions with Dr. J to once a month, and I emailed her when too many things became just too much, because, for all of us, they do, sometimes.

On June 9, 2015, the day it finally happened, I got back to the office, looked down at my phone, and saw a text from my mom.

Grandma is in the hospital. She's having trouble breathing.

* * *

I hustled through the emergency room that I had rushed through so many times before, knowing exactly where to go. I saw my mother first, at the foot of the hospital bed, crying. Grandma had an oxygen mask on, and underneath it, she was wearing bright pink lipstick.

She had an oxygen mask on, and she was wearing bright pink lipstick.

"It's ok," I said to my mom, kissing her on the head.

I went over to Grandma, pulling a chair next to the bed. I whispered, "It's ok. I love you."

A male nurse eventually came in, kicked the locks off of the wheels of the bed, and rolled her toward the elevator.

"How old are you, young lady?" he asked her, even though she obviously couldn't answer.

"She is ninety-eight," I said proudly, giving him a look like, *can you believe it?*

The very last thing Grandma ever said to anyone was to my father, the next morning, as he wet her lips with a small sponge.

She mouthed, "Thank you."

But by the time I got there she was just trembling and gripping the side of the bed, making noises with her throat but not much else. The hospital Chaplan came to read her last rites, and my mother and I cried. I held Grandma's hand, but it was not her hand. I kissed her forehead, but it was not her forehead, not really. Days had turned into months and years that I watched little parts of her rise up, up, and away, and I kissed them each goodbye, mourning in slow, painful increments, and loving what was left to love. Tears quietly came anyway, but I knew that she had left already.

By the time the arrangements were made for hospice care, and by the time my father and I had to convince my mother that morphine was the best thing for her, to minimize any suffering, I didn't feel that fear and all consuming despair that I'd always expected to feel when the time finally came. I had gotten so much extra time with her, so much borrowed time.

My mother's birthday, you'll recall, is June 11, and we convinced her to leave the apartment to have lunch so we could celebrate, just a little, even though it didn't feel like a day for celebrating. We walked over to Front Street and ate sandwiches and pasta at an Italian restaurant where, of course, my dad knew the owner, and some other restaurant owners had dropped by in time to sing "Happy Birthday" and clank their knives against glasses.

As we ate cake, I noticed a big bug, some awful creature with a zillion legs crawling up the side of the wall.

I called the waiter over, who gingerly scooped it up in a napkin and walked outside with it. We watched out the window as he tried once, twice, three times to transfer the bug from a napkin onto a small pine tree. He thought he had gotten it on the third time, but on the way back in, he began to crumple up the napkin—with the bug still crawling on it.

"Shh . . . don't tell him," my mom said, giggling.

At 4:30 a.m. the next day, we got the call.

It was officially June 12, which meant that Grandma had honored my aunt's request, to wait until after Mom's birthday had passed. Grandma had held out for twelve hours longer than the forty-eight hours they projected, defying, as she always had, every doctor's prognosis, leaving on her own terms.

The wake was on Monday, a cloudy day with the occasional few needle-pricks of noncommittal rain. We kept the casket open just for us, just for the family, because she wouldn't have wanted other people to see her that way. I thought she looked beautiful, though, wearing the sparkly, glamorous dress she had worn to my mother's wedding, one that had been made by hand with special beads just for her. I recognized it from the pictures.

Father Jim came, the same priest who had Baptized me and given me my first Communion, and said a few words. Then, he prompted me to get up and read the words I'd written, which made everyone cry all over again. When my dad tried to give him a check, he first shooed it away, saying it wasn't necessary, and when my dad said, "Please," Father Jim said, "Okay, put it in the book," and shut the Bible around it.

The funeral director was over an hour late to bring her to the cemetery. Like my grandpa, she had requested not to be buried in the ground, but above it. My father, mother, Lee, and I drove past the rows of graves up there in the Bronx until we parked right behind Aunt Fran and Uncle John, in front of a wall covered in marble markings. It was like an outdoor morgue, but with coffins and flowers.

There was a hole in the wall about five spaces up from the ground, right next to my grandfather's stone, which had been engraved with his name. A green curtain covering the opening she would go into, and a small crane had been positioned underneath it. The funeral director said a few words, and we each held a flower. We tucked our roses into the coffin, and, for the first time on that cloudy day, the sun broke through the clouds. She was loaded onto this mechanical lift, up onto the wall, slowly, to the sound of *beep, beep, beep*, like a tow truck backing up.

Then, the sun disappeared again.

It wasn't until we were driving back to the city that I realized. *You are my sunshine.*

After we turned the lights off to go to sleep, I said to Lee, in the darkness, "You know how I always look for the good in situations? How I've always been able to look back at really bad stuff and think, 'Here's the good thing that came out of it?' I've never been able to do that with what happened to my grandma. It was just so much suffering."

Lee turned on his side to face me.

"From what you've told me, it seems like the more painful it was to be there, the more often you were there. You found ways to comfort her and to get past your own hurt to help comfort someone else."

"I guess . . ." I said.

"I think that made you a softer, gentler person, one you probably wouldn't have become to the extent that you did. And, if she weren't as sick, you may not have been so diligent about being around all the time."

I reached over to pick up Wiley, setting him down on my chest so that his wet nose poked right up against mine. He wiggled up even further, so that his tiny head nestled right into the space between my neck and my shoulder.

Wiley is our rescue dog, a chubby, tan and white little Chihuahua mix whose body gets warm quickly and emits the faint smell of corn chips after he's been laying down for a while. He has been like my shadow, attached to my hip ever since we first picked him up from his third home in two years. Initially, he was found as a stray in Oklahoma, taken in by the rescue president, flown to the East Coast to be fostered in Brooklyn, then adopted out to this family, who decided that, after a year, they had dog allergies.

Wiley stopped shaking within a few minutes of getting in the car with me, Lee, and my father. After taking a huge dump the second he hit the sidewalk, Wiley let us lead him inside, and he hopped onto the couch. We hopped on with him. He situated himself so that he was sitting on both of our laps at once. Picking up the tip sheet they gave us about helping rescue dogs adjust, I read, *"He may be afraid of your newspaper, shoe, anything else that maybe have been used to 'teach' him things."*

It could have, hypothetically, been a banana that he was hit with, and nobody would have known why he would start whimpering at the sight of a simple banana.

Whatever it may have been, there was a time, hypothetically, that he couldn't protect himself, and couldn't escape. Only he would ever really know what those triggers were. Lucky for Wiley, with love, patience, proper medical treatment, he got a chance at a second life. A group of people rallied around him and said, *"Your little life matters this much."*

He loves to be tucked in and smooshed by our bodies. If we aren't around, he will build a tiny fortress with blankets and pillows. He just wants to feel protected, held by a warm presence, in a way that I think all of us do. Despite all that he's been through, he still trusts that I won't let anything happen to him, that I won't leave him, which is why he no longer cries when we leave the house. His favorite place is right between my legs, occupying the space between the "V" they make when they fall open. It's the same protective cocoon I used to build myself when I was a toddler, wiggling my way in and moving my mom's shins around, hooking one on each leg, even when she started to protest that I was "getting too big for that."

Wiley, like other dogs saved from the worst conditions, was able to transform almost entirely.

In this way, dogs like Wiley aren't so different from us.

* * *

Four years after my initial round of interviews, I met back up with some of my former classmates again to find out how they were doing.

Christine was working at a community and youth organization in New York, helping kids have a better chance at success despite the circumstances they're born into. Sarah, too, had become a teacher, but for college kids.

Greg was back at his parents' house in the West Village working on his music in the basement by night and on film production by day. He had tried his hand at alcohol recovery himself, but had found psychedelic drugs to be helpful, so did not choose the path of total sobriety. He eventually met a therapist he found helpful, Dr. Ken, who he said accepted him no matter what he thought or said, and showed him compassion.

Greg still struggles with the concept of feeling safe, but has found comfort staying close to some of his old friends from I.S.89.

Charles got his Master's Degree in Design and Urban Ecologies from The New School, a program that focused on finding the medium between public policy, urban intervention, and social involvement. He has been working as a photo editor and a freelance cartographer, and was on the team that created the first digital map of New York City's Urban Renewal Plans, which had been on display at the Queens Museum in 2015.

Syd had tried his hand at being an EMT while living up in Nyack, something that gave him hope and purpose. He liked the adrenaline rush of being the first on the scene. That all ended one day when he had to actually hold a woman's face together. A year later, he was riding his bike when a man in a car hit him and drove off, leaving him hospitalized with a concussion and unable to recall most of his memories for months. He went on to find a job as an IT consultant in Battery Park, the first job he actually liked. He, like Greg, swears by the power of psychedelic drugs, which he maintains helped him get past his own "mental blocks."

"How has the drinking been?" I asked.

"I usually only have one, if at all," he said.

"How about the weed?"

"Much better. An eighth used to last me a day, now it lasts at least two weeks."

Thomas and I were reunited for the first time in twelve years when we met for dinner in midtown, and I was blown away when I pulled back from our hug. That mousy, quiet kid showed up in a tailored suit, very much a grown-up, nursing one single gin and tonic through the entire meal. His dog, Eddie, made it to age fourteen, even though he developed cancer, which the vet believed to be caused by his exposure to the attacks. He lived a happy life until then.

"Christine and I went to the top of One World Trade Center yesterday," he said.

"How was that?"

"It felt like the most safe and the most dangerous place in the world at the same time."

"Do you feel like you've pretty much been out of the woods, living in Florida?"

"It's better than being in New York. This would be a rough go for me, I think. I'm not good in crowds. But, I still struggle with anxiety. I'm always on edge. I walk into my office and think, *how would I get out if something happened,* and I don't think anyone else is thinking about that. I'm always in that mindset, even if I don't need to be."

"And you never went to therapy?"

"Nope."

"Why?"

"I'm not sure. Maybe I didn't want to have to relive that day again."

"You're telling me you haven't relived that day since then?"

"In my mind, almost every day. But I don't want to talk about it out loud."

Michael and I decided to meet on a rainy afternoon two days before Christmas, at a coffee shop on Bleecker Street. He was much taller than I remembered, and had grown out his hair and a mustache.

"Four years!" I exclaimed as we settled into our seats.

"Has it really been four years?" he asked.

"Yep. The last time we talked was right after bin Laden was killed. I remember, because I remember how you said that you thought death was easy, so torture was better, this way he'd have to suffer."

"Yeah, that sounds about right. I think I thought his death would bring some sort of closure, but it hasn't. Nothing is going to change what he did."

Shortly after we'd last met in 2011, Michael moved to Bangkok to teach English as a Second Language for two years, then moved to Las Vegas to teach fifth grade there, after he heard about the teaching shortage.

"The work is good for me," he said, sipping his green tea. "Kids at that age are brutally honest. It keeps me busy, but it's not stressful. There's not a lot of overwhelming pressure on me."

He told me about how he had given his kids an article to read about children in Africa, one that mentions PTSD.

"I was shocked at how the kids responded. I had never seen so much class participation. One girl got in a car accident with her grandmother. Other kids said they were scared when they heard gunshots at night, wondering if they were going to be okay. Violence is a big problem in Las Vegas. This was the first time I got them so interested in talking."

"What about you, do you still experience any of the things you were struggling with back in high school?"

"Actually, when I got back here from Thailand, I started having panic attacks. But then when I went to Vegas, it stopped. Now, they're starting again. It even happened in a bar a couple of weeks ago. It was just too crowded."

"Have you seen anyone about it?"

"I saw an ad on the subway for the 9/11 Health Fund, so I called them. I had to call the guidance counselor from I.S. 89 to get the paperwork, and they did a physical screening of me, and a psychological screening. The woman who interviewed me said, 'It's probably PTSD, so we'll say it is, this way you qualify for free services.' I haven't pursued it yet, though."

"How come?"

"I think I'm doing okay now. If it happens again I know I can call. I haven't heard from them or anything."

"Do you know what the symptoms of PTSD actually are? Has anyone explained it to you?"

He paused, took another long sip of tea, and looked out the window at the rain collecting in small puddles.

"You know what, not really. I was having nightmares when I got back to New York after Bangkok, I've been more fearful of bad things happening. I had a lot of trouble sleeping, and when I slept, I would have these wild nightmares that stayed with me during the day."

"That sounds really rough," I said.

"This might sound crazy, but sometimes I feel like I'm in the movie *Final Destination*, always narrowly escaping death. Two days after I left Bangkok, this building was bombed, a place that I ate lunch across the street from every day. Two days ago, there was a car accident on the most populated strip of Las Vegas—that woman who drove her car onto the sidewalk and injured thirty-seven people. I'm there all the time. That could have been me."

"How has the drinking been? I know you had a couple of incidents in high school," I said.

"In college I drank more, but it wasn't because of the depression or anything. It's because everyone was binge drinking. It was fun, to escape. I still drink. I choose to get drunk, if I want to. I stopped smoking weed eight months ago."

"That's great," I said, toasting the air with my Winter Tea Latte. "I've been sober four years myself."

"Wow, that's awesome. Yeah . . . I mean, there were times I thought I was an alcoholic, but then I could go long enough without drinking to prove to myself that I wasn't, like a couple of weeks."

* * *

I considered myself pretty lucky that Lee didn't really drink. He did, socially, before he met me, but realized that he "kind of dug" living the sober life with me, save for a very occasional beer or glass of wine. As we filed into the cocktail hour at Columbia University for his coworker's wedding, I recognized a familiar face. The last time I saw Lacey, one of his coworker's dates, she was at a bar in Brooklyn drinking seltzer.

"You look so familiar!" I declared when we were introduced. When I noticed it was seltzer, I said, in a voice so only she could hear, "Maybe that's where I know you from," and winked.

Now, I was sidling up to the bar to order a Pellegrino, catching Lacey's eye and making some comment about how it was a "good year."

But when I looked at her glass, I saw that she definitely wasn't drinking Pellegrino.

I cleared my throat and started chatting with the woman standing next to me at the bar. Behind me, I could overhear

Lee saying, "We go to a restaurant, she makes friends with the waiter, and they go have coffee. She joins a gym, and the next day, all of the trainers are standing in a circle listening to her tell a funny story. . . ."

I smiled to myself and look back at Lacey, feeling odd about being the only one in the room with insider information. *This is not going to be good.* I could have called shot for shot what unfolded in front of me that night; the third glass, the fourth glass, the sloppy way Lacey literally hung on her date during the speeches, the way she completely face-planted at the end of the night on the dance floor. As Lee and I looked out over the skyline, watching it turn from indigo blue to a near black as the night went on, I felt grounded, like we were solid, as everyone else slowly started to lose their inhibition around us.

As I stared out the cab window on the way home, passing the Apollo Theater and holding Lee's hand, I thought about what it meant to go home with a clear head. I thought about how glad I was that I went to the wedding, even though I didn't want to. When you have friends, and a family, and a career, you go to things you don't want to go to. That's what you did when you wanted to keep them all. You got to stand there in your own skin and socialize with people who were not potential adversaries, but potential friends.

Epilogue

So many people walk around with a meaningless life. They seem half-asleep, even when they're busy doing things they think are important. This is because they're chasing the wrong things. The way you get meaning into your life is to devote yourself to loving others, devote yourself to your community around you, and devote yourself to creating something that gives you purpose and meaning.

—Mitch Albom, *Tuesdays with Morrie*

At some point I will sit across from Dr. J and tell her that I feel like I felt when I was eighteen again.

"It's all too much. My body and my brain are just saying 'We've had it.' I'm edgy and I'm down, I'm nervous and I can't sleep, and it's been two months. For ten weeks, actually, I've been put on and off of these medications to try and prevent the migraines, and they're giving me all these hormonal side effects and changing my mood, and I'm supposed to wait for my body to 'adjust' and it doesn't seem to. So now I've discontinued it, and I'm still out of balance because now my body's adjusting to that."

This calm person I've been for the greater part of two solid years, this wise-minded adult who could always turn to the actions that brought her back to balance when the stress of life becomes a little too much—yoga, exercise, bubble baths, helping someone else, meditating, calling friends, calling people in my network—would once more become overpowered by medications.

"But you're not eighteen again. You have to catch yourself in these moments and take five minutes. Just five minutes to deep breathe," Dr. J will say. "This is a lot for anyone."

"This" would be finalizing a book. "This" would be attempting, with no prior business experience whatsoever, to start-up a news service exclusively focused on inspiring and hopeful stories about people who are trying to make the future better. "This" was dealing with chronic pain, for almost ten years, by then, trying tons of doctors and medications and therapies and getting nowhere. "This" would be Lee's family officially announcing they won't be attending our wedding (a consideration that became official after he brought me back to that restaurant on Fifty-Fourth and Madison Avenue and popped the question, to which I smiled said yes, giggling and kissing him through a horrible migraine) because he left the Orthodox Jewish Community when he was twenty years old, and then half-Jewish me came along to put the nail in the coffin.

"This" was doing it all stone-cold sober.

My current sponsor, who also has PTSD, will similarly remind me that it *will* pass, that for a very, very long time, my higher self—and my brain, and my body, and my nervous system—have all lived in harmony, almost seamlessly. So when times of big stress come on, it may trigger this PTSD, especially when there are greater forces at work in my body. I just have to take five minutes, breathe, and tell myself that I'm okay, even if transmitters in my body are trying to trick me into thinking that I'm not.

I will have to fight that heavy feeling, the sensation that darkness is collecting inside of me again. I will have to push away the idea that people who disagree with Lee's decision will try to find us and hurt us or ruin our wedding. I will have to slow down enough to realize that I am not any of these feelings, and that as much as FEAR can stand for False Evidence Appearing Real, it can also stand for Face Everything And Recover.

There will still be beautiful moments in those two long months before the roller coaster finally comes to a stop and my hormones readjust in the midst of these trial-and-error hormone pills that are supposed to help with my migraines. I will put on what will become my wedding dress and instantly think about how much Grandma would have loved it, and my mother will tell me, in the loving way I knew she would, not to worry that it is over budget, she will figure it out, and my maid of honor, one of the truly dear friends I've made over time, will clap and cheer.

I will feel like I'm on my last legs but take a very long, "express-is-running-local" 2 train ride uptown to meet a friend for dinner, one that I've had for five years now, and I won't need to take a Klonopin to be able to do it. We'll laugh and talk over meatballs and soda for two hours, and I'll be able to experience that joy in its entirety.

Lee will go away on business for a few nights, and I will realize upon our happy reunion that I never once wondered what he was doing or even called him, whereas once upon a time it would be 24/7 check-ins, a need for reassurance and constant contact.

I will find a team of people who believe in my dream to bring positive news stories to the world and prepare to go toe-to-toe with the negative and terrifying headlines that still plague everyone today. We'll try to figure it all out together, from the ground up.

* * *

I'm sitting with Estelle, an old lady I visit with. She was one of the women that belonged to the group my grandma "socialized" in. Their home health aids would bring them to the community room or to each other's apartments to have cake and "party," something that stopped when my grandmother died.

Some people have a hard time knowing what to say or do in these situations, with the elderly, but I've picked up this ability to ask questions and make conversation where other people would fall short, silent, and awkward.

"What's your favorite place in the world?" I ask her.

"I don't know," she says. "What about you?"

"I think it would have to be Paris," I say.

"It's bad, what's happening in Paris now," she says. She can't see, but she listens to the news on TV. "Who are the people doing this?"

I clear my throat, and say, "I think they're called ISIS."

"What's that?"

"An Islamic state," I say, not wanting to follow this conversation thread for too long.

"The religion tells them to do that?"

"Well, technically not. Islam is a peaceful religion. They're misinterpreting it. I think anyone who hurts people in the name of religion is abusing that reason."

"Oh," she says, wiping her nose slowly with a tissue and taking this information in. "It seems that bad things are happening everywhere."

"Yes, but also, good things are happening too."

"You don't hear about that."

"I know, and I'm working on it."

I try to explain to her that the journalism I do is "only on the computer, not in a newspaper." I tell her there are a lot of people doing good things out there and that my job is to shine a light on what they are doing to help, that I try to get them attention by writing about them so even more people can help.

She nods, her head falling into her chest, her eyes closing.

"Listen, I've got a defrosted chicken in the kitchen and a hungry man on his way home, but I'll see you soon, ok?"

"Ok, thank you for coming to see me. I didn't have any visitors this week."

"Its my pleasure," I say. "Can I give you a hug?"

"Of course," she says as she accepts my hug.

"I want you to be happy, okay?"

"You make me happy," she says.

"She doesn't say that to nobody," her home health aid chimes in.

I think about our conversation, about how there are days when, if I'm stupid enough to turn on the news, I worry about how dangerous and dark the outside world still is. There are mass shootings, there are people who behave like they have no souls, there are more terrorist attacks. But there is a new filter, almost like a translucent window shade, that is gold, not black. It allows me to see, in between those dark places and nasty people, the good things, and the good people, and the potential for better.

That night, the news, as usual, is not good. I flip through the newspaper, reading about how, after the recent attacks in Paris, ISIS threats were now prevalent in NYC, still the number-one terrorist target in the entire world. Lee walks in around 7:00 p.m., bringing the cold in with him. Wiley immediately begins hopping around on his hind legs to greet him. I start bringing our food to the table, and say, as casually as I can, "If anything ever happens, just get home. We may lose cell signals, so just get here. Don't go underground, though. Get in a cab or on a bus, or just run."

"Someone else was talking about this at work," he says. "Did something happen?"

"Talking about what?"

"Preparedness," he says. "Did they name a specific place?"

"Yes," I sigh as I curl up on the couch and rest my head in my hand, elbow propped up against a throw pillow. "Times Square and Herald Square."

Six blocks from your office.

Lee whips out his phone, asking, "Do you mind if I watch this video?" ISIS had released a video that all of the news sites were posting, which was freaking everybody out.

"No," I say. "In fact, you can bring it over here."

He joins me on the couch, and I ask him to put his headphones in, because I don't want to hear. I rub Wiley's stomach instead, talking to him in the silly way we talk to babies and dogs, glancing at the screen occasionally. Some days, we just spend hours cooing over this baby, marveling at him like he's our own flesh and blood.

"I think we should leave," Lee concludes, pulling his big blue headphones off.

"And go where?"

"Florida," he says. "Nothing happens there. Nobody cares about Florida."

"That's what Thomas said," I chuckle. "That's why he went there after 9/11."

At some point, I would like to leave—as much as I love this city and dread the sting of being a New Yorker living somewhere else—I don't want to live in the same place my entire life."

"So, let's go," he says. "Babe, we have to take this seriously. What's to prevent them from doing this?"

"The same thing that has been for the last fourteen years," I say calmly, cradling Wiley's head in my lap. "Nothing. Maybe it's a real threat, maybe it isn't. But we can't run every time we get scared."

The 9/11 Tribute Center, located across the street from the World Trade Center since 2006, invites visitors to share their thoughts at the end of their experience in their galleries. Here are three comments from those notes (originally published in *9/11: The World Speaks*).

My three young daughters asked if they were safe. I reassured them living in rural Pennsylvania was safe ... but they watched flight 93 fly low over their playground in Ligonier, PA. It crashed three miles beyond. God Bless all of USA.
—*Anonymous. Pennsylvania*

I am a history teacher. Last year my students said, "What's the big deal about 9/11?"
—*Anonymous, Missouri*

Everyone has a story! <u>NEVER</u> stop listening
—*Anonymous, South Africa*

Afterword

Helaina reached out to me as she began her journey to learn more about the condition that rocked her existence and her identity, shattering any sense that life could be within her control. At the time, I was organizing a conference on Trauma & Resilience for the National Association for the Advancement of Psychoanalysis (NAAP).

A young undergraduate, she bravely called me in 2011 to ask about the conference and to see if we could talk. I learned that Helaina was a middle schooler on 9/11 whose only thought was to survive, flee, and get home, an escape that sounded like the stories of many survivors of the disaster—until she described its aftermath. She and her classmates were eventually disbursed throughout the city school system. They were separated from each other and attended class as silent refugees from the Towers, fearful and socially isolated. This created what we now know as a secondary traumatization, impacting emotional and interpersonal development.

Years later, as Helaina began to interview her classmates about their experiences, she learned that many of them, like herself, had suffered impaired psychological development expressed in many symptoms.

What is astonishing in the stories of survivors is the degree of emotional resilience we often find. Research shows that, among the protective factors that influence development are strong early family ties, an ability to access interpersonal resources, a quest to problem solve, and a capacity to grow through adversity. Helaina, and many of the "9/11" children, encountered the struggle of forced adaptation after an overwhelming experience. Their fragilities were often attributed to troubled developmental adjustment, rather than to the squelched parts of healthy egos attempting to symbolically describe stories of traumatization. It was not only the experience of that awful September day, but its pervasive undercurrent in everyday existence, that challenged healthy maturation for the 9/11 children.

How, I wondered, had the authorities, the adults in their world, allowed this to happen to these children? How could they imagine stifling the survivors could have any positive effect? How could an array of clinicians have not have truly understood Helaina's condition as post-traumatic stress disorder (PTSD)? Despite the outrage, I realized it was not a completely unfamiliar pattern. We have many recorded examples of survivors from terror and disaster feeling silenced or ostracized. We now understand that their presence can have a profoundly destabilizing effect on those around them, triggering guilt, deep anxiety, and too frequently, resentment.

There are several successful methods—and combinations thereof—available to help young children who experience trauma, with cognitive behavioral therapy, psychoanalytic psychotherapy, and art therapy among them. CBT gives the child an opportunity to look differently at their experiences and to develop tools to cope with and manage the intrusive, debilitating thoughts that are a part of PTSD. Psychoanalytic Psychotherapy and Art Therapy also provide forums for the child to process high stressor emotional experiences through symbolic communication, allowing the devastating experience to lose its center stage power in the child's mind. They offer a safe haven for developing coping skills and capacity for interpersonal resource development, without the threat of re-traumatizing through enforced focus on the crises.

Therefore, it is important to be aware of the various signs of PTSD among children at the onset, such as nightmares, unusual worrying about family members leaving the house, denial of the event, sudden unusual outbursts of anger, a tendency toward isolation, excessive daydreaming or distractibility, increased anxiety, sudden outbursts of crying, and secretiveness. Early and continued intervention is crucial when it is known that exposure to an overwhelming event has occurred, or when noticing symptoms such as those mentioned above.

Helaina has become an outspoken advocate for herself and her fellow survivors. Her willingness to reach out regardless of the risk of rejection is just one example of how we can grow resilient within adversity. Her journey throws an optimistic light on the rocky road from trauma response to resilient growth.

We may always live with the reverberating reminders over-whelming experience, whether from persistent developmental trauma, abuse, or environmental disaster, but, as Helaina's story shows, there is always hope when you ask for help.

—Patricia Harte Bratt, PhD
Director, Academy of Clinical and
Applied Psychoanalysis (ACAP)
President, National Association for
the Advancement of Psychoanalysis (NAAP)
Author: *Reciprocal Resilience: Surprising
Benefits for Clinicians of Listening to Stories of Trauma*
patbratt@comcast.net

About the Author

Helaina Hovitz is a journalist and editor specializing in positive and inspiring stories. She has written for the *New York Times, Salon, The New York Observer, Forbes, Huffington Post, Teen Vogue*, and *Newsday* and is hard at work on her latest venture, a news service called *Headlines for the Hopeful*. She lives with her fiancé and their rescue dog, Wiley.

Photo: Justin McCallum

If you believe that you or someone you know may be living with post-traumatic stress disorder, alcoholism, drug addiction, depression, or any other mental health issue, please visit www.HelainaHovitz.com for a list of Recovery Resources.

Everyone's journey is different, and Helaina hopes she can help you find a solid place to start yours.